# Basic
# Library
# Skills

*Fifth edition*

# Basic Library Skills

*Fifth Edition*

Carolyn Wolf

McFarland & Company, Inc., Publishers
*Jefferson, North Carolina, and London*

LIBRARY OF CONGRESS CATALOGUING-IN-PUBLICATION DATA

Wolf, Carolyn E., 1941–
    Basic library skills / Carolyn Wolf. — 5th ed.
      p.    cm.
    Includes bibliographical references and index.

    ISBN 0-7864-2635-7 (softcover : 50# alkaline paper) ∞

    1. Libraries — Handbooks, manuals, etc.  2. Library
research — United States — Handbooks, manuals, etc.
3. Libraries and the Internet.  I. Title.
Z710.W64   2006
025.5'6 — dc22                2006000196

British Library Cataloguing-in-Publication data are available

Cover illustration ©2006 Blend Images

Manufactured in the United States of America

*McFarland & Company, Inc., Publishers
 Box 611, Jefferson, North Carolina 28640
 www.mcfarlandpub.com*

In loving memory
of Richard I. Wolf

# Preface and Acknowledgments

This text is designed to be a self-contained short course in the use of the library, not an exhaustive treatment of the subject. The intent is to provide a quick and easy way to learn to do library research. One could use it as an adjunct to a course in library usage or as part of an introductory English composition course. Also, it might serve as a self-paced instructional sequence for all students. Students have used the first four editions of this book as the major text in a college course in library usage. An author used the text in a graduate course in research methods. These courses included at least 15 hours of classroom instruction. The student should master basic library skills in about 35 to 40 hours. This will vary according to the intellectual skills of the student and his or her study technique. Furthermore, the self-paced design of the text allows students to learn the material at individual speeds.

The author has included only material that is considered essential for mastery of basic library skills. One cannot learn to use the library by working through the text only. Mastery demands "hands on" experience and practice in the library. The concepts in the text are generalizable to all libraries. Materials that were deemed to be too specific were omitted. The author determined which skills were needed by library users. Each chapter lists the performance skills, called *objectives*. These statements tell the student what is to be learned in the chapter. After studying the materials in each chapter the student should be able to perform the objectives. These objectives are practical and have immediate application. The author omitted theoretical or abstract materials unrelated to specific tasks.

Learning psychologists have discovered that students learn more efficiently if they are presented with and attend to stated objectives. Therefore, it is recommended that students attend to the objectives before studying each chapter.

The *exercises* give students hands-on experience by applying rules stated in the text to situations that approach real "research problems." Students also will find the *new or unusual terms* found in the text listed at the back of the chapter. They should be able to define these after studying the text. Bibliographies of examples used in the text and other resources are also included after each chapter.

Finally, the library is the essence of the educational institution. It is unfortunate that some students have negative feelings toward the library. These feelings will become more positive as students learn to use the library. That is the goal of this text.

The author would like to thank the following individuals and libraries for their assistance in updating this text: Pam Stocking, Head Librarian at the Ellenville (NY) Public Library, the reference staff at Manatee Community College in Venice, Florida and my fellow employees at the Frances T. Bourne Jacaranda Public Library (Venice, Fl), Venice Public Library (Venice, Fl) and Selby Public Library (Sarasota, Fl).

The author would like to thank the H. W. Wilson Company, Marquis Publications, Hartwick College and OCLC Online Computer Library Center for permission to use examples of their publications.

Hartwick College library web page courtesy of Hartwick College, Stevens-German Library, Yager Hall, Oneota, NY 13820 USA.

Page from Who's Who in America, 59th ed., reprinted by permission.

WorldCat and FirstSearch screen shots are used with permission of OCLC Online Computer Library Center, Inc. WorldCat and FirstSearch are registered trademarks of OCLC Online Computer Library Center Inc.

Bibliographic Index 1996, p. 29. Copyright (c) 1996 by the H.W. Wilson Company. Material reproduced with permission of the publisher.

Book Review Digest 2003, p. 478. Copyright (c) 2003 by the H.W. Wilson Company. Material reproduced with permission of the publisher.

Short Story Index Supplement 1979–1983, p. 791. Copyright (c) 1979–1983 by the H.W. Wilson Company. Material reproduced with permission of the publisher.

Fiction Catalog 14th edition, p. 653. Copyright (c) 2001 by the H.W. Wilson Company. Material reproduced with permission of the publisher.

Biographical Index 9/90–8/91, p. 198. Copyright (c) 1991 by the H.W. Wilson Company. Material reproduced with permission of the publisher.

Current Biography April 2005, p. 1. Copyright (c) 2005 by the H.W. Wilson Company. Material reproduced with permission of the publisher.

Current Biography Yearbook 2000, p. 665. Copyright (c) 2000 by the H.W. Wilson Company. Material reproduced with permission of the publisher.

All WilsonWeb screen shots copyright (c) 2005 by the H.W. Wilson Company. Material reproduced with permission of the publisher.

# Table of Contents

# Introduction: A Brief Historical Perspective

The earliest books, especially those written on papyrus, were scrolls. Users stored them in earthen jars to protect them from water, insects and fire. Early civilizations, such as the Egyptians, had libraries and librarians to store these scrolls. The library at Alexandria, Egypt, was one of the largest of the ancient libraries and contained more than 700,000 scrolls. Julius Caesar destroyed most of the library in 47 B.C., and the Christians further damaged it in A.D. 391. Ancient books contain references to the library, part of which still stands, and one may find book titles and the names of some librarians on the walls.

Discoverers have found other ancient libraries. The Library of Assurbanipal at Nineveh, dated at 668–626 B.C., contained about 25,000 clay tablets. Archaeologists have recovered many of these tablets, and about 21,000 of them, whole or fragmentary, are in the British Museum. Many other ancient libraries were destroyed by war and invading barbarians. During the Dark or Middle Ages, the monastic libraries preserved much of the classical literature and knowledge. The monks copied books in the scriptorium, a writing room–library combination. Many books were not only copied but translated from Greek and other languages. Early medieval universities were located near monasteries that had libraries. Students waited long periods of time and paid large sums of money to scribes who copied books for them.

The invention of printing by movable type is generally credited to Johannes Gutenberg of Mainz, Germany, sometime between 1450 and 1455. Scholars believe that Gutenberg printed the first complete book, a Bible, in 1456. The art of printing spread rapidly across Europe and arrived in the New World in 1539. With the spread of the technology of printing came uses other than the reproduction of Bibles, Psalters and other religious books. Broadsheets, pamphlets, newssheets and other forms of spreading information and news were developed. American colonists printed the first book in 1639.

During the mid–18th century came the formation of national libraries. The British Museum, a library and museum, was founded in 1733. The nucleus of the library was the personal collections of Sir Robert Cotton, Robert Harley, Earl of Oxford, and Sir Hans Sloan. The holdings were enlarged in 1757 with the addition of the Royal Library, books collected by the kings from Edward IV to George II. The United States Congress founded the Library of Congress in 1800 as a research library. The British burned the library in 1814 during the attack on Washington. The collection was rebuilt around the personal library of Thomas Jefferson, who was also instrumental in convincing other book collectors to send their personal collections to the library.

Copyright offices have been established in national libraries for developing the national libraries and insuring the completeness of its collection (at a somewhat small cost to the government).

The first public library in the United States was founded in 1833 in Petersborough, New Hampshire. The first major public library was established in Boston in 1852 but was not opened until 1854. In the 1900s, Andrew Carnegie began donating money to communities throughout the country for the construction of libraries. These libraries were to be open to the public free of charge. Often Carnegie built libraries in small rural communities that would have been unable to build their libraries without this financial assistance. Many of these libraries are still in use today.

In 1969 the term "media center" came into general use for the school library. Most of today's institutional libraries are truly media centers, offering non-print resources (such as audio and video recordings, computer software and DVD's) besides traditional printed material. By the mid 1970s library networks, such as OCLC, were formed and libraries began to automate (computerize) their catalogs and share their resources. As computer technology improved and costs decreased more libraries joined networks and more library functions were automated. By the late 1990s most libraries were using computerized catalogs and circulation systems and providing access to their catalogs via the Internet. With the high costs and diversity of materials it is necessary to share resources. Such sharing enables libraries to fulfill their mission; to serve as repositories to recorded history and culture, making information readily available for the individual.

As scanning technology has improved, projects to digitize printed matter have emerged. Many institutions and private groups are involved in the preservation of printed materials in a digitized form. The resulting digitized books or those produced only in digital form are called e-books. For more information on e-books see Chapter 11.

## *Suggested Readings*

Cater, John, ed. *Printing and the Mind of Man: A Descriptive Catalogue Illustrating the Impact of Print on the Evolution of Western Civilization During Five Centuries.* New York: Holt, Rinehart and Winston, 1967.

Christ, Karl. *The Handbook of Medieval Library History.* Metuchen, NJ: Scarecrow, 1984.

Clement, Richard W. *The Book in America: With Images from the Library of Congress.* Golden, CO: Fulcrum Publications, 1996.

Diringer, David. *The Book Before Printing: Ancient, Medieval and Oriental.* New York: Dover, 1982 (reprint of 1953 ed.).

Dunkin, Paul Shaner. *Tales of Melvil's Mouser; or Much Ado About Libraries.* New York: R. R. Bowker, 1970.

Goodrum, Charles A. *The Library of Congress.* New York: Praeger, 1974.

_____. *Treasures of the Library of Congress.* New York: H. N. Abrams, 1980.

Hobson, Anthony Robert Alwyn. *Great Libraries.* London: Weidenfeld & Nicholson, 1970.

Jackson, Donald. *The Story of Writing.* New York: Taplinger, 1981.

Jones, Theodore. *Carnegie Libraries Across America: A Public Legacy.* New York: John Wiley, 1977.

Katz, William A. *Dahl's History of the Book.* 3rd rev. ed. Metuchen, NJ: Scarecrow, 1995.

Keep, Austin Baxter. *The Library in Colonial America.* New York: B. Franklin, 1970.

McMurtrie, Douglas C. *The Book: The Story of Printing and Bookmaking.* New York: Covici, Friede, 1937.

Musmann, Klaus. *Technological Innovations in Libraries, 1860–1960: An Anecdotal History.* Westport, CT: Greenwood Press, 1993.

New York Public Library. *Censorship: 500 Years of Conflict.* New York: Oxford University Press, 1984.

Oswald, John Clyde. *Benjamin Franklin, Printer.* Detroit: Gale Research Company, 1974.

Rosenberry, Cecil R. *For the Government and People of This State: A History of the New York State Library.* Albany: University of the State of New York, 1970.

Winkler, Paul A. *Reader in the History of Books and Printing.* Englewood, CO: Information Handling Services, 1978.

# 1

# A Walking Tour
# of the Library

## *Objectives*

After studying this chapter the student shall be able to
- locate the various facilities of the library in a quick and efficient manner
- draw a map indicating where these facilities are
- identify relevant staff members and the services each provides
- find the location of each staff member and show this on the map
- list the hours the library is open and when its constituent services are available
- state the policies of the library in terms of borrowing regulations, open and closed stacks, overdue fines, and the general regulations regarding the use of the building

## *General Information*

The aim of this chapter is to help the student identify and locate basic services offered by the library. To use the library extensively, the student should familiarize himself with its layout, facilities, resources and staff. To do this, a walking tour is essential. Many libraries give official tours by staff members. If these are not available, then the student should take his own tour.

As the student walks through the library he or she should note where all services and materials are located. For future reference a map or schematic diagram is helpful. Since each library is unique, the location of these components will vary greatly. The student should therefore diagram the library that they will use. Some libraries provide maps. These may be very specific or somewhat incomplete. In the latter case, additional information may be added.

The next stop on the walking tour is the circulation desk, since it is the "hub" where most of the business of the library is conducted. The main function of the circulation desk is to keep books moving in and out of the library. Students should familiarize themselves with the rules for book circulation (length of loan period, identification required when checking out books) and the policy for fines and lost books.

Some libraries now have self checkout kiosks. One will probably be located near the circulation desk. Others may be scattered around the library. Most items can be checked out at the kiosk avoiding a line at the circulation desk. Many libraries use a locking devise on the CD and DVD cases. If your library uses these locks it will be necessary to check out these materials at the circulation desk where the locks are removed.

Libraries usually have a special system for reserve materials, which may include books, journal articles, tapes and other sources that are set aside for use by students in their courses. There may be special restrictions on the use of these materials. If this reserve area is not located near the circulation desk, a point should be made to find it.

A critical area of the library is the reference section. The reference librarian's main function is to provide help in using the reference materials provided by the library. This person can locate sources to be consulted to answer specific questions. The reference desk is usually located near the entrance or the circulation desk.

On the next stop of the walking tour, the student should locate the catalog. Nearly everything the library has is listed here. (The use of the catalog is explained in Chapter 2.) The catalog is usually located near the reference desk. Most libraries have given up the card catalog and are using computer terminals (Online Public Access — OPAC) and some use microfiche cards for older holdings. If the library has "closed" and removed its card catalog, then find the computer terminals or microfiche copy (COM) of the catalog. A "closed" catalog means that no cards have been added after the "closed" date and the student must consult the OPACs or COM catalog for recent additions to the library's collection. Libraries are working towards inputting all their holdings into the computerized catalog. Those who have finished this "retrospective" work have removed the card catalog and the microfiche.

Compact shelving saves space, but its operation may require the assistance of a library staff member.

A brief walk through the bookshelves (stacks) will enable the user to get a general overview of how the books are grouped. Notice should be taken of the numbering system and how it relates to the catalog. Since the use of the catalog is thoroughly explained in Chapter 2 just a brief overview is necessary during the tour. The student could randomly select a book from the catalog to see if it can be located on the shelves. Special sections, such as fiction, new books, recorded books (cassettes or DVDs) and rare books, should be located and added to the map.

Most libraries have a separate area or special reading room for periodicals, magazines and journals. There is usually a periodicals desk or office, which may be staffed by a librarian or student assistants to aid in locating or identifying specific items. Most libraries do not permit the free circulation of periodicals since they have heavy use for short periods of time. The rules for the use of the periodical sections should be studied as they vary between libraries. Some libraries keep back files of newspapers or microfilms of them. The student should locate where these are kept and find out how to use the microfilm readers. Overcrowded libraries may use compact shelves for periodicals. Usually a library staff member will operate these stacks.

A recently burgeoning part of library services is "nonprint" (or nonbook") materials. The materials include microprint formats (microfilm, microfiche), audio and video tapes, records, slides, videodiscs, CDs, DVDs, computer software and 16mm and 35mm films. Unfortunately, these materials may be underused because students think they are difficult to use. Students should familiarize themselves with all the materials that are available and with how to operate the equipment. A valuable use of time might be just looking at an example from these specific materials and operating the equipment. The location of the materials and the equipment should be noted on the library map.

An important adjunct of the library is the copying service. One should find where services are, how to use them with the various types of materials, and any charges connected with their use. If the machines are coin operated, change should be brought to the library, as some librarians find it distracting and time-consuming to make change! Some libraries do have machines that make change. Some libraries have machines which dispense prepaid cards for use with the copy machines. There may be special copying areas in the library. These should be located and indicated on the map. The prudent use of copying is suggested, and copyright laws should be followed. The student should not make multiple copies of copyrighted materials without permission of the publisher since it is illegal to do so.

The location of certain items that may not appear essential can make the use of the library a more pleasant and efficient experience. Such items include stairs and elevators, lavatories, water fountains, pencil sharpeners, paper cutters and telephones. These should be shown on the map. The student should also include the location of listening rooms for records, CDs and tapes and special areas for typewriters, computers and calculators.

The student should become familiar with the staff of the library. They are there for the user's benefit and are usually eager to help. It is important to remember that the library aides are employed to help find information and expect to be called upon. To the librarian there is no such thing as a "stupid question."

Libraries generally divide their staff into two major departments, pub-

*Opposite:* Browsing in the stacks.

The workroom of most libraries is often crowded and the staff rarely seen by most library users.

lic services and technical services. The public services employees are "up front" and interact with the library patrons or visitors. They work at the circulation, reference, reserve and periodical desks. Knowing the names of the people who work in the public services areas may be useful. The technical services employees are the "behind-the-scenes" staff. They are usually divided into two departments, cataloging and acquisitions. The acquisitions staff is responsible for purchasing books, periodicals, non-print and other materials and may be consulted if students wish the library to purchase materials on an individual basis. The cataloging staff is responsible for adding new acquisitions to the catalog and making resources ready for the shelves and circulation. Finally, the head librarian supervises all staff and is available to solve problems that cannot be handled by the staff. The name and location of the head librarian's office should be noted.

The rules, regulations and policies of the library are instituted and maintained for the benefit of the users. A copy of the library manual should be obtained and some of these questions should be answered by referring to the manual: What services are available at what hours? What are the borrowing regulations? What are the rules for the reserve materials? What are the fines for overdue books? What is the policy on lost books? Does the library permit smoking, eating or drinking and where are these things permitted? What are the security precautions? (Knowing these may avoid embarrassment when leaving the library.)

After the tour the student should complete a map containing the following locations:

| | |
|---|---|
| 1. circulation desk | 15. catalog |
| 2. reference desk | 16. special collections |
| 3. reserve desk | 17. rare book room |
| 4. reference section | 18. lavatories |
| 5. periodicals section | 19. water fountains |
| 6. reading room | 20. pencil sharpener(s) |
| 7. book stacks | 21. stairs and elevators |
| 8. newspapers | 22. exits |
| 9. microfilm section | 23. smoking areas |
| 10. readers | 24. computers for public use |
| 11. copying machines | 25. computer software |
| 12. head librarian's office | 26. atlases |
| 13. cataloging department | 27. public telephones |
| 14. acquisitions department | 28. self check kiosk |

A list of people who work in the library should contain at least the names of the following:

1. head librarian
2. circulation department head
3. reference department head
4. periodicals department head
5. cataloging department head
6. acquisitions department head

# Exercises for Chapter 1

1. Complete a map locating the facilities listed earlier.
2. List the name(s) of the person(s) responsible for various library services.

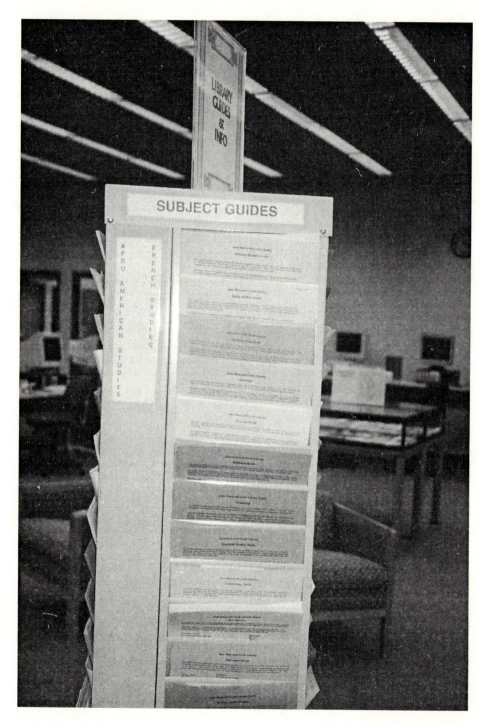

3. Complete the following chart of library hours:

|  | Library Opens | Library Closes |
|---|---|---|
| Sunday |  |  |
| Monday |  |  |
| Tuesday |  |  |
| Wednesday |  |  |
| Thursday |  |  |
| Friday |  |  |
| Saturday |  |  |

4. (A) For what period of time may an open shelf book be charged out?
   (B) A reserve book?
5. (A) What is the *daily* fine for an overdue book?
   (B) What is the *hourly* fine for an overdue book?
6. Does the library have closed stacks? If so, how do you get books?

## Important Terms in Chapter 1

| | |
|---|---|
| *circulation* | *periodicals* |
| *"closed catalog"* | *public services* |
| *reserve* | *technical services* |
| *reference* | *stacks* |

**Opposite:** Librarians prepare bibliographies on various topics to assist students in their research.

# 2

# The Catalog and Cataloging Systems

## *Objectives*

After studying this chapter the student shall be able to
- use call numbers to locate materials anywhere in the library
- use either the Dewey Decimal system or the Library of Congress system to locate materials
- interpret all the information found in catalog entries

## *The Catalog*

Catalogs contain all the books owned by a particular library. Trying to use the library without referring to the catalog is like looking for the proverbial needle in a haystack. Besides showing what a library owns, the catalog supplies information about each holding. Most libraries catalog their pamphlets, records, tapes, microforms and other resources as well as books. A card catalog is a series of cabinets filled with 3 × 5 cards in drawers.

Most libraries are no longer using a card catalog. Some have the same information on microfiche, magnetic tape or CDs. Most libraries use a computerized catalog, often referred to as an OPAC or Online Public Access Catalog. Microfiche catalogs are frequently called COM (computer output microfiche) and are computer-produced. With easy and often high speed access to the Internet few if any libraries are still producing COM catalogs. Libraries generally have their catalog on magnetic tape or CD, which require the use of a computer terminal. Libraries locate terminals throughout the library and sometimes in locations outside the library. In general, most libraries allow access to the catalog via the internet. Additional information about OPACs will be found in Chapter 3.

The library lists most items in the catalog by subject, by author and by title. Older fiction and autobiography, however, usually do not have subject entries. In addition to the traditional entries to the catalog many vendors provide additional access points, such as the use of keyword searches.

## *The Catalog Contents*

When you consult the catalog you will find the following types of information (* if applicable).

1. author's name
2. birth and death dates*
3. title
4. subtitle*
5. coauthor's name*
6. notes on editor, compiler, illustrator*
7. edition number*
8. place of publication
9. publishing company
10. date of publication or copyright
11. subject headings*
12. other added entries*
13. summary or detailed CONTENTS of the book*

See figures 2.1, 2.2 and 2.3 for the entry of the previous edition of this book as found in three different catalogs. Note that the left margin of each entry includes a "tag" or term describing the information on that line. Figure 2.1 is the briefest entry but still provides the basic information about the book PLUS the libraries in the Sarasota County Library System that own the book. In addition to the locations, the entry includes the call number (Dewey number 025.56 WOL) PLUS the status of the book. In this case, both copies are on the shelf and available for circulation.

Figure 2.2 is for the same title, but from the Library of Congress cat-

SUNCAT Library Catalog

| PREVIOUS RECORD | NEXT RECORD | RETURN TO BROWSE | ANOTHER SEARCH | START OVER | MARC DISPLAY |

REQUEST

AUTHOR    wolf, carolyn e                    View Entire Collection    Search

Record 2 of 2

| Author | Wolf, Carolyn E., 1941- |
| Title | **Basic library skills / by Carolyn Wolf.** |
| Pub info | Jefferson, N.C. : McFarland, c1999. |

| LOCATION | CALL # | STATUS |
|----------|--------|--------|
| Jacaranda Nonfiction | 025.56 WOL | ON SHELF |
| North Sarasota Nonfiction | 025.56 WOL | ON SHELF |

| Edition | 4th ed. |
| Descript | xiv, 208 p. : ill. ; 23 cm. |
| Bibliog. | Includes bibliographical references and index. |
| Subject | Library research -- United States. |
| ISBN | 0786406690 |

| PREVIOUS RECORD | NEXT RECORD | RETURN TO BROWSE | ANOTHER SEARCH | START OVER | MARC DISPLAY |

REQUEST

## Sarasota County Libraries

Figure 2.1

alog. Note that this entry includes more information than the entry in figure 2.1. This entry also includes the Library of Congress call number, Z710W64 1999. The library also has two copies and instructions for requesting this title are included.

Figure 2.3 is the entry found in the OCLC databasae **WorldCat.** This entry has the most detailed information, including the contents of the book, both Dewey and LC call numbers and how many member libraries worldwide own a copy.

Students tend to ignore information other than author, title, call number and publication information. Information in the tags Descriptions, Biblio., and Notes can provide clues for locating books that include charts, tables, illustration, maps, charts, etc. Collation information such as number of pages, size (height in cm) and format (paper, microfiche, e-book, etc.) is also included. This information provides information about location of the title in the library. Some libraries put large (oversized) books in an area with extra large shelves.

Since 1999 (when the last edition of this book was published) the

The Library of Congress                    >> Go to Library of Congress Authorities

# LIBRARY OF CONGRESS ONLINE CATALOG

**Help ❶** | **New Search** | **Search History** | **Headings List** | **Titles List** | **Request an Item** | **Account Status** | **Other Databases** | **Start Over**

DATABASE: Library of Congress Online Catalog
YOU SEARCHED: Author/Creator Browse = wolf, carolyn e
SEARCH RESULTS: Displaying 2 of 7.

◀ **Previous   Next ▶**

Brief Record | Subjects/Content | Full Record | MARC Tags

*Basic library skills / by Carolyn Wolf.*

**LC Control Number:** 99018567
   **Type of Material:** Text (Book, Microform, Electronic, etc.)
   **Personal Name:** Wolf, Carolyn E., 1941-
   **Main Title:** Basic library skills / by Carolyn Wolf.
**Edition Information:** 4th ed.
  **Published/Created:** Jefferson, N.C. : McFarland, c1999.
    **Description:** xiv, 208 p. : ill. ; 23 cm.
      **ISBN:** 0786406690 (alk. paper)
    **Notes:** Includes bibliographical references and index.
    **Subjects:** Library research--United States.
 **LC Classification:** Z710 .W64 1999
 **Dewey Class No.:** 025.5/6 21
 **Geog. Area Code:** n-us---

**CALL NUMBER:** Z710 .W64 1999
        Copy 1
 -- **Request in:** Jefferson or Adams Bldg General or Area Studies Reading Rms
   -- **Status:** Not Charged

**CALL NUMBER:** Z710 .W64 1999
        Copy 2
 -- **Request in:** Jefferson or Adams Bldg General or Area Studies Reading Rms
   -- **Status:** Not Charged

**DATABASE NAME:** Library of Congress Online Catalog

◀ **Previous   Next ▶**

http://catalog.loc.gov/cgi-bin/Pwebrecon.cgi?v3=2&ti=1,2&SEQ=20050716154143&Sear...   7/16/2005

Figure 2.2

## Basic library skills /

Carolyn E **Wolf**

**1999 4th ed.**
**English** ◇ Book xiv, 208 p. : ill. ; 23 cm.
Jefferson, N.C. : McFarland, ; ISBN: 0786406690 (alk. paper)

GET THIS ITEM

**Availability:** **FirstSearch indicates your institution owns the item.**
    • Libraries worldwide that own item: 457    ⓡ SARASOTA CNTY LIBR SYST

FIND RELATED

**More Like This:** Search for versions with same title and author | Advanced options ...

**Title:** **Basic library skills /**
**Author(s):** Wolf, Carolyn E., 1941-
**Publication:** Jefferson, N.C. : McFarland,
        **Edition:** 4th ed.
**Year:** 1999
**Description:** xiv, 208 p. : ill. ; 23 cm.
**Language:** English
**Contents:** A walking tour of the library -- The catalog and cataloging systems -- On-line public access catalogs -- Subject headings -- Bibliography -- Book reviews and the parts of a book -- General information sources -- Periodicals and newspapers -- On-line database searching, cd-rom indexes and reference sources -- Literature and criticism -- Governmental information and government documents -- Biography -- Business, career and consumer information -- Nonprint materials and special services -- On-line computer use in school libraries -- Hints for writing papers.
**Standard No:** **ISBN:** 0786406690 (alk. paper) **LCCN:** 99-18567

SUBJECT(S)

**Descriptor:** Library research -- United States.
        Library orientation.
        Information services -- User education.
**Note(s):** Includes bibliographical references and index.
**Class Descriptors:** LC: Z710; Dewey: 025.5/6
**Responsibility:** by Carolyn Wolf.
**Document Type:** Book
**Entry:** 19990120
**Update:** 19991116
**Accession No:** OCLC: 40723753
**Database:** WorldCat

Figure 2.3

"look" of entries in OPACs, especially those in OCLC and the Library of Congress have changed dramatically.

Using Figures 2.1, 2.2 and 2.3 compare the subject headings. Look at the tag SUBJECT in figure 2.1 and 2.2. The heading assigned is *Library research — United States.* Figure 2.3 includes three subject descriptors. The additional descriptors are *Library orientation and Information Services —*

*User education.* Online catalogs always provide subject searching. If additional sources with the same subject are needed the student can either do a subject search or click on the subject heading (if the catalog includes links).

Some large universities, such as Cornell University, and other large libraries many still have a card catalog for their older holdings. If this is the case a note will appear on the screen instructing users to consult the card catalog for materials acquired by the library before a specific date. The card catalog can be searched using the author's name, the title of the book or by subject. If a subject search is done, the searcher must know the exact subject heading(s) assigned by the Library of Congress. For additional information about Library of Congress subject headings see chapter 4. Each document listed in the card catalog will have a card for the author, the title and one card for each subject heading assigned to that title. If there are joint authors, each joint author will also have a card. The call number of the book will be located at the upper left side of the card. Many libraries entered the subject heading in red type. If you need to use a card catalog and encounter problems ask a librarian for assistance.

## *The Call Number*

Libraries use either the Dewey Decimal Classification System or the Library of Congress Classification System. The call number on the computer screen shows which system is being used. A Library of Congress call number begins with one, two or three *letters* whereas the call number in the Dewey Decimal system starts with a *number*. Melvil Dewey devised the decimal system in the 19th century while a student at Amherst College. The Amherst Library was in disorder (as were most large libraries of the time) and it was impossible to find specific books. Dewey used a numerical system to arrange the books and submitted it to the Amherst Library Committee for consideration. Many libraries throughout the world still use his system. Dewey also devised the card catalog system of filing information, a series of drawers of 3 × 5 cards, and each card having a hole in the center near the bottom of the card. A rod went through the holes and kept the cards in their proper place even if the drawer was dropped. The rod was easily removed so that additional cards for new materials could be added in the correct place. A simple and effective method for keeping the catalog updated.

Understanding of the Dewey system helps to find books by browsing and is also helpful in selecting books using the catalog. Dewey divided all knowledge into nine categories, numbering them 100 through 900, and put all the general reference works (dictionaries, encyclopedias, newspapers, etc.) into the category 000. Figure 2.4 shows Dewey's general system headings.

### Figure 2.4

000 General Works
100 Philosophy and Psychology
200 Religion
300 Social Science
400 Language
500 Pure Science
600 Technology (Applied Science)
700 The Arts
800 Literature
900 History

Each of these general categories is broken down into nine specific categories and each of these into nine or more specific categories. Then, by adding a decimal point, the system can be expanded continuously. Figure 2.5 contains an example of the 500 category broken down into subcategories.

### Figure 2.5

500 Pure Science
510 Mathematics
520 Astronomy and Allied Science
530 Physics
540 Chemistry and Allied Science
550 Science of the Earth and the Other Worlds
560 Paleontology — Paleozoology
570 Life Sciences
580 Botanical Sciences
590 Zoological Sciences
    591 Zoology
    592 Invertebrates (animal plankton and neuston)
    593 Protozoa and Other Simple Animals
    594 Mollusca and Molluscoidea
    595 Other Invertebrates
    596 Chordata Vertebrata (craniata, vertebrates)

597 Cold Blooded Vertebrates — Pisces (fish)
598 Aves (birds)
599 Mammalia (mammals)
    599.1 Momotremata
    599.2 Marsupialia
    599.3 Unguiculata
    599.4 Chiroptera (bats)
    599.5 Cetacea and Sirenia
    599.6 Paenungulata
    599.7 Fernugulata and Tubulidentata
    599.8 Primates
    599.9 Hominidae (humankind and forebears)

For instance, 540 contains Chemistry and Allied Sciences; 590 contains Zoological Sciences. Subcategory 590 can be broken down into the types of Zoological Sciences, such as 591 for (general) Zoology and 599 for Mammals. Likewise 599 can be broken down by using decimals, 599.1 *Monotremata* and 599.9 *Hominidae*. Similarly the .9 categories could be broken down into .91, .92 and so on depending on the specificity needed. A manual is available that contains all the categories in the Dewey system.

As useful as the Dewey system is, it is inefficient for large libraries. Around the turn of the twentieth century the Library of Congress, which used no real classification system, was chaotic. Users could not access many materials. Many other materials were hopelessly lost. In 1899 Herbert Putnam was appointed librarian of Congress and began an effort to get the library's materials in order. A study showed that the Dewey system was ineffectual in dealing with such a large library. The staff and other librarians continued devising a classification system that would be usable with the library's unorganized and rapidly growing collection.

Besides devising the classification system for the Library of Congress, Putnam felt that it was not really necessary for every library to read and catalog the same books. He thought it would be preferable for the Library of Congress to do that work and then share its work with other libraries. He also offered to sell copies of the cards printed by the Library of Congress for its own collection. Librarians eagerly received his ideas since cataloging and card production are time-consuming tasks. Libraries worldwide use the cataloging produced by the Library of Congress.

The Library of Congress system uses one of 21 letters of the alphabet as the first letter of the classification number. A second or third letter may be added to make up the first part of the classification or call number.

Using letters provides more categories than the Dewey system. The system leaves some letters unassigned to provide for undiscovered knowledge. Other letters like O are not used because they may be easily confused with the number 0 (zero). The second line of the LC call number is a number from 1 to 9999. Often these two lines make up the subject part of the call number.

**Figure 2.6**

| | |
|---|---|
| A | General Works |
| B | Philosophy, Psychology, Religion |
| C | History — Auxiliary Sciences |
| D | History — Except America |
| E–F | America |
| G | Geography, Anthropology, Sports |
| H | Social Sciences |
| J | Political Sciences |
| K | Law |
| L | Education |
| M | Music |
| N | Fine Arts |
| P | Language |
| Q | Science |
| R | Medicine |
| S | Agriculture, Plant and Animal Industry |
| T | Technology |
| U | Military Sciences |
| V | Naval Sciences |
| Z | Bibliography, Libraries, Library Science |

**Figure 2.7**

| | |
|---|---|
| N | Fine Arts |
| NA | Architecture |
| NB | Sculpture |
| NC | Graphic Arts, Drawing and Design |
| ND | Painting |
| NE | Engraving |
| NK | Art Applied to Industry, Decoration and Ornament |

Figure 2.6 contains the general categories in the LC system. For example, B contains Philosophy, Psychology and Religion and N contains Fine Arts. Fine Arts, N, can be further subdivided by adding a second letter. For

example, in Figure 2.7 NA is Architecture and NE is Engraving. Also further categories can be devised by adding numbers on the next line, as illustrated in Figure 2.8 (this figure shows just the beginning of the NE tables). As is the case in the Dewey system, the LC system has manuals describing all the various categories.

**Figure 2.8**

NE ENGRAVING
  1 periodicals
    10 Yearbooks
    20 Encyclopedias
    25 Dictionaries
    30 Directories
      Exhibitions (by Place)
    40 International
    45 Others
      Museums, Collections
      Public (Art Galleries, Print Departments, etc.)
    53 American
    55 European
      Private
    57 United States
    59
      Sales Catalogs
    63 Before 1801
    65 Auction Catalaogs, 1801–
    70 Dealers' Catalogs 1801–
    75 Publishers' Catalogs 1801–

To review, the first line of the Dewey number and (generally) the first two lines of the LC number refer to the topic of the book. These call numbers then provide a means of keeping all the books on the same topic in the same section of the library. Both systems also include another line of the call number for the particular author found under the subject indicated. The author line starts with the first letter of the author's last name (see Figures 2.1, 2.2 and 2.3 again: W for Wolf). This letter then may be followed by a number of additional numbers. These numbers provide finer discriminations, that may be necessary in extremely large libraries but will not be further discussed here. Thus the first line of the call number in Dewey and usually the first two lines in LC denote the subject of the book.

The next line (often the last line) is the alphabetic listing of authors within that subject. This system makes it convenient to "browse" through the stacks and to find information without using the catalog. The call numbers also can be thought of as the "address" of the book: it tells the user exactly where that specific book can be found in the library.

To locate materials, the call number in the catalog must be matched with the shelf area location. The book's call number must be copied exactly as it appears in the catalog since each item has a unique number. Once the individual becomes familiar with the location of the shelves, a piece of material can be located quickly, since librarians mark the shelves with a label at one or both ends of the stack.

It should be noted that some libraries have an "oversized" book section. Books that are too large for the regular shelves are put in special sections. For example, many art books are oversized and may be found in this section. If the student is unable to locate materials on the shelves, he or she should **ask the librarian**. The librarian will be able to tell the student if a particular book is on reserve, out in circulation or in some special section. Many libraries will recall books in circulation or put a "hold" (held/reserves upon return for the person requesting) on the book; when the book is returned the requesting individual is notified.

## *Filing Rules—Alphabetizing*

An understanding of some of the rules for filing in the catalog may facilitate the use of the catalog. In the old card catalogs there were many filing rules that are no longer followed by computer catalogs. For example in the card catalog personal names beginning with **Mac** and **Mc** were interfiled (filed together) as if they were all spelled **Mac**. Words which begin with **mac** (e.g., machete) were interfiled with the personal names. Computerized catalogs file exactly as the word or name is spelled. For those personal names where exact spelling (Mc or Mac) was not known the card catalog simplified the search. Just one example of the "old" system being more user friendly than the "new" system. If "A," "An" or "The" is the first word of the title the computer ignores it. If it appears any place in the title other than the first word, it is considered when filing. If the title is in a foreign language and the title begins with the equivalent of "a," "an" or "the" (for example, Der, Das, La, Le), the word is ignored. Words which may be written as one word, two words or hyphenated may be found under any form but not always. Numerals and numbers are filed by "computer rules" which those not familiar with computers might find difficult to understand. For example

**Figure 2.9**

1
101
11
2
2000
3

When using most catalogs some, but not all, of the "old" rules for filing cards in a catalog are observed but are invisible to the user.

## Exercises for Chapter 2

1. Using the catalog find the call numbers of the following books. Record the call numbers and then locate the books on the shelves.
    (A)  *McGraw-Hill Encyclopedia of Science and Technology*
    (B)  *Oxford English Dictionary*
    (C)  *World Almanac and Book of Facts*
    (D)  *Guide to the Presidency*
    (E)  *Famous First Facts*
2. Using figures 2.4 and 2.5, give the most specific call number you can for the following books:
    (A)  *Basic Astronomy*
    (B)  *Introduction to Human Anatomy*
    (C)  *The Great Apes of Africa*
    (D)  *Encyclopedia Americana*
3. Using figures 2.6, 2.7 and 2.8, give the most specific category you can find for the following books:
    (A)  *Custer's Last Stand*
    (B)  *A History of American Education*
    (C)  *Paintings of Pablo Picasso*
    (D)  *Early Copper Engravings*
    (E)  *Pediatric Surgery*
    (F)  *New York Times Encyclopedia of Sports*
4. The following questions should be answered by consulting the catalog entry reproduced in Figure 2.10.
    (A)  What is the publication date?

*Indians of North and South America. a bibliography based on the collection...*

**C Control Number:** 97003590

    **Type of Material:** Text (Book, Microform, Electronic, etc.)

    **Personal Name:** Wolf, Carolyn E., 1941-

    **Main Title:** Indians of North and South America. Second supplement : a bibliography based on the collection at the Willard E. Yager Library-Museum, Hartwick College, Oneonta, NY / Carolyn Wolf.

    **Published/Created:** Lanham, Md. : Scarecrow Press, 1997.

    **Related Names:** Willard E. Yager Library-Museum.

    **Description:** 492 p. 23 cm.

    **ISBN:** 0810833018 (alk. paper)

    **Notes:** Includes indexes.

    **Subjects:** Willard E. Yager Library-Museum--Catalogs.
    Indians--Bibliography--Catalogs.

**LC Classification:** Z1209 .W83 1988 E58

**Dewey Class No.:** 016.970/00497 21

**Geog. Area Code:** n------ s------ n-us-ny

**CALL NUMBER:** Z1209 .W83 1988 Alc
        Copy 1

    **-- Request in:** Reference - Main Reading Room (Jefferson, LJ100)

    **-- Status:** Not Charged

**Figure 2.10**

(B)   In what city was this book published?
(C)   What is the LC call number?
(D)   What is the author's name?
(E)   What is the Dewey call number?
(F)   How many subject headings have been assigned to this book?
(G)   What is the title of this book?
(H)   Does this book have illustrations?
(I)   Who published this book?
(J)   Is this book available for check-out?

# *Important Terms in Chapter 2*

| | |
|---|---|
| *microfiche* | *catalog* |
| *COM* | *subject headings* |
| *tags* | *Dewey system* |
| *LC system* | *OPAC* |
| *Descriptors* | |

## Important Books for Chapter 2

American Library Association. *ALA Filing Rules.* Chicago: American
Library Association, 1980.

_____. *ALA Rules for Filing Catalog Cards,* 2nd ed. Prep. by ALA Editor-
ial committee. Subcommittee on the ALA Rules for Filing Catalog
Cards. Pauline A. Seely, chairman and editor. Chicago: American
Library Association, 1968.

Comaromi, John P., ed., and Margaret J. Warren, asst. ed. *Manual on the
Use of the Dewey Decimal Classification,* 19th ed. Albany, NY: Forest
Press/Lake Placid Education Foundation, 1980. The 20th edition, 1993,
is also available on CD-ROM from OCLC (the 120th year celebration).

Dewey, Melvil. *A Classification and Subject Index, for Cataloging and
Arranging the Books and Pamphlets of a Library.* New York: Gordon
Press, 1979. (Reprint of the 1876 ed. published in Amherst, MA.)

Jefferson, Thomas. *Thomas Jefferson's Library: A Catalog with the Entries
in His Own Hand.* Edited by James Gilreath and Douglas L. Wilson.
Washington, Library of Congress: GPO, 1989.

United States. Library of Congress. Subject Cataloging Division. *Classification; Classes A–Z.* Washington, DC: GPO, 1971–.

# 3

# Online Public
# Access Catalogs

## *Objectives*

After studying this chapter the student shall be able to

- recognize and use Boolean operators
- identify different search procedures for OPACs
- access OPACs via the Internet

## *Definitions*

**Online**— A computers ability to interact with another computer at another location.

**OPAC**—(Online Public Access Catalog) The library's computerized catalog that replaces the card catalog and is available to anyone using the library. Most library catalogs are available via the internet.

**CD-ROM**—(Compact Disk—Read Only Memory) An optical disk, single sided, with read only memory. Many contain audio, video or data impressed at time of manufacture.

**Remote Access**— Communicating with another computer by phone line, DSL or cable modem.

**Dial-Up**— Using a telephone line to "dial" or call another computer.

**Keyword**— A significant word in a title, subject or author's name.

**KWIC**—(Keyword in Context) A type of indexing that allows searching by any term in any part of the record.

**Boolean Operators**—(and, or, not, near, with, except, in) Terms used to narrow or broaden searches.

**MaRC**—(Machine Readable Cataloging) The cataloging of library resources using standardized rules and symbols which various computer programs can read, then print and reorganize the data as desired.

**Bar Code**—A series of lines varying in thickness, making up a code that is read by an optical scanner.

**Gateway**—Means of connecting one computer terminal of a network with another terminal or computer of a different network.

**Protocol**—A set of formats or conventions that allow computers to communicate over data transmission (phone, DSL, fiber optic or cable) lines.

**Cable Modem**—A device which allows a computer to access the internet via a TV cable system.

**DSL**—A high speed means of accessing the internet.

**Network**—An interconnection of computers or nodes by communication facilities (phone lines, DSL, fiber optic or cable ).

**LAN**—(Local Area Network) A means of connecting computers that share programs, data, databases, often used in offices, schools, etc.

**Internet**—an outgrowth of the ARPAnet (a U.S. Defense Department experimental network) and other networks. Currently it is a cooperative system connecting computer networks worldwide. Every user of every computer on the Internet has an address. Addresses have suffixes, which provide information about the location or type of network. For example

.com — a company

.gov — a governmental agency or office

.edu — an educational site in the U.S.

.net — a network

.mil — military

.ca — Canada

.Uk — Great Britain

**World Wide Web (WWW)**—a loosely organized set of computer sites that provide free information that anyone world wide can read via the Internet. Most sites use HTTP (HyperText Transfer Protocol).

**Telnet**—a program that allows one computer to act as a terminal for a remote computer network via the Internet. Telnet provides a direct path to the remote computer.

**Vendor**—a supplier of services, equipment or supplies.

Public catalogs are located throughout the library.

## General Information

Most, if not all libraries have "closed" their card catalogs and are no longer adding cards. These libraries have a COM catalog (see Chapter 2) or an online catalog, usually called an OPAC (Online Public Access Catalog). The libraries that have public access catalogs also will have open computer terminals and some form of instruction on how to search the online catalog. Online catalogs can now be found in public libraries, public school libraries (elementary through high school), college and university libraries and special libraries. Many of these online catalogs provide more access points in searching than the old card catalog. Libraries that have officially "closed" their card catalog often do not physically remove the cards. Some libraries *must* keep their old card catalogs, since the old cards are not yet stored in the computer database. Both card catalog and database must be consulted. The Cornell University Library Catalog is an example of this situation (see Figure 3.7) A note is included for searchers to consult the card catalog in Olin Library for materials acquired before 1973. Libraries are gradually entering their older records into their OPAC. When the conversion of data is complete the card catalog (and/or COM) is discarded.

Libraries which have an OPAC have generally automated (computerized) all the library's operations: circulation, cataloging, periodical check-in and binding, reserves and other daily library procedures. All the daily operations then appear in the public catalog. Thus, when searching the catalog the student is informed of the status of the item, such as "on the shelf," "out in circulation," "on reserve," "on order," or "at the bindery." The catalog also shows the latest issue of a periodical that the library has received and on some systems what date the next issue is expected to arrive. Some circulation systems will generate overdue notices to remind patrons that books should be returned.

Most OPACs allow remote access, that is, if you know the web address it is possible access the library catalog from a computer outside the library via the internet. Then one searches the library's catalog as if you were in the library. Some OPACs have a "gateway" or system allowing the user to access other computers or remote periodical indexes. There is sometimes a charge for using this type of "gateway." Some libraries have bulletin boards or newsletters with information about the school or community that can be accessed from the OPAC "gateway."

Libraries using OPACs generally have printed instructions at the terminal and provide online help. If the student has difficulty while searching, a help command gives additional onscreen instructions. Some terminals attached to the OPAC will have printers. Library cards have bar codes or magnetic strips (similar to those on credit cards) and a valid card is required to check items out of the library.

## Searching the OPAC

OPACs allow searching by author, title, and subject as well as author/title combinations, keywords and call number. Some catalogs have additional access points which are discussed in other chapters. In each case it is necssary to follow the directions for that particular system. Some systems use a series of menus from which the user selects the desired type of search. See figures 3.1 and 3.2 for the basic search menus of two different libraries. Other systems require the user to type in a command to select the type of desired search. Often a mnemonic system is employed. Because the computer can read all the words in each entry it is possible to provide additional points of access. It is possible to do a keyword search, one on which the computer looks for a word anyplace it appears in the record. Some systems allow free text keyword searching, that is the systems search

# Welcome to SUNCAT
### Sarasota Universal Catalog

| Library Web Page | View Your Patron Record |
|---|---|
| Suggestions For The Library | Books The Library Should Acquire |

### Search The Catalog by:

| TITLE | KEYWORD |
|---|---|
| SUBJECT | AUTHOR / TITLE |
| AUTHOR | CALL NUMBER |

**HELP & Frequently Asked Questions**

**Note**: You must use a Java-capable browser to view your circulation record or request items @home customers, click here.

## Sarasota County Libraries

Figure 3.1

home        search        calendar        contact us        apply        giving

**ABOUT HARTWICK    ACADEMICS    ADMISSIONS    ATHLETICS    CAMPUS LIFE    NEWS**

hartwick - liberal arts in practice - academics - the stevens-german library - technic

HARTWICK
*at 1797*

**LIBRARY CATALOG**
**FIND PERIODICALS**
**ELECTRONIC RESOURCES**
**WEB SUBJECT GUIDES**

# Library Catalog
Search the Web Catalog at the Stevens-German Library

| Title | Keywords |
|---|---|
| Author | Subject Headings |
| Author / Title | Call Numbers |

| Reserves | New Books | What's New | E-Books |
|---|---|---|---|
| View Your Own Record | Electronic Resources | Other Libraries | Video Titles    Music ( |

Figure 3.2

for that word anyplace in the record. Some systems also allow the use of Boolean searching in the keyword search and may provide searching by ISBN, ISSN or OCLC number. Some systems allow searching by call number, a means of browsing the shelves without going to the shelf. This is particularly useful if the library has closed stacks. Some systems allow searches to be revised without starting over, a blessing for those who can't type. Some systems allow the limiting of a search by date, a range of dates, language or format (print, CD, audio recording, video, DVD, etc.).

When doing an author search, the author's name should be searched last name first. It is generally not necessary to put commas between names. One may enter just the last name or as many letters of the last name as are known (a truncated or shortened term). Some systems require the entry of a special symbol to show a truncated entry, e.g., "?," "*" or "#." For example it is possible to enter **Green?** The system will then display *all* the authors whose last name begins with those letters and the student can then choose the desired entry. For example — Green, Greenblat, Greene, Greenstone, Greentree, etc. When searching by author, it is sometimes possible to enter alternative spellings using Boolean operators and doing just one search, e.g., Green OR Greene. This is preferable to using the truncated search as it eliminates all except the two possible spellings of the name.

Title searches also allow the student to enter as many words as are known and the OPAC will display on the screen *all* the books that start with those words (see Figure 3.3 titles beginning with the word "**parrots**" on page 35). The desired title can then be selected from the list. It is sometimes permissible to use truncated words in title searches. Note that the search found 11 title with a total of 25 entries. Only the first 8 are displayed on the screen.

Subject searches may present the most difficulty as some systems require that the subject entered match *exactly* with Library of Congress subject headings. Incorrect subject headings may lead to no matches.

Also, if the student has not consulted LCSH (Library of Congress Subject Headings, see Chapter 4) guessing correct headings is even more difficult. Some systems are "kinder" ("user friendly") than others and instead of saying "no match," provide an alphabetical list of terms that surround the heading entered. Some systems also provide cross references and show the number of entries for each cross reference. This feature allows the student to choose other subjects without rekeying the search. See figure 3.4 for an example of a subject search on parrots. Note that the search located 16 subjects starting with the word **Parrots** and see references are also included. Only the first 8 subjects are displayed on the screen.

```
You searched for the TITLE: parrots              SUNCAT:All Locations
11 TITLES found, with 25 entries; TITLES 1-8 are:

   1   Parrots  ............................................  13 entries
   2   Parrots A Guide To Parrots Of The World  ..............  1 entry
   3   Parrots And Parakeets As Pets  ........................  1 entry
   4   Parrots Everything About Purchase Acclimation Nutrition  1 entry
   5   Parrots Everything About Purchase Care Feeding And Hous  1 entry
   6   Parrots Lament And Other True Tales Of Animal Intrigue   3 entries
   7   Parrots Life For Me  ..................................  1 entry
   8   Parrots Look Whos Talking  ............................  1 entry
```

```
Please type the NUMBER of the item you want to see, OR
F > Go FORWARD                        A > ANOTHER Search by TITLE
W > Same search as WORD search        P > PRINT
N > NEW Search                        + > ADDITIONAL options
Choose one  (1-8,F,W,N,A,P,D,T,L,J,Y,M,X,+)
```

**Figure 3.3**

```
You searched for the SUBJECT: parrots            SUNCAT:All Locations
16 SUBJECTS found, with 113 entries; SUBJECTS 1-8 are:

   1   Parrots --> See Related Subjects  ....................   7 entries
   2   Parrots  .............................................  53 entries
   3   Parrots Anecdotes  ...................................   3 entries
   4   Parrots Behavior  ....................................   5 entries
   5   Parrots Behavior Fiction  ............................   1 entry
   6   Parrots Breeding  ....................................   2 entries
   7   Parrots California San Francisco  ....................   1 entry
   8   Parrots Dictionaries  ................................   1 entry
```

```
Please type the NUMBER of the item you want to see, OR
F > Go FORWARD                        A > ANOTHER Search by SUBJECT
W > Same search as WORD search        P > PRINT
N > NEW Search                        + > ADDITIONAL options
Choose one  (1-8,F,W,N,A,P,D,T,L,J,Y,X,+)
```

**Figure 3.4**

Some systems allow the student to combine the author's name and the book title in one search. If the author's name is common or the author has published many books (e.g. Shakespeare) this option provides fewer "hits" and is more likely to display the desired title with fewer steps.

Keyword searches often produce the largest number of entries and so it is necessary to devise a good search strategy. See the following section on Boolean searching.

## Boolean Searching

In those OPACs that include Boolean search capabilities the Boolean operators generally include "and," "or," and "not." Boolean searches can be done in other types of databases such as periodical indexes or via online vendors such as DIALOG, LexisNexis or BRS. These systems add additional operators such as "with" and "near."

The use of the "and" operator serves to narrow a search by looking for entries that contain **both** terms, e.g., North "and" South. The "or" operator serves to enlarge the search by looking for entries that contain **either** of the terms, North "or" South. The "not" search narrows a search by eliminating from the search all citations with the undesired term, North "not" South. The "not" operator should be used with caution as it might eliminate desired entries (see Figure 3.5).

## Accessing OPACs via the Internet

Libraries that have OPACs have a home page on the Internet (World Wide Web). See figure 3.6 for the Library of Congress home page. In general the home page gives information about the library, such as its location, hours and services. The home page should be accessible using a web browser. Libraries use different systems for operating their OPAC. Among the most popular vendors are NOTIS, DRA, III, Dynix, and GEAC. Each system has different searching techniques.

To locate libraries with online catalogs around the world use *www.lib-dex.com*. This site provides a world wide directory of library home pages, web based OPACs, Friends of the Library pages and library e-commerce. Countries are listed alphabetically. When searching for libraries in the United States, chose USA option not United States of America. The USA list is arrangeed alphabetically by state. Each state is subdivided by type of library, including academic, armed forces, business,government, law, public, etc. Click on the library and the page displays information about the library and a link to the library catalog. The information included is the full name of the institution, location (city/county/state), the type of library (academic, military, etc) and the system vendor (such as iii or DYNIX). For searching, follow the screen directions/links. Some libraries may require an ID number or bar code number to search some or all of the services listed on the home page.

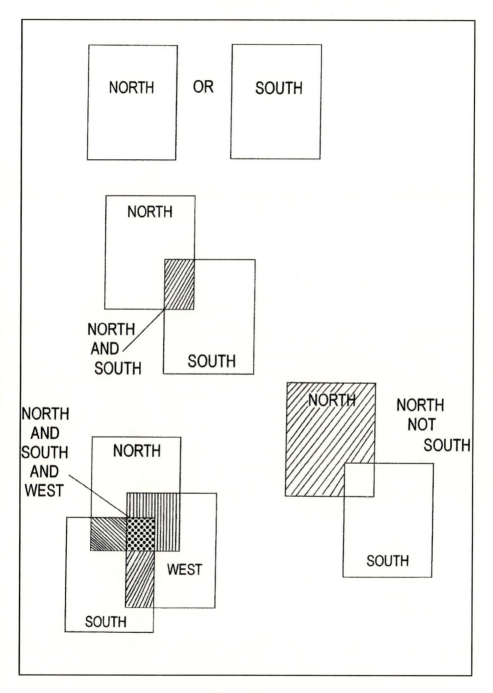

Figure 3.5

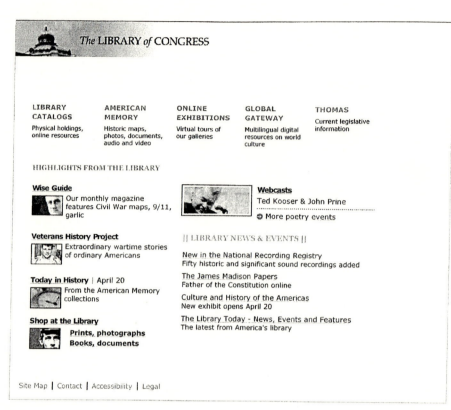

**Figure 3.6**

## Exercises for Chapter 3

1. Do an author search for Richard Warren.
   (A) First try just his last name.
   (B) Record (or print) the results.
   (C) Try his full name.
   (D) Was there a difference in the results?
   (E) Was there a difference in the time it took for the system to search?
2. Do a title search for Richard Warren's *A Purpose Driven Life.*
   (A) Try the search first using just the first word of the title. Record (or print) your results.
   (B) Try the search again using the first couple of words of the title. How did your results differ from previous title search?
3. Suppose you did not know the exact title of the book in question 2 but did know "driven life" was in the title.

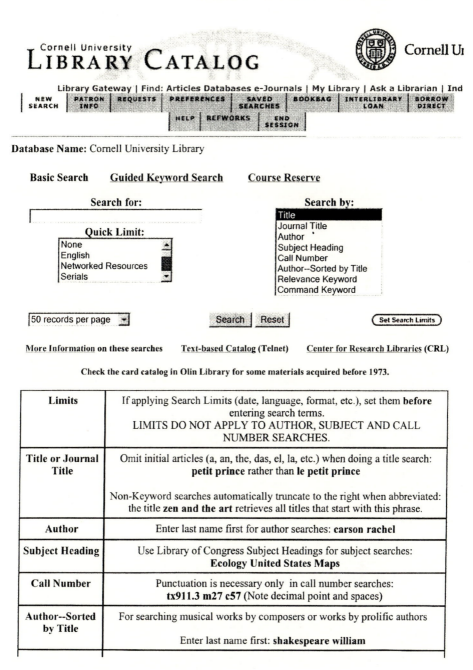

Figure 3.7, page 1

| Relevance Keyword | Use quotes to search phrases **"artificial intelligence"** |
|---|---|
| | Use + to mark essential terms: +**cornell** |
| | Use ! to exclude terms: **java !indonesia** |
| | Use ? with partial words to find variant endings: **manage?** finds manager, managers, management, etc. |
| | **Do not use Boolean operators**: and, or, not.. |
| **Command Keyword** | Use quotes to search phrases: **"artificial intelligence"** |
| | Combine search terms with Boolean operators: **and, or, not.** |
| | Use parentheses to group terms in complex searches: **(residence or home or housing) and (elderly or aged)** |
| | Use ? with partial words to find variant endings: **manage?** finds manager, managers, management, etc. |
| | Use field codes to refine your search: **kpub cornell** retrieves materials published by Cornell. |

<u>More Information</u> **on these searches**

---

**New Search** <u>Patron Info</u>  <u>Requests</u>  <u>Preferences</u>  SavedSearches  <u>Bookbag</u>    <u>Interlibrary</u>
<u>Loan</u>  <u>Borrow Direct</u>  <u>Help</u>  <u>RefWorks</u>  <u>Exit</u>

<u>Ask a Librarian</u> | <u>Report a Problem Connecting</u> | <u>Send us Feedback</u>
<u>CU Info</u> | <u>Cornell University Homepage</u>

Cornell University Library

**Figure 3.7, page 2**

(A)  How would you search for this title? Try your solution.

(B)  Did it work? If not, can you give an explanation?

4.  Try a subject search for books on Christian living.

(A)  What subject did you enter? Was it successful?

(B)  Record (or print) your results. How would you use information from this search to find additional books?

(C)  Call up a complete record from this search. What is its status?

(D)  Does the library have more than one copy? If you are using a public library system, does the system show locations by branch libraries?

5. If the system you are using allows Boolean searching, search Warren AND Life
   (A) Try various combinations of the books by Warren, using various words in the titles. Record (or print) your results.
   (B) Try other combinations that are of interest to you. What did you discover?

## Important Terms for Chapter 3

| | |
|---|---|
| *OPAC* | *CD-ROM* |
| *keyword* | *Boolean operators* |
| *bar code* | *network* |
| *LAN* | *user friendly* |
| *truncated* | *Internet* |
| | *vendor    World Wide Web (WWW)* |

## Important Books for Chapter 3

Crawford, Walt, et al. *Bibliographic Displays in the On-Line Catalog.* Boston: G. K. Hall, 1986.

*Dial-In.* An annual guide to library online public access catalogs in North America. Westport, CT: Meckler, 1991–.

*Dictionary of Computing.* 3rd ed. New York: Oxford University Press, 1990.

Fayen, Emily G. *The On-Line Catalog: Improving Public Access to Library Materials.* Boston: G. K. Hall, 1983.

Glossbrenner, Alfred. *The Complete Handbook of Personal Computer Communications.* 3rd ed. New York: St. Martin's Press, 1989.

*Manual of Online Search Strategies.* 2nd ed. New York: Toronto: G. K. Hall; Maxwell Macmillan Canada, 1992.

Matthews, Joseph R. *Access to On-Line Catalogs.* 2nd ed. New York: Neal Schuman, 1985.

Olson, Hope A. and John J. Boll. *Subject Analysis in Online Catalogs.* 2nd ed. Englewood, Co.: Libraries Unlimited, 2001.

*OPAC Directory 1994: An Annual Guide to Internet Accessible Online Public Access Catalogs.* Westport, Conn.: Meckler, 1994.

Peters, Thomas. *The Online Catalog: A Critical Examination of Public Use.* Jefferson, NC: McFarland, 1991.

Yee, Martha M. and Sara Shatford Layne. *Improving Online Public Access Catalogs.* Chicago: American Library Association, 1998.

# 4

# Subject Headings

## Objectives

After studying this chapter the student shall be able to

- use *Library of Congress Subject Headings*
- find correct subject headings for a particular topic
- use various forms of cross references correctly

## General Information

Often, students looking for material in the library do not have specific titles or authors in hand and need to use subject headings instead. This is particularly true during the early stages of a search. Frequently, students guess the appropriate heading to use. A proper and specific subject heading is essential for the efficient use of the card catalog, online catalog (OPAC), CD-ROMs, and periodical indexes. Using a heading that seems logical but is inappropriate wastes effort, especially when using OPACs. For example, searching for information on the battles of the American Civil War, one might use initially the heading **Civil War**. Titles about the Civil War are found more appropriately under **United States — History — Civil War, 1861–1865**.

The dates of events are also important since citations are arranged chronologically within groups. Thus entries **United States — History — Revolution, 1775–1783** and **United States — History — Colonial Period, ca. 1600–1774** both appear before the Civil War entry because they precede

Even librarians need to put their heads together to solve research problems.

it in time. Some catalogs contain cross-references to help minimize this problem. These are of two types: the *see* and the *see also* reference, which lists other closely related subjects.

To help find the correct subject heading when cross-references are not available, searchers need to find additional headings. Users should consult one or more special books that help to discover appropriate subject headings. The most comprehensive of these is *Library of Congress Subject Headings* (LCSH), a five-volume work conspicuous by its bright red cover. Well-equipped libraries use this five-volume work as the "bible" of subject headings and often place this work at the reference desk, in the reference section or near the OPAC terminals. Other books of subject headings that are not as comprehensive are the: *Sears List of Subject Headings*; *Subject Cross Reference Guide*; and *Cross Reference Index*.

Libraries also may have books of subject headings for *specific indexes or subjects*. For example: *Thesaurus of Psychological Indexing Terms* and *A to Zoo: Subject Access to Children's Picture Books*.

Consulting such works before using the catalog will save time and frustration and may provide additional headings, more specific or descriptive than the headings originally checked. Some headings, particularly in the *Library of Congress* work, may contain voluminous entries, filling an entire column or more. See Figure 4.1 for the subject **Legends** that continues on to a second column in LCSH. This means the subject is very broad and the user might consider specifying a narrower topic. This is particularly important in writing term papers. Problems in writing term papers often begin by selecting topics that are too comprehensive.

## Using Library of Congress Subject Headings (LCSH)

The LCSH is the list of subject headings assigned by the Library of Congress to books in its collection. It reflects the changes and growth in the collection since the development of the LC Classification system in 1898. The 14th edition was published in 1991 and is the first edition to use abbreviations introduced with computer thesaurus in the mid–1980s. The 24th edition was published in 2001. The introductory material in the front of Volume 1 contains explanations and instruction on how headings are arranged and assigned.

Subject headings may be one word or several words. A one word subject heading is usually a noun, with concepts using the singular form and objects using plural forms:

authorship (concept — singular)
soils (object — plural)

Two word headings are generally an adjective and a noun and may be inverted, especially if the adjective describes a language or a nationality. In recent years the natural word order is the preferred form except for language, national or ethnic adjectives. Older headings are more likely to be in inverted word order. Examples are:

authorship, disputed
coach horses
churches, Anglican
Camsa language
dramatists, Italian
public records

Names of geographic places are usually inverted to put the significant word first, e.g., Michigan, Lake. Headings with more than two words may include conjunctions and prepositional phrases. Headings with reciprocal relations or generally used associated ideas may be combined. Those head-

UF  Adventure of Link (Game)
    Legend of Zelda II (Game)
    Zelda (Game)
    Zelda II (Game)  *[Former heading]*
BT  Video games
Legend of Zelda II (Game)
USE  Legend of Zelda (Game)
**Legendmaker (Game)**
    *[GV1469.62.L45]*
BT  Fantasy games
Legendreidae
USE  Spathidiidae
Legendre's coefficients
USE  Legendre's functions
Legendre's equation
USE  Legendre's functions
**Legendre's functions**
    *[QA406]*
UF  Functions, Legendre's
    Legendre's coefficients
    Legendre's equation
BT  Spherical harmonics
**Legendre's polynomials**
UF  Polynomials, Legendre's
BT  Orthogonal polynomials
**Legends**  *(May Subd Geog)*
    *[N7760 (Iconography)]*
    *[PN683-PN687 (Medieval literature)]*
    *[PZ8.1 (Juvenile)]*
UF  Folk tales
    Traditions
    Urban legends
BT  Exempla
    Fiction
    Folk literature
    Homiletical illustrations
    Literature
    Tales
SA  *subdivision* Legends *under subjects,*
    *e.g.* Martyrs—Legends; Mary,
    Blessed Virgin, Saint—Legends
NT  Chansons de geste
    Fables
    Heldensage
    Mythology
— Jews
    USE  Legends, Jewish
— Africa
    NT  Adamastor (Legendary character)
— Canary Islands
— China
    NT  Chiyou (Legendary character)
        Fu Hsi (Legendary character)
        Huangdi (Legendary character)
        Yen-ti (Legendary character)
— Egypt
    NT  Eudoxia (Legendary character)
— England
    NT  Mark, King of Cornwall
            (Legendary character)
        William of Palerne (Legendary
            character)
— Europe
    NT  Adamastor (Legendary character)
        Milon d'Angers
— France
    NT  Bluebeard (Legendary character)
        Raoul de Cambrai (Legendary
            character)
        William of Palerne (Legendary
            character)
— Germany
    NT  Mephistopheles (Legendary
            character)
— Greece
    NT  Aeneas (Legendary character)
        Cocalus (Legendary character)
        Dido (Legendary character)
        Diotima (Legendary character)
        Euthymos (Legendary character)
        Minos (Legendary character)

— India
    NT  Nura Yaithim Konu (Legendary
            character)
— Indonesia
    NT  Ratul Kidul (Legendary character)
— Iraq
    NT  Pyramus (Legendary character)
        Thisbe (Legendary character)
— Ireland
— Italy
    NT  Cocalus (Legendary character)
— Middle East
    NT  Sindbad the Sailor (Legendary
            character)
— Mongolia
    NT  Man'badar (Legendary character)
— Polynesia
    NT  Tawhaki (Legendary character)
— Romania
    NT  Manole, Master (Legendary
            character)
— Rome
    NT  Aeneas (Legendary character)
        Andronicus, Titus (Legendary
            character)
        Dido (Legendary character)
        Roman charity (Legend)
— Scotland
    NT  Bean, Sawney (Legendary
            character)
— Spain
    NT  Bernardo del Carpio (Legendary
            character)
        Florinda (Legendary character)
        Infantes of Lara
        Lovers of Teruel (Legend)
— Thailand
    NT  Cama (Legendary character)
— Ukraine
    NT  Kiï (Legendary character)
— Vietnam
    NT  Bà Chúa Kho (Legendary
            character)
**Legends, Buddhist**  *(May Subd Geog)*
UF  Buddhist legends
NT  Miao-shan (Legendary character)
**Legends, Buddhist, in literature**
    *(Not Subd Geog)*
**Legends, Christian**  *(May Subd Geog)*
UF  Christian legends
Legends, Hasidic
USE  Hasidim—Legends
**Legends, Hindu**  *(May Subd Geog)*
UF  Hindu legends
**Legends, Islamic**
    *[BP137-BP137.5]*
UF  Islamic legends
    Legends, Muslim
    Muslim legends
NT  Khidr (Legendary character)
**Legends, Jaina**  *(May Subd Geog)*
UF  Jaina legends
NT  Meghakumāra (Legendary character)
**Legends, Jewish**
    Here are entered collections of and works about
    Jewish legends, including comprehensive works cov-
    ering both Old Testament legends and post-Biblical
    Jewish legends. Works on legends in the Bible and on
    extra-Biblical legends about Biblical characters and
    events are entered under Bible—Legends. Works lim-
    ited to legends in or about the Old or New Testament
    are entered under Bible. O.T.—Legends or Bible.
    N.T.—Legends.
UF  Jewish legends
    Jews—Legends
    Legends—Jews
RT  Bible. O.T.—Legends
NT  Aggada
    Golem
    Hasidim—Legends
    Midrash—Legends

Legends, Muslim
    USE  Legends, Islamic
**Legends, Shinto**  *(May Subd Geog)*
UF  Shinto legends
**Legends in art**  *(Not Subd Geog)*
**Legends in literature**  *(Not Subd G[eog])*
**Legenne family**  *(Not Subd Geog)*
**Leger family**  *(Not Subd Geog)*
RT  Saint Leger family
Legerdemain
USE  Juggling
    Magic tricks
Legerdemainists
USE  Magicians
**Legeriomycetaceae**  *(May Subd Ge[og])*
    *[QK621.L]*
UF  Genistellaceae
BT  Harpellales
**Legerton family**  *(Not Subd Geog)*
**Legg-Calvé-Perthes disease**
    *(May Subd Geog)*
    *[RJ482.O8]*
UF  Calvé-Legg-Perthes syndrom[e]
    Coxa plana
    Legg-Perthes disease
    Osteochondritis deformans ju[...]
    Perthes-Calvé-Legg-Waldens[...]
        syndrome
    Perthes disease
    Pseudocoxalgia
    Waldenström's syndrome
BT  Hip joint—Diseases
    Osteochondrosis
    Pediatric orthopedics
**Legg family**  *(Not Subd Geog)*
UF  Leg family
    Legge family
    Leggs family
Legg-Perthes disease
USE  Legg-Calvé-Perthes disease
Leggan family
USE  Ligon family
Legge family
USE  Legg family
Leggieri Theater (San Gimignano, Ita[...])
USE  Teatro dei Leggieri (San Gim[...]
    Italy)
Leggin family
USE  Ligon family
**Leggings**  *(May Subd Geog)*
BT  Clothing and dress
Leggon family
USE  Ligon family
Leggs family
USE  Legg family
**Leggs United (Fictitious characters)**
    *(Not Subd Geog)*
**Leghorns (Poultry)**  *(May Subd Ge[og])*
    *[SF489.L5]*
BT  Chicken breeds
Leghoya (African people)
USE  Ghoya (African people)
**Legibility (Printing)**  *(May Subd G[eog])*
    *[Z250.A4]*
UF  Readability (Printing)
BT  Printing
    Reading, Psychology of
Legin family
USE  Ligon family
**Legind Lake (Denmark)**
UF  Lake Legind (Denmark)
    Legind Sø (Denmark)
BT  Lakes—Denmark
Legind Sø (Denmark)
USE  Legind Lake (Denmark)
Legionary ants
USE  Eciton
**Legionella**  *(May Subd Geog)*
BT  Legionellaceae
NT  Legionella pneumophila

**Figure 4.1**

ings with prepositional phrases may be in the *inverted format*. Examples are:

charity laws and legislation
bites and stings
Antietam, Battle of, 1862
bachelor of arts degree
technology and civilization

Place names may also be used as subject headings and subheadings. Over the years the format for place names has changed as have the rules to assign subject headings for place names. In addition, many places have changed their names. Thus place names in card catalogs and even in OPACs are inconsistent and diligent searching is necessary to locate all desired information. An example of a geographic heading that is confusing for users of any type of the catalog is George, Lake (not Lake George) but Lake George Region. Examples of place name changes include colonies that have become independent nations and changed their name, territories conquered in war resulting in city or country name changes, name changes in cities when governments change such as St. Petersburg–Petrograd–Leningrad, a city known by three different names in the 2oth century. In 1991, the citizens voted to change the name back to St. Petersburg.

Cross references are always helpful in directing students from incorrect headings to correct headings. Also helpful are cross references between similar headings or between broad and narrow headings. Many libraries, catalogs, and indexes use *see* and *see also* headings. The *see* reference directs the student from an incorrect heading to a correct heading. The 20th and later editions of LCSH and many computer thesauri have substituted the term **use** for *see*. The function remains the same, directing the user to the correct heading.

The *see also* (or SA) reference directs the student to other headings that are related. Recent computer thesauri and LCSH are supplementing the *see also* reference with additional breakdowns as follows:

RT = related term
BT = broader term
NT =narrower term
UF = use from, a cross reference from the *use* reference

The inclusion of the UF in a list means that terms designated with UF are *not* good subject headings and should not be used when searching. In Figure 4.1 for the subject heading **Legends,** note that UF references include

*Folk tales; Traditions* and *Urban legends.* These headings are not to be used and if the user looked, for example, under *Folk tales* LCSH says *USE Legends.* The BT or broader terms for the subject heading **Legends** include *Exempla; Fiction; Folk literature; Homiletica illustrations; Literature* and *Tales.* The RT or related term for **Legends, Jewish** is *Bible. O.T.— Legends.* The note for SA (see also) for **Legends** says "*subdivision* **Legends** *under subjects,* e.g. Martyrs — Legends; Mary, Blessed Virgin, Saint — Legends. The list for NT or narrower terms under **Legends** includes Chansons de geste; Fables; Heldensage; and Mythology. For examples of a **use** reference see Figure 4.1 *Legends— Jews* USE *Legends, Jewish.* LCSH also includes a variety of notes with the subject headings and their subdivisions. Often the beginning or subject class number (see Chapter 2) of the call number is included. See Figure 4.1 **Legends** and note the call numbers N7760 (Iconography), PN683-PN687 (Medieval literature) and PZ8.1 (Juvenile). Also note that there are call numbers included with some of the subdivisions, (see Figure 4. 1) e.g. **Legends, Islamic** is BP137-BP137.5. With this information the student can go to the shelves and browse to see which books the library has on the subject. Having part of the call number is also useful with those OPACs that have a call number browse search option. Another type of note that may be included is a scope note — one that explains what is included or excluded in that particular subject heading. See Figure 4.1 for **Legends,** note that this heading says (May *Subd Geog* ). See Figure 4.1 **Legends, Jewish** for a scope note that begins "Here are entered collections of and works about Jewish legends..."

There are generally four types of subdivisions used by the Library of Congress:

1. topical — ones that limit the concept
       semiconductors — failures
2. form — includes the literary form
       addresses, essays, lectures
       periodical
       abstracts
       collected works
3. chronological — shows time period(s)
       Sicily — civilization — 15th century
       Sri Lanka — history — 1505-1948
4. geographical — shows places
       Legends — China (Figure 4.1)

The countries that are exceptions to this rule are the United States, Canada, Russia and Great Britain. These countries have more specific breakdowns, using names of states, provinces, regions, constituent countries and republics instead of just the name of the country, e.g. public buildings — Washington, D.C.

Not all possible subdivisions are listed in LCSH. Subdivisions are marked by a dash that eliminates the need to repeat the main heading. If a subdivision has a subdivision there will be two dashes.

## Searching the Catalog

If you are searching the subject heading in the card catalog you can browse easily through the cards and find singular and plural forms of the term and other headings beginning with the same word. In most OPACs a user starts a subject search from the menu or with a command s= or su=. Some OPACs allow free text searching (see Chapter 3). In others the subject term entered into the computer must be an *exact* match to a Library of Congress subject heading. Problems could be singular vs. plural forms of the word, inverted terms, etc. Searching any catalog by subject is limited by the number of subject terms assigned and by the imprecise use of some headings and the changes in terminology through time. Some OPACs have a subject browse option. This option gives all the subheadings for that subject, some of which might not be listed in LCSH. For example, many subjects can include geographical subdivisions but all the possible geographical subheadings will **not** be listed in LSCH, only a note that the subject might have geographical subheadings.

## Exercises for Chapter 4

1. Using *Library of Congress Subject Headings*, look up the subject **Last Supper**. Record call number, any notes, cross references, subheadings or other subjects beginning with the term **Last Supper**.
2. Using *Library of Congress Subject Headings* find the correct subject heading(s) needed to locate information about the conflicts between the Jews and the Palestinians and or other Arab groups.
3. Using *Library of Congress Subject Headings* locate and record one or two examples of subject headings that use or contain the following:
   (A)  chronological subdivisions

   (B)   geographical subdivisions
   (C)   scope note(s)
   (D)   class note(s)
   (E)   multiple cross references

4. Using your example in question 3E, trace and record all cross references to BT, NT, RT, SA, UF and USE. Is the example in 3E a topic usable for a term paper? Why or why not?

## *Important Terms in Chapter 4*

**cross reference**
*"see" reference*
*"see also" reference*
*"BT" reference*
*"NT" reference*
*"RT" reference*
*"USE" reference*
*"UF" reference*
*LCSH*

## *Important Books for Chapter 4*

Atkins, Thomas V. *Cross Reference Index: A Guide to Search Terms.* New York: Bowker, 1984, 1989.

Bade, David W. *Misinformation and Meaning in Library Catalogs.* Chicago: D.W. Bade, 2003.

Booth, Barbara, and Michael Blair. *Thesaurus of Sociological Indexing Terms.* 5th ed. Bethesda, MD.: Cambridge Scientific Abstracts, 1999.

Chan, Lois Mai. *Library of Congress Subject Headings: principles and applications.* 4th ed. Westport, Conn.: Libraries Unlimited, 2005.

Lima, Carolyn W. and John A. Lima. *"A to Zoo" Subject Access to Children's Picture Books.* 6th ed. New York: R. R. Bowker, 2001.

*Sears List of Subject Headings.* 18th ed. New York: H. W. Wilson, 2004.

*Subject Guide to Books in Print.* New York: R. R. Bowker, 1998–. Annual. Electronic source, on disc including book reviews.

*Thesaurus of Psychological Index Terms.* 10th ed. Alvin Walker, ed. Arlington, VA: American Psychological Association, 2005.

United States. Library of Congress. Subject Cataloging Division. *Library of Congress Subject Headings.* Washington, D.C.: Library of Congress, 27th ed. 2004.

# 5

# Bibliography

## *Objectives*

After studying this chapter the student shall be able to

- distinguish between the two types of bibliography, book length and short lists
- figure out where to find lists of available published books and how to use these lists
- use the *National Union Catalog*, the *Cumulative Book Index* and the *Bibliographic Index* to locate materials
- distinguish between annotated bibliographies and the other types and how to find materials in them
- recognize an appropriate format for writing bibliographies
- locate bibliographies on specific topics

## *General Information*

After defining a topic the writer will find a bibliography an essential part of research. *Webster's Third New International Dictionary of the English Language Unabridged* (1971) defines bibliography as follows:

**1a:** the history, identification, or analytical and systematic description or classification of writings or publications considered as material objects **b:** the investigation or determination of the relationships of varying texts or multiple editions of a single work or a related group of works — called also *analytic bibliography, descriptive bibliography*. **2 :**

| Sort | Related Subjects | Related Authors | Limit | E-mail | Print | Export | Help | WorldCat results for: kw: bibliography and kw: frost and kw: robert and yr: 2000-2004 and la= "eng" and dt= "bks" (Save Search) Records found: 10 Rank by: Number of Libraries | WorldCat |

◄ |1  ►
Prev           Next

Limit results: Any Audience ▾  Any Content ▾  Any Format ▾  Search  ?

☐ 1.  ◈ **The Cambridge companion to Robert Frost /**
Author: Faggen, Robert. **Publication:** New York : Cambridge University Press, 2001
Document: English : Book ⊕ Internet Resource
**Libraries Worldwide**: 764
More Like This: Search for versions with same title and author | Advanced options ...
⊕ See more details for locating this item

☐ 2.  ◈ **American short-story writers since World War II.**
**Fourth series /**
Author: Meanor, Patrick.; McNicholas, Joseph.
**Publication:** Detroit : Gale Group, 2001
Document: English : Book
**Libraries Worldwide**: 573
More Like This: Search for versions with same title and author | Advanced options ...
⊕ See more details for locating this item

☐ 3.  ◈ **Great American writers :**
**twentieth century /**
Author: Shuman, R. Baird
**Publication:** New York : Marshall Cavendish, 2002
Document: English : Book
**Libraries Worldwide**: 346
More Like This: Search for versions with same title and author | Advanced options ...
⊕ See more details for locating this item

☐ 4.  ◈ **Encyclopedia of Catholic literature /**
Author: Reichardt, Mary R.
**Publication:** Westport, Conn. : Greenwood Press, 2004
Document: English : Book
**Libraries Worldwide**: 195
More Like This: Search for versions with same title and author | Advanced options ...
⊕ See more details for locating this item

☐ 5.  ◈ **A dab of Dickens & a touch of Twain :**
**literary lives from Shakespeare's old England to Frost's New**
**England /**
Author: Engel, Elliot, 1948-
**Publication:** New York : Pocket Books, 2002
Document: English : Book
**Libraries Worldwide**: 106
More Like This: Search for versions with same title and author | Advanced options ...
⊕ See more details for locating this item

☐ 6.  ◈ **Poems by Robert Frost /**
Author: Frost, Robert, 1874-1963.; Frost, Robert,

Figure 5.1

a list or catalog, often descriptive or critical notes, of writings related to a particular subject, period or author «a *b*— of modern poetry» «a *b*— of the 17th century»; *also* a list of works *b*— of Walt Whitman» «a publisher's *b*—»3 : the works, or a list of them, mentioned in a text or consulted by an author in a production of that text — usu. Included as an appendix to the work «a *b*— of 40 books and articles» 4 : the study of bibliography or bibliographic methods «an intensive course in *b*—»

Most students are familiar with bibliographies that are citations of the works used by an author in writing a book or paper (see definition 3 above). Yet, bibliographies such as those found in definition 2 are extremely useful to the sophisticated searcher. Libraries have many bibliographies of this type that are invaluable when preparing a list of materials on a topic.

Bibliographies may be book length, containing thousands of entries, or may be only several pages in length. For instance, the *Indians of North and South America* by Carolyn Wolf is a comprehensive bibliography containing over 4,200 sources of information on that topic.

On the other hand, some bibliographies are listings of the works by a particular author, some *about* a particular author and some are both. For example the bibliography by Joan Crane, *Willa Cather: A Bibliography*, is just a list of works by Willa Cather. Yet the bibliography by John A. Stoler, *Daniel Defoe: An Annotated Bibliography of Modern Criticism, 1900–1980*, contains a list of works by Defoe *and* a list of critical analysis of Defoe's works. When using the catalog the student does a subject search. A keyword search may also produce acceptable results. Figure 5.1 shows a World-Cat search done for bibliographies on Robert Frost published between 2000 and 2004 in English in book format. The search found 10 titles. Figure 5.2 shows the results of a similar search done on the Library of Congress online catalog. A subject search for Frost, Robert, 1874–1963 — Bibliography netted 13 entries of which the first few are shown.

Other bibliographies are topical. Subjects or authors' names will be arranged alphabetically. Sometimes the student will find bibliographies that contain both subjects and authors in one alphabetical listing. Another category of bibliographies is determined by geographical area. Some of these contain items about or published in a specific country, while others may be regional or international in scope. Further, a distinction may be made on the time period with which the bibliography deals. For instance, a bibliography might contain only works of Russian authors of the 19th century.

DATABASE: Library of Congress Online Catalog
YOU SEARCHED: Subject Browse = Frost, Robert, 1874-1963 Bibliography.
SEARCH RESULTS: Displaying 1 through 13 of 13.

◀ Previous   Next ▶

Resort results by: [Date (Descending) ▼]

Add Limits to
Search Results

| # | Subject Heading | Name: Main Author, Creator, etc. | Full Title | Date |
|---|---|---|---|---|
| ☐ [1] | Frost, Robert, 1874-1963 Bibliography. | Byers, Edna Hanley, [from old catalog] | Robert Frost at Agnes Scott College. | 1963 |
| | ACCESS: Jefferson or Adams Bldg General or Area Studies Reading Rms | | | CALL NUMBER: Z8317.78 .B9 |
| ☐ [2] | Frost, Robert, 1874-1963 Bibliography. | Clymer, William Branford Shubrick. | Robert Frost, a bibliography, by W. B. Shubrick Clymer and Charles R. Green; foreword by David Lambuth. | 1937 |
| | ACCESS: Jefferson or Adams Bldg General or Area Studies Reading Rms | | | CALL NUMBER: Z8317.78 .C64 |
| ☐ [3] | Frost, Robert, 1874-1963 Bibliography. | Cramer, Jeffrey S., 1955- | Robert Frost among his poems : a literary companion to the poet's own biographical contexts and associations / by Jeffrey S. Cramer. | 1996 |
| | SELECT TITLE FOR HOLDINGS INFORMATION | | | |
| ☐ [4] | Frost, Robert, 1874-1963 Bibliography. | Dartmouth college. Library. | Fifty years of Robert Frost; | 1944 |
| | ACCESS: Jefferson or Adams Bldg General or Area Studies Reading Rms | | | CALL NUMBER: Z8317.78 .D3 |
| ☐ [5] | Frost, Robert, 1874-1963 Bibliography. | Greiner, Donald J. | Merrill checklist of Robert Frost, compiled by Donald J. Greiner. | 1969 |
| | ACCESS: Jefferson or Adams Bldg General or Area Studies Reading Rms | | | CALL NUMBER: Z8317.78 .G74 |
| ☐ [6] | Frost, Robert, 1874-1963 Bibliography. | Greiner, Donald J. | Robert Frost [by] Donald J. Greiner. | 1974 |

Figure 5.2

Some bibliographies are detailed lists of other bibliographies. A logical starting point for researching a particular topic is to consult one of these comprehensive bibliographies. Then one should see if the library has or can obtain the most useful ones. There is an extensive section in the catalog under the subject bibliography that lists most of the bibliographies in the library.

Also, bibliographies can be located under a specific subject heading that has the subheading "bibliography"—for example, air pollution–bibliography contains references to lists of information on air pollution.

The following are books that are either bibliographies or contain useful information about bibliographies.

## *Books in Print*

*Books in Print* (BIP in library lingo) is a current list of books published by *major* American publishers. Students will find a set in all libraries, book stores and other large stores with a book department. BIP is a listing of books *available for purchase.* This listing could include a book written 50 years ago if it is still available for purchase from the publisher. A book published a year ago that is no longer available for purchase will not be listed. BIP is published annually and the new edition generally is available in the fall. Most libraries will have a CD-ROM copy or an online subscription. Figure 5.3 shows the results of a search of Books in print done using FirstSearch. The search found 382 records for John Grisham. To see the complete record, click on the record.

*Books in Print* includes scholarly, popular, adult, juvenile, reprint editions and all other types of books, provided they are published or exclusively distributed in the United States and are available to the trade or to the public for single or multiple copy purchase according to the preface to BIP.

BIP has author, title, subject and publisher sections arranged alphabetically. The subject section, *Subject Guide to Books in Print*, is useful in preparing a list of books on a specific topic. The author section is a listing of the authors found in the subject section and the title section is a listing of the titles in the subject section. The publisher volume is a directory of included publishers.

The entries in BIP include the author(s) name(s), title, publisher, date of publication, price of the book, and other ordering information for libraries and book stores. The ordering information is primarily useful for

## Books in Print List of Records

- Click on a title to see the detailed record.
- Click on a checkbox to mark a record to be e-mailed or printed in Marked Records.

| Home | Databases | Searching | Results | Resource Sharing | Staff View \| My Account \| Options \| Comments \| **Exit** |
|------|-----------|-----------|---------|------------------|------------------------------------------------|

| | | | | | | Hide tips |

List of Records    Detailed Record    Marked Records    Saved Records    Go to page    ▼

**Books in Print** results for: **au: grisham, and au: john. (Save Search)**
Records found: **382**

Sort    Related Subjects    Related Authors    Limit    E-mail    Print    Export    Help

Find related:    Books etc. (WorldCat)    Articles (ArticleFirst)    Journal Articles (ECO)    Previous Searches

◀ 1 ▶
Prev    Next

☐ 1.   **Bleachers [sound recording]**
**Author:** Grisham, John, 1955-, Author, Read by; Cristil, Jack **Publication:** New York :RH Audio [Imprint]Random House Audio Publishing Group; Westminster :Random House, Incorporated [Distributor]; Sept. 2003
**Document:** English : Audio recording
⊕ See more details for locating this item

☐ 2.   **The Street Lawyer [sound recording]**
**Author:** Grisham, John, 1955-, Author; Beck, Michael **Publication:** New York :RH Audio [Imprint] Random House Audio Publishing Group; Westminster :Random House, Incorporated [Distributor]; Feb. 1998
**Document:** English : Audio recording
⊕ See more details for locating this item

☐ 3.   **The Partner [sound recording]**
**Author:** Grisham, John, 1955-, Author; Muller, Frank **Publication:** New York :RH Audio [Imprint] Random House Audio Publishing Group; Westminster :Random House, Incorporated [Distributor]; Feb. 1997
**Document:** English : Audio recording
⊕ See more details for locating this item

☐ 4.   **The Client [sound recording]**
**Author:** Grisham, John, 1955-, Author; Brown, Blair **Publication:** New York :RH Audio [Imprint] Random House Audio Publishing Group; Westminster :Random House, Incorporated [Distributor]; Feb. 1993
**Document:** English : Audio recording; Book
⊕ See more details for locating this item

☐ 5.   **The Street Lawyer [sound recording]**
**Author:** Grisham, John, 1955-, Author; Muller, Frank **Publication:** New York :RH Audio [Imprint] Random House Audio Publishing Group; Westminster :Random House, Incorporated [Distributor]; Feb. 1998
**Document:** English : Audio recording
⊕ See more details for locating this item

☐ 6.   **John Grisham Boxed Set**
**Author:** Grisham, John, 1955-, Author
**Publication:** New York : Dell Publishing; Westminster : Random House, Incorporated [Distributor], Oct. 2002

Figure 5.3

library staff but may be used by the student to order books directly from the publisher.

## Library of Congress Catalog of Printed Cards and the National Union Catalog

The *Library of Congress Catalog of Printed Cards*, commonly called the *LC Cat*, was first published in 1942 and covered the period 1898 (when cards were first printed) to 1942. Supplements in monthly, quarterly, annual and five-year accumulations have appeared since. The *LC Cat* is a reproduction of the author cards printed by the Library of Congress. The *LC Cat* is not a complete list of books at the Library of Congress because the library has books for which cards have never been printed.

Many major libraries in the United States and Canada have supplied the Library of Congress with cards of local, unusual or foreign publications that they have added to their collections. The Library of Congress has interfiled these cards with the cards they have printed, and have thus maintained a "National Union [Card] Catalog" in their Washington, D.C. main building. Each library supplying information has a letter code and the code is added to the card supplied to the Library of Congress. When several libraries supply the same information, the code for each library is added.

In 1956 the Library of Congress changed the scope of the *LC Cat* to include all the entries supplied by other libraries. The title was changed to *National Union Catalog*, NUC for short, to reflect the change in scope. The codes for all the libraries supplying information are printed after the entry. This helps to locate libraries having a copy of a particular book, which may then be borrowed through interlibrary loan (see Chapter 15).

In 1968 a commercial publisher, Mansell, began a major undertaking, the printing of the *National Union Catalog, Pre-1956 Imprints*. This catalog lists in one alphabet all the cards printed by the Library of Congress from 1898 to 1956 and all the cards supplied by other libraries up to 1956. All three categories, *LC Cat*, *NUC*, and *NUC Pre-56 Imprints* are primarily author listings.

In 1950 the Library of Congress began printing a subject approach to *LC Cat* called *Library of Congress, Books — Subjects*. It was published quarterly with annual and five-year accumulations and is arranged by the subject headings assigned to each book by the Library of Congress. The last cumulative set is 1970 to 1974. Annual volumes continued until 1982.

Beginning in 1983 the microfiche NUC contains both authors and subjects in one alphabet.

The Library of Congress now contributes all its new entries to OCLC's main database. The National Library of Canada and other national libraries contribute their new entries to OCLC's main database. All OCLC members contribute their holding to WorldCat (main database) making it an extremely comprehensive online bibliography. See Figure 5.1 for a WorldCat search for bibliographies.

## Cumulative Book Index

The *Cumulative Book Index* (CBI) is an author-title-subject world list of books published in English. It also includes some government documents, pamphlets and privately published items. All entries are in a single alphabetical list. The entries include the author(s), title, publisher, date of publication, price and other information for ordering from the publisher.

## Bibliographic Index

The *Bibliographic Index* is a bibliography of bibliographies. It is a list of bibliographies arranged by subject and where they may be found. If, for example the student desires a bibliography on prehistoric agriculture, it may be found under that subject, **Agriculture, Prehistoric** (Figure 5.4). The bibliographies included in *Bibliographic Index* may be a complete book length listing or a bibliography after a journal article, book or chapter of a book. *Bibliographic Index* is also available via WilsonWeb (see chapter 9).

## Annotated Bibliographies

Certain bibliographies are annotated — that is, they describe the books included. Some of these are lists of reference works with annotations. All libraries have bibliographies of this type and it is essential to consult them to find the best reference books on a subject.

The *Guide to Reference Books*, edited by Robert Balay (11th edition, 1996), is an excellent example and is available in all libraries. Students will

**United States**
*History*
Mooney, P. H. and Hunt, S. A. A repertoire of interpretations: master frames and ideological continuity in U.S. agrarian mobilization. *Sociol Q* v37 p194-7 Wint '96
Olmstead, A. L. and Rhode, P. W. Beyond the threshold: an analysis of the characteristics and behavior of early reaper adopters. *J Econ Hist* v55 p54-7 Mr '95

**Zambia**
Moore, Henrietta L., and Vaughan, Megan. Cutting down trees; gender, nutrition, and agricultural change in the Northern Province of Zambia, 1890-1990. Heinemann (Portsmouth); Currey, J. 1994 p255-66

**Zimbabwe**
Eicher, C. K. Zimbabwe's maize-based green revolution: preconditions for replication. *World Dev* v23 p815-17 My '95

**Agriculture, Cooperative**
*See also*
Collective farms
Deininger, K. Collective agricultural production: a solution for transition economies? *World Dev* v23 p1332-4 Ag '95

**Israel**
*See also*
Moshavim

**Peru**
Mejía, José Manuel. Cooperativas azucareras; crisis y alternativas. (Colección Textos, 1) Instituto de Investigaciónes Cambio & Desarrollo (Peru) 1992 p149-65

**Agriculture, Prehistoric**
*See also*
Agriculture—Origin
Prehistoric peoples—Food
Corn and culture in the prehistoric New World; edited by Sissel Johannessen and Christine A. Hastorf. (University of Minnesota publications in anthropology, no5) Westview Press 1994 p545-623
Oyuela-Caycedo, A. The study of collector variability in the transition to sedentary food producers in northern Colombia. *J World Prehist* v10 p88-93 Mr '96
Rowley-Conwy, P. Making first farmers younger: the West European evidence. *Curr Anthropol* v36 p352-3 Ap '95
Schurr, M. R. and Schoeninger, M. J. Associations between agricultural intensification and social complexity: an example from the prehistoric Ohio Valley. *J Anthropol Archaeol* v14 p335-9 S '95
Van Andel, T. H. and Runnels, C. N. The earliest farmers in Europe. *Antiquity* v69 p498-500 S '95

**Agriculture, Primitive** *See* Traditional farming

**Agriculture and energy**
Potoki antropogennoĭ énergii v agroékosistemakh; bibliograficheskiĭ ukazatel' literatury za 1979-1988 gg; [sostaviteli, G.A. Bulatkin et al.] Biblioteka po estestvennym naukam RAN 1992 124p

**Agriculture and state**
*See also*
Land reform
Rural development
Surplus agricultural commodities

**Figure 5.4**

find it useful to read the few introductory pages in the front of the volume. Other similar guides are available; some are general, like the *Guide to Reference Books*, and others cover only specific subjects such as astronomy or American history. A few of these guides have been published in inexpensive paperback and would be a useful addition to any student's personal library. See the list after this chapter for additional examples.

After completing the exercises after this chapter the student will have discovered that there are many different formats for bibliographies. When preparing a bibliography of one's own for an assignment, a specific format may be desired. The sensible way to decide the appropriate format is to ask the teacher if he or she has any preference. Most formats include the information in generally the same order shown here, but punctuation and spacing and other details differ.

Author (last name first). *Title*, edition number. Place of Publication: Name of Publisher, date of publication.

The most important thing to remember is to be consistent, using the same order, punctuation and spacing throughout the bibliography.

Listed below are some popular term paper guides and style sheets. They all give instruction for, and examples of, bibliographic format. Additionally these guides provide invaluable information to the term paper writer, and all students should own one.

## *Term Paper Guides* (see also Chapter 17)

*The Chicago Manual of Style*, 15th ed. Chicago: University of Chicago Press, 2003.

Fleischer, Eugene B. *A Style Manual for Citing Microfilm and Non-Print Media*. Chicago: American Library Association, 1978.

Lester, James D. *Writing Research Papers: a complete guide*. 11th ed. New York: Pearson/Longman, 2005.

*MLA Handbook for Writers of Research Papers, Theses and Dissertations*, 4th ed. Edited by Joseph Gibaldi and Walter S. Achtert, New York: Modern Language Association, 1995.

Shields, Nancy E. and Mary W. Uhle. *Where Credit is Due: a guide to proper citing of sources, print and non-print*. 2nd ed. Lanham, MD.: Scarecrow Press, 1997.

Thurston, Marjorie H., and Eugene S. Wright. *The Preparation of Term Papers and Reports*, 6th ed. Minneapolis: Burgess Publishing Company, 1970.

Turabian, Kate L. *Manual for Writers of Term Papers, Theses and Dissertations.* 6th ed. Chicago: University of Chicago Press, 1996.

VanLeunen, Mary-Claire. *A Handbook for Scholars.* 2nd ed. New York: Alfred A. Knopf, 1992.

## *Exercises for Chapter 5*

1. Find the bibliographies in your library for the two authors listed below. Answer the questions about both authors. If you have problems using the catalog or locating the books on the shelves, ask the librarian.
   (A) Edgar Allan Poe (choose subject on the OPAC menu -POE, EDGAR ALLAN 1809–1849 — BIBLIOGRAPHY) and then try a keyword search and compare the results:
       1. How many bibliographies does your library have on Poe?
       2. In what section of the library are the bibliographies located?
       3. Are the bibliographies of works *about* Poe, of works *by* Poe, or both?
       4. Do any of these bibliographies circulate?
   (B) D. H. Lawrence (choose subject on the OPAC menu LAWRENCE, DAVID HERBERT 1885–1930 — BIBLIOGRAPHY) then try a keyword search and compare the results:
       1. How many bibliographies does your library have on Lawrence?
       2. In what section of the library are the bibliographies located?
       3. Are the bibliographies of works *about* Lawrence, of works *by* Lawrence, or both?
       4. Do any of these bibliographies circulate?
2. If available in your library, read the preface to BIP, CBI and *LC Cat.*
   (A) Using the **author** section of BIP:
       1. Count and record the number of entries for Dean R. Koontz.
       2. What information is provided about each book?
   (B) Using CBI for 1989:
       1. Count and record the number of entries for Stephen King.
       2. What information is provided in each entry?
       3. Does this information differ from BIP? If so, how?

(C) Using NUC (**authors**), check the 1973–1977 accumulation for Stephen King.
    1. Count and record the number of entries.
    2. Check annual volumes or microfiche edition, if available.
    3. How do the entries differ from those in CBI and BIP?

3. The following questions are based on Princess Diana as a subject.
  (A)    Using the *Subject Guide to Books in Print*, count and record the number of entries.
  (B)    Using the last five years of CBI, count and record the number of entries.
  (C)    Under what heading(s) would you look for information about Princess Diana in a guide to reference books?
  (D)    Check WorldCat using subject and word and search for Princess Diana. Also search using Princess of Wales. Record your results.
  (E)    Which of the sources checked provided the best information?

## Important Terms in Chapter 5

This chapter has described only a few bibliographies that can be useful in identifying materials not located by using the catalog. The following list includes these plus a few more. Libraries will have many more bibliographies than those listed below. They may be found by using the subject approach to the catalog and by asking the reference librarian.

> BIP
> *NUC*
> *CBI*
> *Books-Subjects*
> *LC Cat*
> Bibliography of Bibliographies

## Important Books for Chapter 5

Aby, Stephen H., et al. *Sociology: A Guide to Reference and Information Sources.* 3rd ed. Westport, Conn.: Libraries Unlimited, 2005.

*American Reference Books Annual*, 1970–, ed. by Bohdan S. Wynar. Littleton, CO: Libraries Unlimited, 1970–.

Baker, William, and Kenneth Womack. *Twentieth-Century Bibliography and Textual Criticism: an annotated bibliography.* Westport, Conn.: Greenwood Press, 2000.

Balay, Robert. *Guide to Reference Books,* 11th ed. Chicago: American Library Association, 1996.

Besterman, Theodore. *A World Bibliography of Bibliographies and of Bibliographical Catalogues, Calendars, Abstracts, Digests, Indexes and the Like.* 4th ed., revised and greatly enlarged. Lausanne, Switzerland: Societas Bibliographica, 1965–1966. 5 vols.

*Bibliographic Index: A Cumulative Bibliography of Bibliographies,* 1937–. New York: H. W. Wilson, 1938–.

*Books in Print: An Author-Title Series Index to the "Publishers' Trade List Annual,"* 1948–. New York: R. R. Bowker, 1948–.

British Museum. Department of Printed Books. *General Catalogue of Printed Books.* Photolithographic edition to 1955. London: Trustees of the British Museum, 1959–66. 263 vols. (Supplements, 1956–1965, 1966–1970, 1971–1975, 1976–1985, 1986–1987, 1988–1989, 1990–1992, 1993–1994, 1995–1996, 1997–1998.)

*Cumulative Book Index.* New York: H. W. Wilson, 1928–.

*National Union Catalog: A Cumulative Author List Representing Library of Congress Printed Cards and Titles Reported by Other American Libraries, 1953–1957.* Ann Arbor, MI: Edwards, 1958. 28 vols. (5 year accumulations from 1958–1977.) *National Union Catalog: Books* 1983–2002 available in microfiche.

*National Union Catalog, Pre–1956 Imprints: A Cumulative Author List Representing Library of Congress Printed Cards and Titles Reported by Other American Libraries.* London: Mansell, 1968–. (610 vols.)

Scott, R. Neil. *Flannery O'Connor: An Annotated Reference Guide to Criticism.* Milledgeville, Ga.: Timberlane Books, 2002.

*Subject Guide to Books in Print: An Index to the "Publishers' Trade List Annual,"* 1957–. New York: R. R. Bowker, 1957–. Currently available in CD-ROM format.

Toomey, Alice E. *A World Bibliography of Bibliographies, 1964–1974: A List of Works Represented by Library of Congress Printed Cards:* ... Totowa, NJ.: Rowman and Littlefield, 1977. A supplement to Theodore Besterman, *A World Bibliography of Bibliographies.*

United States. Library of Congress. *A Catalog of Books Represented by Library of Congress Printed Cards, Issued to July 31, 1942.* Ann Arbor, MI: Edwards, 1942–1946. 167 vols. (Supplements cover years 1942–1952.)

Walford, Albert John. *Walford's Guide to Reference Materials,* 5th ed. London: Library Association, 1980–. (Vol. 1, 1989, v. 2 1989, v. 3 1991.)

# 6

# Book Reviews and the Parts of a Book

## Objectives

After studying this chapter the student shall be able to

- find book reviews using available sources
- identify and use the different parts of a book

## Book Reviews

After compiling a list of books on a topic, students may want to choose only several relevant ones for the term paper or other project. There are many types of book review sources and not all libraries will have all the sources.

Most books are reviewed in newspapers, periodicals and on the internet. The trick is to find the appropriate review for a specific book. Some professional journals contain no articles, just book reviews. Some examples of these are *Choice*, *New York Review of Books*, and *Booklist*. Other journals, such as *Library Journal* and *Publishers Weekly*, include many reviews as well as articles covering many topics. Specialized periodicals such as *Journal of American History* review books only in that specialty.

Newspapers often include book reviews. The *New York Times* is the most useful source of newspaper book reviews. It includes book reviews in its daily paper besides the Book Review Section of the Sunday edition.

Reviews appearing in the *New York Times* may be located by using the *New York Times Index* under the subject heading book reviews. There is a list of the books reviewed arranged alphabetically by the author's last name. Anthologies — collections of works by many authors, usually poems or short stories — are reviewed and listed alphabetically by the title and found after the author list. The *New York Times Index* shows the date of the review, then page number of the edition and the column number of that page. Roman numerals or letters identify the section number of the edition. A typical listing follows:

| Ja | 6 | III (or B) | 19: | 3 |
|---|---|---|---|---|
| [month: | [day] | [section] | [page] | [column] |
| January] | | | | |

The most efficient process for finding book reviews is to use the indexes to periodicals, either print copy or online databases. Some of these indexes specialize in book reviews, for example; *Book Review Index, Index to Book Reviews in the Humanities, Book Review Index to Social Science Periodicals* and *Current Book Review Citations*. Most libraries own at least one of the above titles. These indexes list the source of the book review, title of the periodical, volume number, date and pages. The titles of the journals containing the reviews are abbreviated and the student must check the abbreviations list at the front of the volume to get the full title of each journal. Another useful source is *Book Review Digest*, which began publishing in 1905 and is issued monthly with annual accumulations. The *Book Review Digest* includes excerpts from reviews besides listing the location of the reviews in journals. It also includes the number of words in the review — which can be a vital clue to its scope (see Figure 6.1). See Figure 6.2 for a WilsonWeb search of *Book Review Digest Plus*. Notes indicate which entries have full text reviews. The introductory page to *Book Review Digest* informs how selections for inclusions are made. To find reviews in professional or specialized journals it is necessary to consult the periodicals indexes for that field. For further discussion of periodical indexes see chapters 8 and 9.

To locate a book review, use the index for the year the book was originally written, not a reprint date. If the review is not located in that year, check the following year, as reviews will appear up to a year or more after the publication date. Not all sources of book reviews include all books and it may be necessary to consult several sources before locating a review.

500                    BOOK REVIEW DIGEST 2002

GRINT, PETER DAMIAN- *See* Damian-Grint, Peter, 1964-

GRISHAM, JOHN. Skipping Christmas. 177p $19.95 2001
    Doubleday
    1. Christmas—Fiction
    ISBN 0-385-50583-3

SUMMARY: This book "tells the story of Luther and Nora
Krank, a pair of affluent suburbanites who decide to take a pass
on Christmas. Luther, a tax accountant, discovers that the previous Christmas set him back about $6,000. Because their only
child is serving in the Peace Corps during the holidays, the
Kranks decide to save money by forgoing the obligatory gifts and
parties and instead taking a Caribbean cruise. But there's a
catch—the Kranks' pushy neighbors . . . embark on a campaign
of psychological warfare designed to snap the couple back into
the holiday spirit." (N Y Times Book Rev)

REVIEW: *Libr J* v126 no20 p170-2 D 2001. Samantha J. Gust
    (50-500w)
    "Grisham astutely captures the way many people spend the
holiday season, from fighting the crowds to commenting on their
neighbors' Christmas trees. A Painted House was Grisham's first
departure from the legal thriller genre, and this further demon-
strates his ability to tell a story with nary a courtroom in sight.
Highly recommended for all public libraries."

REVIEW: *N Y Times Book Rev* v106 no51 p17 D 23 2001.
    Adam Mazmanian (50-500w)
    "Grisham marshals his considerable skills as a thriller writer to
evoke the urgency with which the forces aligned against the
Kranks gathers strength as Christmas approaches. The result is an
odd mixture of tension, suburban comedy and schmaltz. Grisham
approximates the bizarro-world mood of an existential nightmare
but puts little of value at stake. The Kranks are just trying to
save a few bucks, not discover what's come to be called the true
meaning of Christmas. As a result, their trials leave a bitter taste
that isn't redeemed by this novel's Hollywood ending."

GRISHAM, JOHN. The summons. 341p $27.95 2002
    Doubleday
    1. Mississippi—Fiction 2. Legal stories
    ISBN 0-385-50382-2        LC 2001-58185

SUMMARY: This novel starts "with a life-altering letter. It in-
structs Ray Atlee, a 43-year-old law professor in Virginia, to return to his family's home in Clinton, a small Mississippi town.
. . . Ray's father, a respected judge, . . . is very ill and he
wants to discuss his estate with his two sons. By the time Ray
gets there, his father has died. . . . [The house] turns out to be
full of cash: $3.12 million packed in 27 boxes. Ray has no idea
where it came from or where it should go." (N Y Times Book
Rev)

REVIEW: *N Y Times Book Rev* v107 no8 p13 F 24 2002 Adam
    Liptak (1000+w)
    "Grisham tells his tale in a bright, knowing style that owes
something to country music. His evocation of small-town life in
rural Mississippi can be deft, but the action that makes up the
bulk of the book is disjointed and repetitive."

REVIEW: *N Y Times (Late N Y Ed)* p E7 F 5 2002. Janet Maslin
    (501-1000w)
    "[Mr. Grisham] successfully returns to form. . . . 'The Sum-
mons' is a swift, no-nonsense story written in a highly effective,
uncluttered fashion. . . . But behind that highly salable simplicity
is enough grounded, reflective intelligence to give this book its
ballast. Mr. Grisham seems genuinely interested in the questions
of conscience that snare Ray, and he makes them matter. As
best-seller lists attest, he knows whereof he speaks."

REVIEW: *Nation* v274 no13 p31-3 Ap 8 2002. David Corn
    (1000+w)
    "The Summons does not advance the unsteady justice-ain't-
equal populism of Grisham's previous work. That's not its mission. But in general Grisham presents the tens of millions who
glide through his popcorn novels with the view—in some books
more than others—that life is often unfair for a reason, unfair by
design, and that special interests are responsible for this. Not
quite a Nation editorial, but better than Sidney Sheldon."

GRISSELL, ERIC. Insects and gardens; in pursuit of a garden
    ecology; with photographs by Carll Goodpasture. 345p col il
    $29.95 2001 Timber Press
    577.5        1. Beneficial insects 2. Garden ecology
    ISBN 0-88192-504-7        LC 00-52791

SUMMARY: The author discusses insects that inhabit gardens,
how they affect the ecology of gardens, and how they interact
with humans. Index.

REVIEW: *Booklist* v97 no22 p2069 Ag 2001. Alice Joyce
    (50-500w)
    "With a captivating blend of humor and candor, this research
entomologist describes in detail the insect orders residing in our
gardens. . . . Maintaining a delightfully readable style, Grissell
concludes with an engagingly thought-provoking section devoted
to relationships between insects and humans. Goodpasture's fine
photographs befit Grissell's effervescent treatise."

REVIEW: *Choice* v39 no9 p1611-12 My 2002. P.K. Lago
    (50-500w)

REVIEW: *Libr J* v126 no17 p100 O 15 2001. Brian Lym
    (50-500w)

REVIEW: *N Y Times Book Rev* v106 no48 p52-3 D 2 2001.
    Verlyn Klinkenborg (50-500w)
    "Some gardeners take more inspiration from the handwashed
prose of a how-to book than they ever could from extreme color
close-ups of quivering anthers and dewy bracts. For those read
ers, there are some extremely handy books this season, like Eric
Grissell's Insects and Gardens."

GROOM, NICK, 1966-, ed. Thomas Chatterton and romantic
    culture. See Thomas Chatterton and romantic culture

GROOME, THOMAS H. What makes us Catholic; eight gifts
    for life. 320p $23.95 2001 HarperSanFrancisco
    282        1. Catholic Church
    ISBN 0-06-063398-0        LC 2001-39770

SUMMARY: This is a guide "to Catholic thought and the Catholic approach to life." (America) Index.

REVIEW: *America* v186 no12 p26-7 Ap 8-15 2002. Paul Wilkes
    (50-500w)
    "What is it about this book that troubles me, with its robust
Catholic cheerleading? . . . Grousing on devices and puffery
aside, when stripped down to its basics, Groome's book contains
a handy précis of Catholic thought. . . . More importantly, when
Professor Groome speaks from the heart at book's end, we have
both a clear call to what Catholicism can mean to a person's
life—and the demands that will be made upon us. . . . By providing four practical spiritual practices (make friends among people who are different, promote peace and compassion for people
who are far away, place no borders on our concern and prayers,
and recognize faith as an ultimate mystery, being ready to say 'I
don't know'), Groome supplies a straightforward primer for a
quite wonderful and holy Catholic life."

REVIEW: *Libr J* v127 no3 p150 F 15 2002. John-Leonard Berg
    (50-500w)

GROSENICK, UTA, ed. Women artists in the 20th and 21st
    century. See Women artists in the 20th and 21st century

GROSH, MARGARET E., ed. Designing household survey
    questionnaires for developing countries. See Designing house-
    hold survey questionnaires for developing countries

GROSS, ARIELA JULIE. Double character; slavery and mas
    tery in the antebellum southern courtroom; [by] Ariela J
    Gross. 263p il $39.50 2000 Princeton Univ. Press
    342.75        1. Slavery—Southern States 2. Courts—South
    ern States
    ISBN 0-691-05957-8        LC 00-35395

SUMMARY: "Gross uses trial court records in South Carolina,
Mississippi, Georgia, Alabama, and Louisiana to examine the
'moment of confrontation' between masters and their slaves. Focusing on the implications of this interaction for understanding
Southern culture, racial ideology, medicine, and law, Gross ar-
gues that the courts first and foremost protected slaveholders' financial investments. But the decisions of Southern courts also re-
inforced whites' understandings of white 'honor' and black 'dis-
honor,' the 'character' of the master class, and alleged peculiari-
ties of the slaves' bodies, health, and behavior." (Choice) Bibliography. Index.

Figure 6.1

Current Search: (grisham, john) <in> ALL

Records: 45

In: Book Review Digest Plus

Link To: ⑤ S·F·X LINCCWeb SFX

60% ☐ 1     *Grisham*, J. The broker. Doubleday, 2005. 357 p.
⑤ S·F·X     Review(s):
          *The New York Times Book Review* v. 110 no. 2 (Jan. 9 2005). [with excerpt]

60% ☐ 2     Bissinger, H. G. Three nights in August. Houghton Mifflin, 2005. 280 p.
⑤ S·F·X     Review(s):
          *The New York Times Book Review* v. 110 no. 18 (May 1 2005). [with excerpt]

60% ☐ 3     *Grisham*, J. The last juror. Century, 2004. 355 p.
⑤ S·F·X     Review(s):
          *New Statesman (London, England: 1996)* v. 133 (Feb. 23 2004). [with full text]

60% ☐ 4     Monks, R. A. G. Reel and rout. Brook Street Press, 2004. 350 p.
⑤ S·F·X     Review(s):
          *The Economist* v. 370 (Jan. 24 2004). [with excerpt]

60% ☐ 5     *Grisham*, J. The last juror. Doubleday, 2004. 355 p.
⑤ S·F·X     Review(s):
          *New Statesman (London, England: 1996)* v. 133 (Feb. 23 2004). [with excerpt, full text]
          *New York Times (Late New York Edition)* (Feb. 2 2004). [with excerpt]
          *Publishers Weekly* v. 251 no. 5 (Feb. 2 2004). [with full text]
          *Tennessee Bar Journal* v. 40 no. 5 (May 2004).

60% ☐ 6     *Grisham*, J. Bleachers. Doubleday, 2003. 163 p.
⑤ S·F·X     Review(s):
          *Entertainment Weekly* no. 727/728 (Sept. 12 2003). [with full text]

60% ☐ 7     *Grisham*, J. The King of Torts. 2003. p. cm
⑤ S·F·X     Review(s):
          *Entertainment Weekly* no. 695 (Feb. 14 2003). [with full text]

60% ☐ 8     *Grisham*, J. Bleachers. Doubleday, 2003. 163 p.
⑤ S·F·X     Review(s):
          *New York Times (Late New York Edition)* (Sept. 22 2003). [with excerpt]
          *School Library Journal* v. 49 no. 12 (Dec. 2003). [with full text]

**Figure 6.2**

# *Online Book Reviews*

Online book stores/suppliers such as **Amazon.com** provide book reviews. Search the site and when the title is identified, click and look for the reviews. The included reviews may be from a source listed above (*Publishers Weekly*), one written by the staff of the site or by customers who have purchased the title.

Book reviews may also be included in the databases or online journals to which the library subscribes. Online indexing services such as *ProQuest* or *InfoTrac* include book reviews. For more information on searching either of these services, see Chapter 9.

## *Parts of a Book*

Most books consist of a title page, preface, introduction, text and appendixes. Each of these parts contains useful information. Knowing where to find this information is helpful.

The title page (usually the first page with printing) gives the following information: (a) title of the book, (b) author(s), (c) publishing company, (d) place of publication, and sometimes (e) the date of publication. The back (or "verso") of the title page also contains useful information. It usually includes a copyright notice (name of the owner and a date frequently with the symbol ©) and sometimes edition and printing information (e.g., 2nd edition, 3rd printing; no such statement usually means it is a first edition). Publishers also include cataloging information including subject headings. The ISBN (International Standard Book Number) identifies the publisher in a prefix (this publisher's is 0-89950-) and the actual book is the digits following (e.g., this book is 2635-7). The ISBN number is used not only for ordering books from the publisher, but as a unique identifier of that book, that edition, etc., among a possible group of very similar titled books. The ISBN is also used as a search key in catalogs, OCLC and other databases.

Most nonfiction books have a preface where the author explains what the purpose of the book is and many include acknowledgments (thanks to certain people for providing permissions, being of help, etc.). Further, many books include an introduction that frequently includes instructions on using the book. This is particularly true of books with many charts and tables. The introduction also may provide background information that makes the text easier to understand or use. The introduction is not necessarily written by the author. Students too frequently ignore a book's introduction, which sometimes leads to confusion in interpreting or using information it provides.

The text is the main body of the work. The appendixes (often spelled "appendices") might include a bibliography, index, maps, charts, graphs, etc., which have been added after the text. Consulting the bibliography will lead to additional sources of information. Using the index will help find information in the text easily and quickly. Some books may have a detailed table of contents in the front of the book that supplements or replaces the index. Most books have some sort of table of contents for locating general categories.

## Book Review Sources

*Book Review Digest, 1905–.* New York: H. W. Wilson, 1905–.
*Book Review Index, 1965–.* Detroit: Gale Research, 1965–.
*Book Review Index to Social Science Periodicals.* Ann Arbor, MI: Pierian Press, 1978–(contents begin with 1964).
*Current Book Review Citation, 1976–1982.* New York: H. W. Wilson, 1976–1982.
*Index to Book Reviews in the Humanities, 1960–.* Detroit: Phillip, Thompson, 1960–.

## Exercises for Chapter 6

1. Look carefully at the title page, back of the title page, table of contents, and index of this book. Note how they are arranged and what information is included.
2. Select one of the books about Princess Diana that you found in BIP or other source (Chapter 5) and look for reviews in the book review sources in your library.

## Important Terms in Chapter 6

**anthologies**
*ISBN*
*New York Times Index*
*Choice*

# 7

# General Information Sources

## Objectives

After studying this chapter the student shall be able to

- distinguish among the various types of dictionaries and determine which is appropriate for a particular word
- use a variety of encyclopedias to research a topic
- list the subject dictionaries and encyclopedias in a particular subject field
- list the handbooks, yearbooks and directories available in a particular field and obtain information available from them
- look up specific information in almanacs and other sources
- find and use gazetteers and atlases

Occasionally students seek answers to specific questions or definitions for particular words. The resources that supply these answers are called *general information sources*. Students have probably used some or all references previously in school, although they didn't know how to use them efficiently. The following discussion concerns the more common sources of general information and some alternate sources.

## General Dictionaries

The most commonly used reference book is the dictionary. Yet students are often unaware that there are different types of dictionaries devised for particular uses. For most purposes a standard abridged desk size dictionary such as *The American Heritage Dictionary* is satisfactory for finding definitions of words, spelling and pronunciation. However, the standard dictionary is abridged, that means that the editors have selected the more commonly used words in the language and omitted many that are uncommon. If the student cannot locate a particular word in the standard dictionary he should consult an unabridged dictionary such as *Webster's Third New International Dictionary of the English Language Unabridged*. This volume contains many of, but not all, the words in the language, including the archaic (out of date) words, slang words and acronyms (words formed by accumulating the first letters of each of several words). These volumes are huge and expensive and are thus unlikely to be found outside of the library. These dictionaries may include special sections in the back that may be useful. A gazetteer is an alphabetical listing of famous or not-so-famous place names. Some sections contain short biographies of famous persons, such as royalty or presidents of the United States. Others contain specialized information such as flags of the countries of the world, population counts and dates of important events. A brief perusal of the back of the dictionary takes only a minute or two, but will save time later. Before using any dictionary the student should consult the directions found in the front of the book to understand the format of definitions and special symbols used, particularly pronunciation symbols.

## Special Dictionaries

Although consulting an abridged or unabridged dictionary may provide all the information that is necessary, other special dictionaries may be checked for additional or more specific information. Some of these specialized volumes are dictionaries of slang, abbreviations, rhyming (containing lists of words that rhyme, especially useful when writing poetry), synonyms (words with the same or similar meanings), antonyms (words that have opposite meaning) and acronyms.

Using dictionaries such as *A Dictionary of Modern English Usage* by Henry Fowler is an essential tool in writing. This dictionary deals with points of grammar, syntax, style, and proper use of words and their spelling and preferred pronunciation and punctuation. It also contains commonly used foreign words and their meanings. There is even a dictionary containing commonly mispronounced words and another with commonly misspelled words. There are many foreign language dictionaries translating words from one language to another as well as dictionaries of archaic languages such as Joseph T. Shipley's *Dictionary of Early English*. A thesaurus is a kind of dictionary that lists synonyms and related words for each entry word. A thesaurus is useful when you know the definition of a word and want another way of expressing it.

## Subject Dictionaries

Dictionaries have been compiled for special subject fields. Often the meaning of words varies when they are found in different subject contexts. For example, the word "mutant" in general usage usually refers to some product of genetic failure; however, the biological meaning of mutant is "any abrupt change in genetic structure," good or bad. These subject dictionaries clarify such subtle differences in meaning. The subject dictionary is considered a secondary source when the standard dictionary does not provide subtle differences.

The definitions supplied in subject dictionaries are devised by experts in that field and may differ from field to field. Subject dictionaries provide a more detailed and specific contextual definition and may provide cross-references to other useful terms. To locate these special dictionaries the subject headings in the catalog should be used. The same rules for subject headings stated in Chapter 4 apply to subject dictionaries. Also the librarian may guide one to the proper heading.

## Encyclopedias

Encyclopedias, like dictionaries, come in a variety of types. The most familiar type is the multi-volume general encyclopedia, such as the *Americana*, *Britannica* or *World Book*. Encyclopedias are also available on CDs and the internet. These may be available at the school library or purchased for use at home with your personal computer. There are also multi-volume encyclopedias in foreign languages, such as *Encyclopedia Universalis* (French), and *Gran Enciclopedia Rialp* (Spanish). Subject encyclopedias in both single volume and multi-volume sets are available. These subject encyclopedias are a valuable source of specific information. They include more detailed explanations than the ones given in general encyclopedias.

Examples of subject encyclopedias found in libraries are: *The Ency-*

**Putting several heads together often helps in solving problems.**

*clopedia of Philosophy, The Catholic Encyclopedia, International Encyclopedia of the Social Sciences, Grove's Dictionary of Music and Musicians, Encyclopedia of World Art* and *McGraw-Hill Encyclopedia of Science and Technology.* These are just a few examples of the hundreds of subject encyclopedias available. Most topical areas have encyclopedias associated with them.

The information in encyclopedias is updated, but not necessarily regularly. Information is added and deleted with new editions. The size of the article may change with new editions depending on new information and space available. Some articles go unchanged for ten years or longer. One must read the introductory statement in an encyclopedia to determine its policy on updating information and its frequency of publishing new editions. Some encyclopedias contain a manual to help in using that particular set. Finally, encyclopedias contain only summaries of important information and should not be considered the final word. One should keep in mind also that articles are usually written by individual experts and may contain opinions with which not every expert agrees.

# Handbooks, Directories...

Everyone, at one time or another needs some bit of information and thinks, "There must be a quick way to find this." There are many reference books that provide specific short answers and facts. Handbooks instruct on how to find and use this information. Handbooks are available on all subjects. It is vital to become familiar with the ones in a major field of interest and students may even wish to purchase one in their chosen field. The *Library Research Guide to Nursing* by Strauch contains information on the use of reference books and the major ones available, lists of indexes and available periodicals published in nursing. The *Handbook of Chemistry and Physics* contains graphs, tables and charts that are used frequently.

Yearbooks contain updated information in particular subject fields. These are extremely valuable, because besides periodicals, they contain the most current information available. *The Annual Review of Psychology* has summaries of selected topics with extensive bibliographies. These topics, however, vary from year to year. Such reviews are excellent starting points for researching topics for a paper since they are current and complete. A student or practitioner in a particular field would be well-advised to purchase or periodically read the annual reviews.

Almanacs are particularly handy in that they provide some unusually specific or obscure information. The *World Almanac* contains data such as the capitals of all the countries of the world, weights and measures used, the birth and death dates of famous persons, zip codes, addresses, population figures, records, and maps and so on. It is also an inexpensive purchase. Besides a dictionary, the almanac is a wise acquisition for the student. Although data are added or changed yearly, an almanac several years old is still valuable. Most libraries own several almanacs, which increases the probability that a particular item of information may be found.

Directories cover many subjects. Of course, the telephone book is a directory. Basically, all directories are lists of names, addresses and phone numbers. Some directories are annotated; that is, they include some explanation about the organization or corporation listed. See the list after this chapter for examples of directories. Information that may not appear in almanacs and encyclopedias may be found in statistical yearbooks, newspaper and periodical indexes.

If current events information is needed and the newspapers are unable to supply the needed information, try another current source such as

*Keesing's Contemporary Archives, Congressional Quarterly Weekly Report* or *Facts on File*. Most libraries will have at least one of these sources. The Internet also provides current information and in some sites information is updated as often as minutely (stock market quotes, for example).

## Atlases and Gazetteers

There are many sources providing geographical information. Encyclopedias, almanacs and telephone directories all provide some geographical information and maps. Further, travel guides are valuable sources of information, including maps and textual information. Some travel guides are commercially produced hardcover books and others are inexpensive paperbacks produced by organizations such as the big oil companies (Mobil and Exxon travel guides, for example). Some organizations such as the American Automobile Association (AAA) also produce comprehensive travel guides. Commercially produced guides, of course, may be somewhat biased.

Commonly used sources of geographical information are atlases and gazetteers. Atlases contain maps and charts with all sorts of geographical information. Consult the map of the library you produced in Chapter 1 to locate atlases in the library. Besides a collection of maps, they frequently contain: 1. Population data; 2. Mileage charts; 3. Statistics on imports and exports; 4. Information on rainfall, agricultural and natural resources; 5. Tourist attractions and national parks; and 6. Photographs of cities and scenery. Gazetteers are lists of place names and people. A gazetteer is very helpful in locating places which have undergone a name change. Gazetteers may be separate volumes or appended to atlases.

## Exercises for Chapter 7

1. Look up and record (briefly) the meaning of "memory" in the following:
    an unabridged dictionary
    an abridged dictionary
    any biological dictionary
    any social sciences dictionary
    any thesaurus
2. Look up and record the meaning(s) of "hip" in the following:

an unabridged dictionary
an abridged dictionary
any slang dictionary
any abbreviations dictionary
any acronyms dictionary

3. (A)   Look up your home state or your hometown in two different encyclopedias (e.g., *Americana* and *World Book* and compare the entries.

   (B)   Look up "organic gardening" in two general encyclopedias and any subject encyclopedia you think may include an entry. Compare the articles and indicate the titles of the encyclopedias you checked.

4. List the subject dictionaries and encyclopedias in your major field of interest. Record the call numbers for future reference.

5. Locate on the shelves all the titles listed in question 4. Indicate which items circulate and which ones are multi-volume sets.

6. Take a term or concept in your major field of interest and look it up in a general encyclopedia and an encyclopedia in that subject. List the term or concept and briefly compare the articles.

7. Using the catalog, make a list of handbooks and guides in your library that deal with your major field of interest.

8. Locate in the catalog and on the shelves the almanacs and telephone directories. Do they circulate? If yes, explain briefly.

9. In general do yearbooks like *Statistical Abstracts of the United States* and the ones published by the United Nations circulate? Explain why or why not.

10. Using almanacs and statistical sources look up your hometown or state and the college you attend (or one you know about).

    (A)   How does this information on your hometown compare to what you found in the encyclopedia earlier?

    (B)   Is the information about the college accurate?

    (C)   Where else might you look for information about colleges?

11. (A)   What kind of information does the telephone directory provide in the yellow pages? The Blue Pages?

    (B)   Are zip codes in the phone book? If yes, where?

    (C)   Are area codes listed in the phone book? If so, where?

    (D)   What information about a community can be obtained by looking through the yellow pages, green pages, blue pages, and other sections?

12. Using the types of sources discussed in this chapter, answer the

**A comfortable spot to read current periodicals.**

following questions. List the sources checked and those which provided information useful in answering the question.

(A)   Using three sources, find the address, zip code and phone number of McGraw-Hill, Inc., publishers.

(B)   Using at least three sources, find the population of Chicago, Illinois.

(C)   Using five sources, list the population, geographical area and political leaders of Canada.

13. Check the catalog and record the titles and call numbers of two gazetteers in your library.

14. Locate the atlases in your library, look through five, and record the types of information they contain in addition to maps.

## Important Terms for Chapter 7

almanacs

*handbooks*

*yearbooks*

*unabridged*
*abridged*
*thesaurus*
*directory*
*atlas*
*gazetteer*
*synonyms*
*antonyms*
*acronyms*

# Important Books for Chapter 7

## DIRECTORIES

*American Art Directory*, v. 1–, 1898–. New York: Bowker, 1899–. Every 3 years, 1952–. Addresses and information about art organizations, and traveling booking agencies.

*Annual Directory of Environmental Information Sources*, 1971–. Boston: National Foundation for Environmental Control, 1971–. Addresses of agencies and organizations, lists of books, documents, reports, periodicals and films on the environment.

*Encyclopedia of Associations*. Detroit: Gale Research, 1956–. Revised approximately every 2 years; 4 vol. Addresses and descriptions of organizations. Also lists defunct organizations.

*National Faculty Directory*, 1970–. Detroit: Gale Research, 1970–. Annual, 3 vols. Names and college or university affiliations of fulltime teaching faculty. Schools not listed did not submit requested information.

*New York State Industrial Directory*, 1959–. New York: State Industrial Directories Corp., 1959–. Annual, Available for each of the 50 states. Names and addresses of industries including company offices, number of employees and products manufactured.

Towell, Julie, and Charles B. Montney. *Directories in Print*. Detroit: Gale Research 1989–. Annual. (Formerly *The Directory of Directories*.) An annotated classified list of directories with title and subject index.

## ALMANACS

Barone, Michael. *Almanac of American Politics*. Washington, D.C.: National Journal, 1972–. Annual. Arranged by state. Includes state and congressional districts, elected officials, campaign financing, congressional committees, etc.

*Information Please Almanac, Atlas and Yearbook, 1947–.* Planned and supervised by Dan Golenpaul Associates. New York: Simon & Schuster, 1947–. Annual. Miscellaneous information, extensive historical and statistical information on the U.S., a general subject index and short biography section.

*Japan Almanac.* Tokyo: Mainichi Newspapers. In English, short articles on many aspects of Japanese history, culture and daily life, statistics and biographies, index.

*The World Almanac and Book of Facts, 1868–.* New York: World Telegram, 1868–. Annual. Now published by Pharos Books and distributed by St. Martin's Press. Up-to-date, reliable statistics; most comprehensive and most frequently used of all U.S. almanacs.

Wright, John W. editor. *2005 New York Times Almanac.* New York, NY: Penguin, 2004.

## ENCYCLOPEDIAS

Barber, Nigel. *Encyclopedia of Ethics in Science and Technology.* New York: Facts on File, 2002.

*The Catholic Encyclopedia: An International Work of References on the Constitution, Doctrine, Discipline and History of the Catholic Church.* New York: Catholic Encyclopedia Press, 1907–1922. 17 vols. Many long articles by experts. In addition to Catholic doctrine articles on general subjects such as literature and history. Somewhat out of date but still valuable. For newer information see the *New Catholic Encyclopedia* 2nd edition published by Thomson/Gale, 2003.

*Encyclopedia of Bioethics.* Stephen G. Post ed. 3rd edition. New York.: Macmillan, 2004, 5 vols. Deals with many aspects of bioethics including such questions as abortion, euthanasia and the definition of death.

*Encyclopedia of Psychology.* Alan E. Kazdin, editor in chief. Washington, D.C.: American Psychological Association; Oxford {Oxfordshire}; New York: Oxford University Press, 2000. 8 volumes.

*Encyclopedia of Sociology.* Edgar F. Borgatta, editor in chief. 2nd edition New York: Macmillan Reference USA, 2000. 5 vols

*Encyclopedia of World Art.* New York: McGraw-Hill, 1959–1968. Fifteen vols. plus two supplementary vols. Long articles with bibliographies. Approximately half of each volume is plates. All areas of art are included as well as all countries and periods.

*International Encyclopedia of the Social Sciences.* David L. Sill, ed. New York: Macmillan and the Free Press, 1968. 18 vols. Articles deal with all aspects of the social sciences, many cross references are included, some biographies and a good index. Updates have been issued as encyclopedias in various areas such as criminal law, justice, Third World, etc. Most of these are 2–4 volumes.

*McGraw-Hill Encyclopedia of Science and Technology.* An international reference work, 9th ed. New York: McGraw-Hill, 2002. 20 vols. Covers all branches of science except medicine and the behavioral sciences. Index volume. The set is kept updated with annual yearbooks.

## YEARBOOKS

*Demographic Yearbook/Annuaire Demographique, 1948–.* New York: United Nations, 1948–. International demographic statistics from approximately 220 countries. This is one of a series of statistical yearbooks compiled by the United Nations.

*Historic Documents of 19XX–.* Washington, DC: Congressional Quarterly, Inc., 1972–. Annual. Chronological arrangement of speeches, letters, reports, etc., of importance. Cumulative index included in each volume. Detailed table of contents.

*Statesman's Yearbook: A Statistical and Historical Account of the States of the World, 1864–.* London, New York: Macmillan, 1864–. Not an almanac but brief and reliable descriptions, statistical information about countries of the world. Includes the countries' leaders, ambassadors and embassies and a bibliography of statistical information for each country.

United Nations. Statistical Office. *Yearbook of International Trade Statistics, 1950–.* New York: United Nations, 1951–. Annual. Provides annual trade statistics, imports and exports, many tables have comparative figures for several years.

United States Bureau of the Census. *Statistical Abstracts of the United States, 1878–.* Washington, D.C.: U.S. Gov. Printing Office, 1879–. Annual. Statistical summaries, most tables cover several years. First source to use national statistics. Leads users to other important statistical sources. Has useful supplements such as *County and City Data Book.*

## HANDBOOKS AND GUIDES

Dolphin, Warren D. *Biological Investigations: Form, Function, Diversity, and Process.* 7th ed. Boston: McGraw-Hill Higher Education, 2005.

*Facts on File Biology Handbook.* The Diagram Group. Rev. ed. New York: Facts on File, 2006.

Frick, Elizabeth. *History: Illustrated Search Strategy and Sources.* 2nd ed. Ann Arbor, MI: Pierian Press, 1995. This is the latest in a series of library research guides from Pierian Press. They include information on selecting topics, organizing term papers, using the literature in the field (includes sample pages of reference sources), computerized literature searching an other aspects of library research.

Gibaldi, Joseph, and Walter S. Achtert. *MLA Handbook for Writers of Research Papers*, 4th ed. New York: Modern Language Association of America, 1995. Widely used standards for preparation of articles, papers and books. This style information is also found in several term paper guides. See the bibliography at the end of Chapter 17.

*Handbook of Chemistry and Physics.* A ready reference book of chemical and physical data. Cleveland: Chemical Rubber, 1913–. 84th ed., 2003.

*South American Handbook.* A yearbook and guide to the countries and resources of South and Central America, Mexico and the West Indies, 1924–. London: Trade and Travel Pubs., 1924–. Descriptions of national history, government, travel and other information on the countries included.

Sweetland, James H. *Fundamental Reference Sources.* 3rd ed. Chicago: American Library Association, 2001.

## SPECIAL DICTIONARIES

Butress, F. A. *World Guide to Abbreviations of Organizations*, 11th ed., Detroit: Gale Research, 1997.

*Chambers Synonyms and Antonyms.* Edited by Martin H. Manser. Edinburgh: Chambers, 2004.

Drucker, Jamie. *What's Up? A Guide to American Collegespeak: Slang & Idioms for TOEFL Students.* Lawrenceville, NJ: Peterson's, 2003.

Ehrlich, Eugene H. *NBC Handbook of Pronunciation.* 4th ed., revised and updated. Introduction by Edwin Newman. New York, N.Y.; Harper-Perennial, 1991.

Fowler, Henry Watson. *Dictionary of Modern English Usage.* With an introduction by Simon Winchester. 1st ed. Oxford; New York: Oxford University Press, 2002.

*International Thesaurus of Refugee Terminology* [electronic source]. UNHCR, the UN Refugee Agency. [Geneva, Switzerland?]: United Nations High Commissioner for Refugees, 2003- . Online thesaurus of indexing terms related to refugee and forced-migration information.

Kacirk, Jeffrey. *Informal English: Puncture Ladies, Egg Harbors, Mississippi Marbles, and Other Curious Words and Phrases of North America.* New York: Simon & Schuster, 2005.

Kipfer, Barbara Ann. *Roget's 21st Century Thesaurus in Dictionary Form: The Essential Reference for Home, School, or Office.* 3rd ed, New York: Delta Trade Paperbacks, 2005.

Most libraries have a collection of phone books for the local area and major cities.

*Merriam-Webster's Rhyming Dictionary.* Springfield, Mass.: Merriam-Webster, 2002.

*Oxford English Dictionary*, 2nd ed. Edited by J. A. Simpson and Edmund S. Weiner. Oxford, England: Oxford University Press, 1989. 20 vols. Also available on CD and online. Online edition is updated quarterly.

*Roget's International Thesaurus.* Edited by Barbara Ann Kipfer; Robert L. Chapman, consulting editor. 6th ed. New York: HarperCollins, 2001.

Seely, John. *Oxford A-Z of Grammar and Punctuation*. New York: Oxford University Press, 2004.

Skeat, Walter W. *An Etymological Dictionary of the English Language*. Mineola, NY: Dover Publications, 2005.

Upton, Clive. *Oxford Rhyming Dictionary*. Oxford, [England]; New York: Oxford University Press, 2004.

## ATLASES AND GAZETTEERS

Alexander, Gerald L. *Guide to Atlases: World, Regional, National, Thematic*. Metuchen, NJ: Scarecrow, 1971. An international listing of atlases published since 1950. A supplement for atlases published 1971–1975 with comprehensive indexes published by Scarecrow Press, 1977.

American Geographical Society of New York. Maps Department. *Index to Maps in Books and Periodicals*. Boston: G. K. Hall, 1969. 10 vols., supplements in 1971, 1976, 1987.

Barraclough, Geoffrey, ed. *The Times Atlas of World History*, 4th rev. ed. Maplewood, NJ: Hammond, 1993.

Byrne, Charles J., *Lunar Orbiter Photographic Atlas of the Near Side of the Moon*. New York: Springer, 2005.

*Chambers World Gazetteer: A Geographical Dictionary*. Edited by David Munro. New York: Cambridge University Press, 1990. Reprint of a 1988 edition with a slightly different title.

Cobb, David A. *Guide to U.S. Map Resources*. 3rd ed. Lanham, Md.: Scarecrow Press, 2005.

*Columbia Gazetteer of the World*. Ed. by Saul B. Cohen. 3 vols. New York: Columbia University Press, 1998.

George Philip & Son. *Oxford Atlas of the World*. 4th ed. New York: Oxford University Press, 1996.

*Goode's World Atlas*. Edward B. Espenshade, Jr., Senior editor, Consultant Joel L. Morrison. 21st ed. Chicago: Rand McNally, 2005.

*Merriam-Webster's Geographical Dictionary*. 3rd ed. Springfield, Mass.: Merriam-Webster, 1997.

Rand McNally and Company. *Rand McNally Premier World Atlas*. Chicago: Rand McNally, 1997.

Shepherd, William Robert. *Historical Atlas*. 9th ed. New York: Barnes & Noble, 1964. Reprinted 1980.

The Times. London. *The Times Atlas of the World: Comprehensive Edition*. 11th ed. London: Times Books, 2003. Considered the best atlas available.

U.S. Board on Geographical Names. *Gazetteer*, no. 130–142. Washington, D.C. GOP, 1974–1977.

# 8

# Periodicals and Newspapers

## Objectives

After studying this chapter the student shall be able to

- identify the different types of periodicals and locate them in the library
- find specific information in periodicals
- distinguish between indexes and abstracts
- locate appropriate indexes and abstracts and use them to find information
- determine how to find periodicals at remote libraries
- find specific information in newspapers

## Periodical Indexes

What is a periodical? What is a journal? What is a magazine? Students and teachers frequently use these terms. While there are slight differences in their meanings, for the purposes of this discussion these terms are identical and will be used interchangeably. They are publications that appear at regular, short intervals and contain articles, stories, poems, and essays about a specific subject, aimed at a specific age group, or at some other grouping determined by the editors.

For some students, the use of periodicals can be frustrating. They can't find anything pertinent in them. This is unfortunate because periodicals are vital in preparing most reports or term papers. The informa-

**Most libraries keep a three-month backfile of newspapers.**

tion in them is usually more current than the information in books. Finding information in periodicals is not hopeless if the student uses the indexes to periodicals as tools.

Everyone has used an index of some sort, and most people are familiar with the indexes at the back of books. Everyone has used the yellow pages of a telephone directory, which is a type of index.

Individual periodicals may include an index for each volume or multi-volume indexes. Yet, these indexes are useful only if one knows which volume is needed. Unfortunately, this is not the typical situation. Therefore, *subject* indexes are more useful than *volume* indexes.

If students need the titles of journals published in a specific subject, they should consult a periodical directory. They are usually arranged by subject or have a subject index. Libraries will have at least one of the following directories: *Magazines for Libraries, The Standard Periodical Directory* or *Ulrich's International Periodical Directory*. Directories of periodicals in broad subjects (e.g. science) are also available. To enable one to find information published in journals, many comprehensive indexes and abstracts are available and are grouped into four categories:

1. *general*, that includes all relevant journals
2. *subject*, that are topic specific
3. *current*, only those of the present year or past two years
4. *retrospective*, covering a specific period of years.

Many are published by the same company and are in the same format. Having learned to use the "Wilson index" format, one can use almost every other index. The major difference between indexes is in which periodicals are included. The formats are similar.

An entry in a Wilson index under a particular subject heading includes:

1. title of the article
2. author's name
3. title of the journal, frequently abbreviated
4. date, which may include day, month and year
5. volume number
6. issue number
7. pages (see Figure 8.1)

Various indexes may not provide the information in the same order but all the information will be included. Indexes are published weekly, biweekly, monthly, quarterly and semiannually.

Perhaps the best known index and the most used is the *Reader's Guide to Periodical Literature* (RGPL), Figure 8.1 H. W. Wilson, publisher. The *Reader's Guide* indexes approximately 220 periodicals of general interest (popular magazines) and contains magazines such as *Life, Sports Illustrated, Time* and *U.S. News*. The *Readers Guide* is current and general. An example of a general, retrospective index is *Poole's Index to Periodical Literature* that covers the years 1802–1906. An example of a current and subject index is the *Business Periodicals Index*, which indexes approximately 300 journals in the fields of business and economics.

## FirstSearch

OCLC's FirstSearch is available from more than 20,000 libraries worldwide. New FirstSearch introduced in 1999 includes 75 databases/indexes covering the fields of humanities, sciences and social studies. Individual libraries contract with OCLC to make some or all of FirstSearch databases available. FirstSearch may be an option on the OPAC or accessed via a terminal devoted to the Internet.

UNITED NATIONS—*cont.*
                **Bosnia and Herzegovina**
    *See also*
    International Criminal Tribunal for the Former Yugoslavia
                **Croatia**
    *See also*
    International Criminal Tribunal for the Former Yugoslavia
                **Developing countries**
    *See also*
    United Nations Development Fund for Women
    United Nations Development Programme
                **Kosovo (Serbia)**
    *See also*
    International Criminal Tribunal for the Former Yugoslavia
                **United States**
    Our girl at the U.N. K. O'Beirne. *National Review* v54 no6
        p20-2 Ap 8 2002
UNITED NATIONS. COMMISSION ON THE STATUS OF
    WOMEN
    Our girl at the U.N. K. O'Beirne. *National Review* v54 no6
        p20-2 Ap 8 2002
UNITED NATIONS. HIGH COMMISSIONER FOR REFU-
    GEES
    West Africa: sex-for-food scandal [report by the UNHCR] S.
        Coleman. *World Press Review* v49 no5 p29 My 2002
UNITED NATIONS. OFFICE OF THE HIGH COMMIS-
    SIONER FOR REFUGEES *See* United Nations. High
    Commissioner for Refugees
UNITED NATIONS. WORLD FOOD PROGRAMME *See*
    World Food Programme
UNITED NATIONS DEVELOPMENT FUND FOR WOMEN
    A conversation with Noeleen Heyzer. D. Todd. por *Choices
        (New York, N.Y.)* v11 no1 p18-19 Mr 2002
    Women's rights and human security [partnerships of women
        uniting for peace in both developed and developing coun-
        tries] M. M. Brown. il *Choices (New York, N.Y.)* v11 no1
        p4 Mr 2002
UNITED NATIONS DEVELOPMENT PROGRAMME
    Afghan nationals in vanguard of UNDP initiative. S. Zulfiqar.
        *Choices (New York, N.Y.)* v11 no1 p23 Mr 2002
    The hard path to gender equality. A. Zaoude. il *Choices (New
        York, N.Y.)* v11 no1 p7 Mr 2002
    MicroStart makes a difference. E. Rabemananoro. il map
        *Choices (New York, N.Y.)* v11 no1 p12-13 Mr 2002
    Nation at the crossroads. D. Lockwood. il map *Choices (New
        York, N.Y.)* v11 no1 p20-1 Mr 2002
    Ray of hope for sex workers and their children. S. Shames. il
        map *Choices (New York, N.Y.)* v11 no1 p14-15 Mr 2002
    Restoring an oasis strengthens communities in Jordan. N.
        Gouede. il map *Choices (New York, N.Y.)* v11 no1 p10-11
        Mr 2002
    The true meaning of wealth. M. Konno. il *Choices (New York,
        N.Y.)* v11 no1 p25 Mr 2002
    Women's rights and human security [partnerships of women
        uniting for peace in both developed and developing coun-
        tries] M. M. Brown. il *Choices (New York, N.Y.)* v11 no1
        p4 Mr 2002
UNITED NATIONS DEVELOPMENT PROGRAMME. THE-
    MATIC TRUST FUND ON GENDER *See* Thematic Trust
    Fund on Gender
UNITED NATIONS ENVIRONMENT PROGRAMME
    Emeralds of the Cauto [women's role in reforestation in
        Cuba's Cauto River Basin] A. D. Pérez. il map *Choices
        (New York, N.Y.)* v11 no1 p8-9 Mr 2002
UNITED NATIONS INTERNATIONAL ATOMIC ENERGY
    AGENCY *See* International Atomic Energy Agency
UNITED ONLINE INC.
    The battle of his life [M. Goldston's turnaround for United
        Online] A. Weintraub. por *Business Week* no3774 p
        EB18-EB19 Mr 18 2002
UNITED STATES
            *See also*
    Americans
    Southern States
    States (U.S.)
    Western States
                **Appropriations and expenditures**
            *See also*
    Budget—United States
    Off-budget programs
    Pork barrel legislation
                **Armed Forces**
            *See also*
    Servicemen
    United States. Army
    United States. Dept. of Defense
    United States. Navy

When in the Rome treaty—get out: amd get out now. L. A.
    Casey and D. B. Rivkin. *National Review* v54 no5 p27-30
    Mr 25 2002
                *Forces in Afghanistan*
    After Anaconda: Al Qaeda regroups. R. Nordland and others.
        il *Newsweek* v139 no12 p6 Mr 25 2002
    Black Hawk up [argument for use of U.S. ground troops in
        Afghanistan] *The New Republic* v226 no11 p9 Mr 25 2002
    'Leave no man behind' [American casualties in Operation An-
        aconda; cover story] E. Thomas. il map *Newsweek* v139
        no11 p22-7 Mr 18 2002
    On the mop-up patrol [special forces and Afghan allies] M.
        Ware. il *Time* v159 no12 p44-5 Mr 25 2002
    Operation Anaconda [battle of Shah-i-Kot; cover story] M. El-
        liott. il map *Time* v159 no11 p34-45 Mr 18 2002
    To the death [Operation Anaconda in Shah-i-Kot Valley, Af-
        ghanistan] B. Fang and M. Mazzetti. il map *U.S. News &
        World Report* v132 no8 p16-20 Mr 18 2002
                *Forces in Georgia (Republic)*
    Is Washington fighting terrorism on too many fronts? [in for-
        mer Soviet republics] P. Starobin. il *Business Week* no3774
        p57 Mr 18 2002
                *Forces in the Philippines*
    'Terrorist cells all over' [U.S. forces in the Philippines; inter-
        view with G. Macapagal-Arroyo] L. Weymouth. por
        *Newsweek* v139 no6 p36 F 11 2002
                *Forces in Vietnam*
            *See also*
    Vietnamese War, 1957-1975—American participation
                *Recruiting, enlistment, etc.*
            *See also*
    Military service, Voluntary
    Uncle Sam wants them. R. Long. *National Review* v54 no5
        p32-3 Mr 25 2002
                *Reserves*
            *See also*
    United States. Naval Reserve
    Serving on two fronts [role of National Guard and Army re-
        servists in war on terrorism] il *People Weekly* v56 no19
        p60-5 N 5 2001
                *Special Forces*
            *See also*
    United States. Special Operations Command
    'Leave no man behind' [American casualties in Operation An-
        aconda; cover story] E. Thomas. il map *Newsweek* v139
        no11 p22-7 Mr 18 2002
    On the mop-up patrol [special forces and Afghan allies] M.
        Ware. il *Time* v159 no12 p44-5 Mr 25 2002
                **Boundaries**
    Border wars. *National Review* v54 no6 p14-15 Ap 8 2002
    May we get serious now? [controlling our borders, at long last]
        J. O'Sullivan. *National Review* v54 no7 p23-4 Ap 22 2002
    The migrant's story. R. Martinez. *The Nation* v274 no13 p6-7,
        24 Ap 8 2002
    Terrorism and trade: America the vulnerable [globalization has
        opened up U.S. borders to terrorism] S. E. Flynn. *Current
        (Washington, D.C.)* no440 p3-9 F 2002
                **Census**
            *See also*
    United States. Bureau of the Census
    Black elected officials increased six-fold since 1970: study. il
        *Jet* v101 no17 p4-5 Ap 15 2002
    Latest census resets U.S. population clock. S. Perkins. *Science
        News* v161 no8 p117-18 F 23 2002
                **Civilization**
            *See also*
    Social change
    United States—Popular culture
    United States—Social conditions
    Among the bourgeoisophobes: why the Europeans and Arabs,
        each in their own way, hate America and Israel [cover story]
        D. Brooks. il *Weekly Standard* v7 no30 p20-7 Ap 15 2002
                **Commerce**
            *See also*
    Balance of trade
    Investments, American
    Pocket protector: Chuck Hagel, the Senate's newest wise man.
        L. F. Kaplan. por *The New Republic* v226 no10 p17-19 Mr
        18 2002
                *Africa*
    How Susie Bayer's T-shirt ended up on Yusuf Mama's back
        [sale of used clothing to Africans] G. Packer. il *The New
        York Times Magazine* p54-9 Mr 31 2002
                *Canada*
            *See also*
    North American Free Trade Agreement

**Figure 8.1**

FirstSearch databases will indicated when and how often they are updated and if full text is available. Three levels of searching, Basic, Advanced and Expert are available. Search statements may contain Boolean operators, wildcards, truncation and plurals. Records may be printed, e-mailed, exported or requested via interlibrary loan. Ask the librarian about your library's policies.

ArticleFirst is one of the FirstSearch databases. As of June 2005 ArticleFirst had 12.7 million records from more than 12,000 sources. Figure 8.2 is a keyword search for osteoporosis in menopausal women published in 2005. Note the search statement at the top of the results list. This search identified 4 articles. Each entry includes the usual citation information PLUS the number of libraries worldwide that hold that particular journal title. Figure 8.3 is a display for the first article on the list of Figure 8.2. Note the tags at the left margin. Pay attention to the Availability tag and the option to search the catalog at your library.

## *CARL UnCover*

Some libraries subscribe to CARL UnCover, an article database at the Colorado Alliance of Research Libraries. This database includes more than 15,000 periodical titles and 5 million articles (full text) dating from the fall of 1988. A variety of search options provide easy and rapid identification of articles. For fast service CARL will FAX the full text, for a fee, minimum cost of $9.50 per article (as of summer 2005). If your library subscribes to CARL be sure to check with the librarian for information on costs, interlibrary loan possibilities and other CARL features.

## *Abstracts*

Annotated indexes, known as abstracts, include additional information. They include all the information found in the index citation plus a brief description or summary of the article. This enables the user to figure out the content of the article without reading it. This may save time, enabling the user to select articles to be read in a quick and easy way. Yet, these abstracts may not always be accurate; caution is the watchword when using abstracts. If the student is unsure, it is advisable to consult the article directly before discarding it. Abstracts may be prepared by the author of the article or by someone else who probably works for the publisher or

## ArticleFirst List of Records

- Click on a title to see the detailed record.
- Click on a checkbox to mark a record to be e-mailed or printed in Marked Records.

| Home | Databases | Searching | Results | Staff View | My Account | Options | Comments |
| | | | | | | | **Exit** | Hide tips |

List of Records    Detailed Record    Marked Records    Saved Records    Go to page ▼

Sort  Related  Limit  E-mail  Print  Export  Help    **ArticleFirst** results for: **(kw: osteoporosis and kw:**
      Authors                                        **women) and kw: menopausal and yr: 2005.**
                                                     **(Save Search)**
                                                     Records found: **4**

Find related:    **Books etc.**         **Articles**         **Journal Articles**         **Previous Searches**
                 (WorldCat)           (ArticleFirst)           (ECO)

◀ 1 ▶
Prev    Next

☐ 1.  **Exercise Effects on Menopausal Risk Factors of Early Postmenopausal
       Women: 3-yr Erlangen Fitness Osteoporosis Prevention Study Results**
       **Author:** Kemmler, Wolfgang; Von Stengel, Simon; Weineck, Jurgen, and others **Source:** Medicine
       and science in sports and exercise. 37, no. 2, (2005): 194 (10 pages) **Libraries Worldwide:** 1108
       ⊕ See more details for locating this item

☐ 2.  **Association of PvuII and XbaI polymorphism of estrogen receptor alpha
       gene with risk of osteoporosis in women of menopausal age. Moscow
       population**
       **Author:** Tagieva, A. N. **Source:** Problemy reproduktsii. 11, no. 1, (2005): 64-67
       **Libraries Worldwide:** 3  ⊕ See more details for locating this item

☐ 3.  **A COMPARISON OF THE EFFECTS OF RALOXIFENE AND ALENDRONATE
       ON LIPID PROFILES AND BONE MINERAL DENSITY IN POST-
       MENOPAUSAL OSTEOPOROTIC WOMEN: A 1 YEAR STUDY**
       **Author:** Kokino, S.; Ozdemir, F.; Demirhag, D. **Source:** Osteoporosis international : a journal
       established as result of cooperation between the European Foundation for Osteoporosis and the
       National Osteoporosis Foundation of the USA. 16, SUPP/3 (2005): P170 **Libraries Worldwide:** 160
       ⊕ See more details for locating this item

☐ 4.  **POTENTIAL COST-EFFECTIVE USE OF SPINE RADIOGRAPHS TO DETECT
       VERTEBRAL DEFORMITY AND SELECT OSTEOPENIC POST-MENOPAUSAL
       WOMEN FOR AMINO-BISPHOSPHONATE THERAPY**
       **Author:** Schousboe, J.; Ensrud, K.; Nyman, J., and others **Source:** Osteoporosis international : a
       journal established as result of cooperation between the European Foundation for Osteoporosis and
       the National Osteoporosis Foundation of the USA. 16, SUPP/3 (2005): OC13
       **Libraries Worldwide:** 160  ⊕ See more details for locating this item

Figure 8.2

abstracting service. To find the title of indexes or abstracts in a specific field in the library, look under the subject (in the catalog) and then look for the subheading indexes or abstracts. For example, chemistry — abstracts — periodicals.

Indexes and abstracts are generally arranged by subject, although some indexes interfile authors with subjects in one alphabet. Others have separate author index and cross-references back to the subject section. The abstracts are usually numbered. Most abstracting services begin each volume with number 1. It is important to consult the proper volume. Most

## ArticleFirst Detailed Record

- Click on a checkbox to mark a record to be e-mailed or printed in Marked Records.

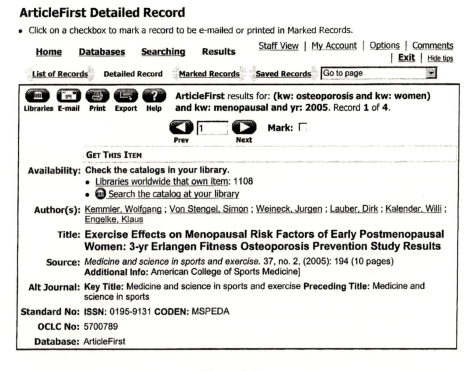

Figure 8.3

abstracting services today are available online and many have digitized their retrospective volumes. Thus those abstracting services have provided additional access to older information to more people, improved the means of accessing the information and preserved information that might have been lost due to deterioration of the paper on which it was printed. Some abstracting services also publish thesauruses of index terms. These thesauruses are as important to consult when searching the index or abstract as consulting LCSH when searching the catalog. The thesaurus for *Psychological Abstracts/PsycINFO* is similar to LCSH in providing B for Broader terms, N for narrower terms, R for related terms, UF and USE, etc.

The ERIC database (a U.S. Government publication, see chapter 12) is available on microfiche and the internet. Figure 8.4 is the beginning of an ERIC entry found using FirstSearch. Each item in ERIC has a unique number, like an abstract number used by other abstracting services. In this case OCLC has provided a TAG — Accession No: to identify this ERIC document. The citation is complete, followed by the abstract. The full text of the document is also available.

## Locating Journals

After the articles in the journals have been identified, the next step is to locate the journals in the library. Using the map constructed in Chapter 1 the location of the periodical stacks can be identified. These stacks usually contain the periodicals in alphabetical order. Each periodical may encompass several shelves. The indexes or abstracts provide the information needed about journal title, volume number, date and pages. The periodical's holdings list for the library is usually a circular or card file, list printed by OCLC, or available by searching the OPAC. This lists all the periodicals the library holds as well as the volumes owned. Journals for current months are usually located in a special section or reading area. Generally, periodicals do not circulate, since they are difficult or impossible to replace and are in high demand by library users.

## Union List of Serials

What if the journal needed is not owned by the library? How can a library that owns the journal be identified? Union lists of serials show which libraries own which journals. They cover a range from local to international. The librarian may be consulted to locate the union lists. Libraries usually own the *Union List of Serials* (ULS), third edition (Figure 8.5) and its supplements, *New Serials Titles* (Figure 8.6). The codes used to identify the holding libraries are the same ones that are used in the *National Union Catalog*. Figure 8.5 from the Union List of Serials, third edition is for the periodical *Ohio bar*. The entry states that the journal is published in Columbus by the Ohio state bar association, and that it began publication on April 3, 1928. Also included are some notes about the history of the publication. Also note that additional information was added by hand after the type was set and before publication. The two columns of letters represent the libraries that own this periodical. The number following each letter code shows the volume number of the beginning volume in the holdings. For this journal most of the libraries' holdings begin with volume 1. The (+) after the volume number shows that the libraries own all volumes after volume 1. A key to the codes is found at the beginning of each volume of the *Union List of Serials*. The *New Serials Titles* (NST) format was the same as NUC (see Figure 8.6). A brief look at the organization of the code will help to identify many libraries without having to consult the list. Generally the code has three letters, the first, the state, the

| | |
|---|---|
| Availability: | • ⓦ Connect to the catalog at your library |
| | FIND RELATED |
| More Like This: | Advanced options ... |
| Accession No: | ED469205 |
| Title: | **Foreign Languages: PreK-12 Sunshine State Standards and Instructional Practices. Florida Curriculum Framework.** |
| Access ERIC: | ❸ FullText |
| Corp Author(s): | Florida State Dept. of Education, Tallahassee. |
| Publication: | U.S.; Florida; 1996-00-00 |
| Description: | 229 p. |
| Language: | English |
| Abstract: | This curriculum framework is a guide for local education communities as they restructure their schools and improve foreign language planning. Grounded in national and state reform efforts, this guide for teachers to help students achieve the Sunshine State Standards, presents broad, overarching ideas for the development of curriculum and instruction. It delineates what knowledge and skills Florida will hold schools accountable for in Grades preK-2 3-5, 6-8, and 9-12. It also highlights strands and standards for foreign languages in five areas: communication (e.g., students engage in conversation, express feelings and emotions, and exchange opinions); culture (students understand the relationship between the perspectives and products of the culture studied and use this knowledge to recognize cultural practices); connections (e.g., students reinforce and further knowledge of other disciplines through foreign language); comparisons (e.g., students recognize that languages have different patterns of communication and apply this knowledge to their own culture); and experiences (students use the language within and beyond the school setting). After an introduction, nine chapters include the following: (1) "Visioning"; (2) "Goal 3 Standards" (from "Florida's System of School Improvement and Accountability); (3) "Foreign Languages Sunshine State Standards"; (4) "Teaching and Learning"; (5) "Curricular Connections through Instruction"; (6) "Assessment"; (7) "The Learning Environment"; (8) "Professional Development"; and (9) "Foreign Language Program Improvement." The ACTFL proficiency guidelines are attached. (SM) |

**Figure 8.4**

second the city and the third the name of the university. Some codes are one or two letters and some four. For example, NNC: N is "New York," thus the first N is for New York State, the second N is for "New York City," and the C is for "Columbia University." Likewise NNU is for "New York University," N for "New York State," N for "New York City" and U for "University." If the second letter is lowercase it is part of the state; CtY, Ct is Connecticut and Y is "Yale." Journal articles needed by students or faculty may be borrowed from other libraries (see Chapter 15 for interlibrary loans).

# *Newspapers*

Although printed information has been available for thousands of years, newspapers as we know them did not develop until the early 17th century. Before then proclamations were read aloud to large crowds and

Ohio short-horn breeders' record. Columbus.
1-3,1878-82‖
DA  1                         MoU     MnU-A
IaAS                          OU
InLP                          OkS     NIC
MAA                           PSt

OHIO association of Union ex-prisoners of war
Proceedings.
CSmH  1884                    OClWHi  1881
OCHP  1881                    WHi  1884

OHIO banker. (Ohio bankers association) Co-
lumbus. 1.1908+
CSt  [29]-[31]                OCl  [13]+
CtY  [19-31]+                 OClW  [22-23]+
IU  [15]+                     OHi  10-12
LNHT  [28-29]                 OO  [5,7,13]
OCU  15+

OHIO bankers' association
Proceedings. 1,1890+
1-21 as Annual convention
CtY   5-6,8-9                 NjP   22-23,25-29,32+
DLC   11,16-17,41-44         NjR   9-10
ICJ   6,27                    OC    15-26
ICU   14-17,22,24-25,27      OCHP  7
                             OClWHi  [10-31]
IU   16-18,20-23             OHi   11
MCM  14-19,21-23             OO    9,19-20
MH-BA  4,18,20-23,25,        OrU   27
  39+                        PU    12
N   27                       TxU   27
NN  12,16-23,25+             WaS   27-30
NNC  1-24,26-30              OCl  29

*See also* Ohio banker

OHIO Baptist. Granville, Ohio. 1,Je 10 1920+
NHC  1-9,16+                  OO  [9-10] KyLSc7]-
OClWHi  1+                    PCA  1+   c 10-12]+

OHIO Baptist bulletin. Granville. Ohio. 1-16,
1905-Je 1920‖
NHC  [3-13]                   OO  [4.13]
OClWHi  [1]-[3-4]-            OU  [10]-16
  [11-12]                     PCA  [2-16]

OHIO Baptist convention
* Proceedings. Granville. 1,1826+
Cover title: Ohio Baptist annual
ICU  [1-91]93+                OCl  116+
KyLS  1826-34,38-39,         ODW  67
  42,57-63,65-74,76,79-       OU   76,89-94
  84,87-1910,12,15-28,
  30-34

OHIO bar. (Ohio state bar association) Colum-
bus. 1,Ap 3 1928+
v1-21 no36,Ap 3 1928-D 13 1948 as the
association's Report. "cited as Ohio bar."
v21 no37,D 20 1948+ contains Ohio law ab-
stract weekly advance sheets, formerly
published separately (not in UL)
Supersedes the association's Bulletin
CU  12+                       N  1-[6]  MoSW-L 7
Ct  1+                        NIC  1+   9-10,13-21
CtY-L  1+                     NNB  1+
DLC  3+                       NNC  1+
FDS  11+                      NcD-L  1+
JCU  [1-10]+                  NcU  [1]-[5]-[7]+
IaU-L  [3,5,9,11]            OClW  1+
MH-L  1+
MdBJ  1-[4-5]                 PPB  1+   OCl c 11]2 +
MiU-L  1+                     WU  7+
                             WaU  1+

OHIO beekeepers' association
Leaflets. np   My 1924+
NIC 1924-[26-27]

OHIO Belgian breeders' association
Eastern Belgian futurity. 1-12.  -1928‖
IU  5-10,12,1921-28

OHIO biological survey. *See under* Ohio state
university

Figure 8.5

TITLE CHANGE
**Occupational compensation survey—pay only. Augusta, Georgia-South Carolina, metropolitan area** / U.S. Department of Labor, Bureau of Labor Statistics. — June 1992-          — Washington, DC : The Bureau : U.S. G.P.O., Supt. of Docs. ¡distributor¡ ;Chicago, IL : Bureau of Labor Statistics, Publications Sales Center ¡distributor¡. 1993-
  v. : 21 x 28 cm. — (Bulletin)
  Annual.
  Title from cover.
  Continues: Area wage survey. Augusta, Georgia-South Carolina, metropolitan area
  Supt. of Docs. no.: L 2.121/10:AU 4/
  GPO: Item 0768-B-10
  1. Wages--Georgia—Augusta Metropolitan Area—Statistics—Periodicals.    2.  Wages—South  Carolina—Aiken County—Statistics—Periodicals.    I. United States.  Bureau of Labor Statistics.  II. Title: Augusta, Georgia-South Carolina, metropolitan area.  III. Series: Bulletin of the United States Bureau of Labor Statistics.
                                       sn 93-27621
                                          AACR 2

InLP  InU  MH-BA  MiU

NEW START
**Occupational compensation survey—pay only. Beaufort County, SC** / U.S. Department of Labor, Bureau of Labor Statistics. — Sept. 1992-          — Washington, DC : The Bureau, 1993-
  v. : 21 x 28 cm.
  Annual.
  Title from caption.
  Supt. of Docs. no.: L 2.122/40:B 38/
  GPO: Item 0768-B-40
  1. Wages—South Carolina—Beaufort County—Statistics—Periodicals.   I. United States.  Bureau of Labor Statistics.  II. Title: Beaufort County, SC.
                                       sn 93-28031
                                          AACR 2
NIC

TITLE CHANGE
**Occupational compensation survey—pay only. Bell County, TX—fast food restaurants** / U.S. Department of Labor, Bureau of Labor Statistics. — Jan. 1993-          — Washington, DC : The Bureau, 1993-
  v. : 21 x 28 cm.
  Annual.
  Title from caption.
  Continues: Fast food restaurants wage survey. Bell County, TX.
  Supt. of Docs. no.: L 2.3/3-3:F 26/BELL/
  GPO: Item 0768-D-01
  1. Wages—Food industry and trade—Texas—Bell County—Statistics—Periodicals.   2. Fast food restaurants—Texas—Bell County—Statistics—Periodicals.    I. United States. Bureau of Labor Statistics.  II. Title: Bell County, TX—fast food restaurants.  III. Title: Bell County, TX, fast food restaurants.
                                       sn 93-28037
                                          AACR 2
NIC

**Figure 8.6**

were posted in the village square. Other ways of transmitting news (besides the town crier and troubadours or ballad singers) included news pamphlets and newsletters. A news pamphlet is usually a short small sheet of paper, folded once to make four pages, and is concerned with one subject. A broadsheet refers to a single sheet of large size paper frequently printed on only one side and posted as one might put up notices on a bulletin board. Broadsheets are also generally involved with one subject. Newsletters usually contain information supplied by one person but on many subjects. Newsletters have been common since the Roman times and are still an important source of information for the researcher. Many corporations produce specific newsletters on various topics. The Carnegie Foundation publishes a periodical newsletter with reports on current research financed by the trust. One should not overlook this source when researching a topic.

Early newspapers were printed sporadically at first, gradually becoming more frequent, once or twice weekly. Some earliest newspapers left one page blank for the reader or subscriber to add news before passing the newspaper to someone else. Church and government official were quick to grasp the influence of newspapers, soon subjecting them to censorship, licensing, taxing and later bribery and prosecution of the editors, printers and writers (reporters). Copies of many early newspapers have survived and the newspapers of the last 350 to 400 years provide historical information, opinions of the times and other information not recorded elsewhere. Many early newspapers in Europe and in the United States invited writers to make unpaid contributions, thus becoming literary and political forums for the intellectuals. By the early 18th century, newspapers had become indispensable in politics and economics and continued to increase despite attempts by governments to control their number and content.

Newspapers in the 20th century have declined in numbers but individual papers have larger circulations. As costs increase, technology for production has become necessary for newspapers to survive. Most newspapers today are composed by computer and printed by photo-offset techniques developed since 1970. The new technology requires less staff and space for composing and printing.

Newspapers are read worldwide and are still a powerful influence on public opinion. They can build or destroy ideas, people or governments and range from the state-controlled propaganda sheets to the free press of the West. Debates about censorship continue. Western papers are expected to play a role in uncovering corruption and scandal, such as the role played by the newspapers in discovering the Watergate scandal. Modern newspapers provide services to researchers. Back issues are kept in a large col-

**Relax and catch up on the latest news.**

lection, the "morgue," and are usually accessible to the consumer. Most newspapers also have a reference library that is used by the reporters and other staff preparing and editing articles. Large newspapers like the *New York Times* have comprehensive reference collections.

The type of information in newspapers falls into three general categories, (1) business and economic news, (2) governmental news, laws, politicians, elections and rulers and (3) social and neighborhood news. Newspapers are important sources of current information. Some are "newspapers of record" in that they print the full text of speeches, public notices and sometimes legislation. If the text of a speech by the governor of New York is needed it will be found in the *New York Times*.

Major newspapers are indexed. All important news and information in the *New York Times* is found by using the *New York Times Index*. The index lists the month, day, section number and page and column number. Other newspaper indexes use the same format. All contain subject entries and personal name entries with cross references. Be sure to check the abbreviations used and additional instructions at the beginning of the index. Library holdings of newspapers are generally on microfilm. For additional information see the section of Chapter 15 on nonprint materials. For additional information about newspapers check the catalog. For additional information about guides and directories, use subject headings guides (Chapter 2) or correct subject headings.

Many newspapers are now available online. Most will include at least the major news stories of the day and perhaps the past week. Most provide access to obituaries however some major newspapers will charge a fee to access information older than one week. Check the website for each newspaper for exact details.

## Exercises for Chapter 8

1. Check the catalog for those subject headings pertinent to your major field of interest. List the indexes and abstracts in your library that relate to that field. If you do not find any listed in the catalog ask the reference librarian.
2. Check a guide to the literature in your major field of interest and record the titles of indexes and abstracts that are published but not available in your library. (Check *Guide to Reference Books* and other titles listed in Chapter 5.)
3. Check the catalog under the heading Periodicals — Directories; list the directories in your library with their call numbers.
4. If available, check the *Reader's Guide to Periodical Literature* (RGPL), v. 61, 2001, v. 56, 1996, v. 44, 1984–1985, look up the subject Investment Fraud. Compare it to RGPL, v. 34, 1974–75 and v. 39, 1979–80 entries for Investment Fraud. Note subheadings and cross-referencing. If *Reader's Guide* is available to you via the internet, search investment fraud and compare your findings with the print edition.
5. Using RGPL, recording the volume number and date, check the entries under the subject Iraq. Note the type of subheadings used and the "see" and "see also" references. Compare the entries for the years 1974–75, 1990–91, 1996–97 and 2004–05. If available, check *Reader's Guide* on line and compare your results to your findings in the paper edition.
6. Check in the *Social Sciences Index*, *Business Periodicals Index* and *Education Index* under the subject heading Iraq. Record the title of index, volume number and year, type of subheadings and cross-references ("see" and "see also"). If your library does not have these indexes, check three other titles. Check at least one online periodical index. Compare the results with your search of the paper indexes.
7. Look in the catalog for the subject Periodicals. Record, with call numbers, those that may be useful, e.g. those listing periodical title abbreviations, bibliographies and indexes.

# Important Terms in Chapter 8

Wilson Index
*abstracts*
*broadsheets*
*ULS*
*NST*
*union lists*
*newsletters*
*Reader's Guide*
*RGPL*

# Important Books for Chapter 8

## DIRECTORIES

*Directory of Electronic Journals, Newsletters, and Academic Discussion Lists.* Washington, D.C.: Association of Research Libraries, Office of Scientific and Academic Publishing, 1991–.

*Internet-Accessible Full-Text Electronic Journals and Periodical Collections for Libraries.* Chicago, Ill: American Library Association, 2000.

LaGuardia, Cheryl, and Katz, William Armstrong. *Magazines for Libraries: For the General Reader and School, Junior College and Public Library.* 13th ed. Providence, NJ: R. R. Bowker, 2004.

*Ulrich's International Periodicals Directory.* New York: R. R. Bowker, 1932–(yearly). 43rd edition published in 2004.

## INDEXES AND ABSTRACTS

*Abstracts in Anthropology.* Westport, CT: Greenwood, v. 1–, 1970–.

*Abstracts of English Studies, 1958–.* Boulder, CO: National Council of Teachers of English, 1958–(monthly). Also available on microfilm.

*Art Index.* New York: H. W. Wilson, v. 1–, 1929–. Available online.

*Bibliography and Index of Geology.* Alexandria, VA: American Geological Institute, v. 32–, 1969–. Earlier volumes published under the title *Bibliography and Index of Geology Exclusive of North America.*

*Business Periodicals Index, 1958–.* New York: H. W. Wilson, 1958–(monthly). Available online.

*Chemical Abstracts, 1907–.* Columbus, OH: American Chemical Society, 107–(weekly).

*Cumulative Index to Nursing and Allied Health Literature.* Glendale, CA:

Glendale Adventist Medical Center, v. 1–, 1956–. Earlier volumes have a slightly different title. Also available on CD-ROM.

*General Science Index.* New York: H. W. Wilson, v. 1–, 1978–. Available online.

*Historical Abstracts.* Santa Barbara, CA: ABC Clio. V. 1–, 1955–. Beginning with v. 17, 1971 it is published in four parts per volume. Available on CD-Rom and online. Beginning with v. 52 (2000) Parts A and B merged. 6 issues per year.

*Humanities Index.* New York: H. W. Wilson, v. 1–, 1971–. Earlier title was Social Sciences and Humanities Index, preceded by the International Index. Available online.

*MLA International Bibliography of Books and Articles on the Modern Languages and Literature.* New York: Modern Language Association of America, 1921–. Beginning with 2000 online subscriptions are available.

*Pooles's Index to Periodical Literature.* Reprinted. Gloucester, MA: Peter Smith, 1963. (7 vols. Covering 1802–1906.)

*Psychological Abstracts, 1927–.* Lancaster, PA: American Psychological Association, 1927–(monthly). Online version is known as *PsychInfo.*

*Reader's Guide to Periodical Literature, 1900–.* New York: H. W. Wilson, 1900–(semi-monthly). Available online.

*Recently Published Articles.* Washington, DC: American Historical Review, v. 1–, 1976–1990. Formerly published as a section of the American Historical Review.

*Social Science Citation Index.* Philadelphia: Institute for Scientific Information, v. 1–, 1973–. The same publisher also issues *Science Citation Index* and *Arts and Humanities Citation Index.*

*Social Sciences Index.* New York: H. W. Wilson, v. 1–, 1974–. Earlier title was *Social Sciences and Humanities Index* which was preceded by International Index. Available online.

*Sociological Abstracts.* San Diego, CA: Sociological Abstracts, v. 1–, 1952–. Available online.

## NEWSPAPER INDEXES

*New York Times Index.* New York: New York Times Co., 1913–. Earlier series index the *New York Times* from September 18, 1951.

*Personal Name Index to the New York Times Index, 1851–1974.* Succa-Sunna, NJ: Roxbury Data Interface, 1976. Supplements to main set have been issued for 1975–2001.

*The Times Index.* Reading, England: Newspaper Archive Developments, 1973–. 1790–1905 indexes as *Palmer's Index to the Times Newspaper.* Indexes to other years published by various publishers.

*Wall Street Journal Index.* New York: Dow Jones, 1958–. Starting in 1981, the index includes *Barron's Index.*

*Washington Post Index.* Ann Arbor, MI: University Microfilms International, 1989–. Earlier volumes published by other publishers. Also available on microfilm.

## UNION LISTS

*New Serials Titles.* New York: R. R. Bowker. A union list of serials commencing publication after December 31, 1949. Sets for the years 1950–1970 (4 vols.), 1971–1975 (2 vols.), 1976–1980 (2 vols.), 1981–1985 (6 vols.), 1986–1989, 1991–1995, 1996–1998 (6 vols.), monthly, quarterly issues and annual volumes.

*Union List of Serials in Libraries in the United States and Canada*, 3d ed. New York: H. W. Wilson, 1965 (5 vols.).

## OTHER HELPFUL BOOKS

Alkire, Leland G., ed. *Periodical Title Abbreviations*, 15th ed. Detroit: Gale Research, 2005. v. 1 by abbreviations, v. 2 by titles

Balay, Robert. *Early Periodical Titles: Bibliographies and Indexes to Literature Published in Periodicals Before 1900.* Lanham, MD: Scarecrow Press, 2000.

# 9

# Online Database Searching and Reference Sources

## Objectives

After studying this chapter the student shall be able to

- Search online databases
- Use Boolean operators and other types of limits in constructing a search
- Know how to access the Internet

## General Information

Searching for specific types of information on the Internet is included in many earlier chapters. There are many ways to access the Internet. Your library may provide access via its catalog. Many public libraries provide free access to the Internet from their catalog in addition to direct connections to one or more of the specific services discussed below. Most academic library catalogs provide access to at least one of the following services in addition to other databases such as FirstSearch (chapter 15).

Whether searching paper indexes or online indexes students must remember that all periodical citations have equal import of value. Further students should discriminate in which citations to pursue. Students should also realize that the library pays a fee to provide access to these databases. If one wished to access these databases in a way other than via a library catalog, charges would be incurred. In general, online indexes (and abstracts) are generally searched in the same manner so only a few popular database suppliers will be discussed.

## *InfoTrac*

InfoTrac is a group of databases available from the catalog of subscribing libraries. The Gale Group (which provides the InfoTrac service) has many databases available. Not every library will subscribe to all databases offered. The databases range from general, such as InfoTrac OneFile to specific, such as Health Reference Center Academic. The level of materials range from Kids Edition K12 to college/graduate level.

Instructions for searching any of the databases is available online via links on the opening page of any database. Each database provides searching by subject, keyword, journal title and Advanced Search. Infotrac also provides a **Relevance Search**. Also available on any opening page is a link to the list of journals and newspapers included plus the dates indexing is available.

When opening any InfoTrac database, the **Subject Guide** Search box appears. The student can type in the subject to be searched. To produce the best results, the students should check those boxes most relevant to the search, such as identifying only those items with complete text, published during a specific time period or only in scholarly journals. Pull down menus are available in some instances. Search results provide the oportunity to print the article or have it emailed to the students inbox. Cross references (generally *see* references) may also be included in the result list. It is possible to change the type of search to a *keyword* or *relevance* search by clicking on the type of search. The search terms do not need to be reentered. A history of all searches conducted in a session are recorded on the screen, simplifying the process of repeating a search or recalling what searches have already been conducted.

InfoTrac databases include ***stop words***, words ignored during searching, for example "a," "the," etc. If the words AND or NOT are included, they are considered Boolean or logical operators. The search is automatically shifted from a subject search to a keyword search. If the subject search is unsuccessful the system provides suggestions and other options. Keyword searches automatically look for the words within two words of each other, in either direction. If the correct spelling in unknown or alternate spellings exist, use the wildcard(s) in constructing the search. Be sure to check the instructions for which wildcard(s) are needed. The **Advanced**

**Search** allows students to construct as simple or complex a search as is needed. Up to three logical (Boolean) operators may be included in the search statement. Be sure to check the drop down menus for options.

A **Relevance Search** is useful when two or more search terms are included. The frequency of use of each term in the article is analyzed. Articles with the highest frequency rate appear at the top of the result list. The Boolean or logical operators **cannot** be used in a **Relevance Search**. Special characters (" ", +, -) are used instead to modify search results. Be sure to check the online instructions when doing relevance searches.

Examples of a few InfoTrac databases and their descriptions as they appeared on the website of the Sarasota County Library System in 2005 follow.

*InfoTrac OneFile* 1980–. According to the Thomson-Gale website (*www.galegroup.com*) as of November 1, 2005, InfoTrac is a one-stop source for news and periodical articles on a wide range of topics: business, computers, current events, economics, education, environmental issues, health care, hobbies, humanities, law, literature and art, politics, science, social science, sports, technology and many general interest topics. Millions of full-text articles, many with images. The index is updated daily.

*Health Reference Center Academic* 1980–. According to the Thomson-Gale website (*www.galegroup.com*) on November 1, 2005, a user of this database can find articles on: Fitness, Pregnancy, Medicine, Nutrition, Diseases, Public Health, Occupational Health and Safety, Alcohol and Drug Abuse, HMOs, Prescription Drugs, etc. The material contained in this database is intended for informational purposes only

*Business Index ASAP* 1980–. According to the Thomson-Gale website (*www.galegroup.com*) on November 1, 2005, this database performs in-depth research on management issues, economic indicators and business theories and practices, as well as on the activities of companies and industries worldwide. Instant access to academic and business journals with full text and images.

## ProQuest Direct

UMI's ProQuest is a database of articles originally published in magazines, newspapers and journals. It can be accessed via the catalog of subscribing libraries. Some subscribing libraries make it available via the internet. It is necessary to enter an ID or bar code number to gain access via the internet.

ProQuest opens to the page for a *Basic* search. At the top of the page are tabs for *Advanced Search, Topic guide* and *Publication Search*. The *Basic Search* provides searchers with options to limit the search. For example, the search can be limited by date or full text articles only. Be sure to look at the options and the drop down menus. The *more search options* link provides at least six additional types of searches.

All search results provide links which might include suggestions for refining the search statement, suggesting similar ideas/concepts, Boolean operators for limiting the search results or browse suggested publications.

If the student does not find exactly what is needed, check the online searching tips. Simple but useful tips include using "quotation marks" to search exact phrases.

ProQuest uses wildcards * and ? The * is used for truncation (shortening) and the ? is used to replace a single letter inside or at the end of a word. An example of the ? to replace a letter is g?ild. This search will find gild, geld and gold. A truncation example is politi*. This could find any or all of the following terms, politic, political, politick, politico and politics. The truncation can also be useful when the exact spelling of a name is unknown. For example, is the name Green or Greene. Students must be aware of unexpected results when using truncation. For example Green* might result in Green, Greene, Greenblatt, Greens, etc.

At the top of the search results list is the total number of documents found. Options are provided for showing items with full text only, scholarly journals only, magazines, trade publications or newspapers. Sorting options are also provided. In addition, there are icons which easily identify items as having text + graphics, a page image in PDF format (requiring Acrobat reader), an abstract or full text. Each citation includes the article title, authors' name, journal (or publication) title with full citation (date, volume, issue number, beginning page number and total number of pages in the article). At the top of the results list is a restatement of the search strategy. If the search produced too many "hits," keep refining the search by adding more terms, limiting by date or type of publication or use of Boolean operators.

Some entries provide an option to have the article translated into another language. The language options for that article are listed as links. Translations are "on the fly" machine translations and are not intended to replace those done by human translators. The HELP option after conducting a search on ProQuest (web site your library accesses is probably *www.proquest.umi.com*) provides information about the above searches.

The Boolean operators available in ProQuest are AND, AND NOT,

**Searching on line can be fully absorbing.**

OR, WITHIN, WITHIN DOC, NOT WITHIN and PRE. To understand any unfamiliar operator, read the instructions in the *search help* section. The *search help* section also provides instructions, with examples, for constructing various detailed search statements. For example, if an author search (to find articles written by a specific person) is needed, the search statement can reflect that. AUTHOR (Tom Brokaw) or AU (Tom Brokaw). Looking for a specific company or organization? The search statement might read CO( Xerox) or COMPANY (Xerox). Please check the search *help section* for the complete list of nearly 40 possibilities.

The *search help* pages include a long list of **stop words**. Stop words are frequently occurring words that are ignored by the computer when it searches. If a word on the stop list is necessary in the construction of the search statement it must be enclosed in quotation marks.

## *WilsonWeb*

All of H.W. Wilson's indexes are available online via WilsonWeb. Many college and universities subscribe to this database. It is possible to select more than one database when designing your search. Options for search construction are available using drop down menus. Basic and advanced searching is included. A master list of indexed journals is available as well as thesaurus. Your search history for the current session is available and you may save, print or e-mail articles. Ask the librarian if you have questions. For detailed information about each available database see Wilson's web site at *www.hwwilson.com.*

## Commercial Vendors of Databases

In addition to the services described above, there are some databases available only through vendors that charge per search or per citation displayed/printed. The charges may also include connect time plus long distance phone charges. DIALOG, BRS and Lexis/Nexis are among the more commonly used suppliers. The vendor assigns a password for access to the database and bills are sent monthly or charged to a deposit account or credit card. Vendors provide regularly updated instructions for searching databases they supply. Most users of these services are corporations and professionals (e.g., lawyers). Some colleges and universities have an educational password to Lexis/Nexis, allowing students and faculty access to most of their extensive legal databases. For this access the schools pays a preset monthly fee. Searching in BRS and DIALOG and other similar services may be available at your library. Ask the librarian if these services are available and what the charges would be. Most schools providing this service require that the librarian do the actual searching.

## Searching or Surfing the Net

As mentioned above, some libraries provide access to the Internet from their catalogs. Individuals may also access the Internet from their personal computer. The method of accessing the Internet is a personal choice. Local companies may provide access or one may choose a large corporate provider (AOL, MSN, ATT, etc.). All providers charge a fee for access to the "net." A web browser is necessary for searching the Internet. Many browsers are available, often at no cost. Popular browsers include NetScape and Microsoft Internet Explorer. Many Internet sites provide menus enabling the user to find information easily. Yahoo and Google are popular sites that continually add and update sources and information. Some sites such as Yahoo also provide free e-mail accounts.

Requesting assistance at the reference desk is always a good idea.

## Exercises for Chapter 9

1. What CD-ROM products does your library subscribe to? Is there a printer attached?
2. Does your library provide online database searching? Who does the searching? Is there a charge?
3. Does your library provide access to the Internet on the catalog?
4. Look up the subjects checked for other indexes. See exercises for Chapter 8. (Iraq, investment fraud)
5. Are any of the online databases available from computers not in the library? If so, how are they accessed?

## Important Terms for Chapter 9

AOL
*Boolean*
*BRS*
*DIALOG*

*Downloading*
*Google*
*Infotrac*
*Logical operators*
*ProQuest*
*Stop words*
*Truncation*
*Vendor*
*Web browser*
*Wild cards*
*Yahoo*

## *Important Books for Chapter 9*

*Best of the Internet* (serial). Indianapolis, Ind.: Que, 2003?–.

*Finding Facts On-Line.* Mechanicsburg, Pa.: Pennsylvania Bar Institute, 2003.

Frey, Donnalyn, and Rick Adams. *!%@, A Directory of Electronic Mail Addresses and Networks.* 4th ed. rev. and updated. Sebastopol, CA: O'Reilly and Associates, 1994.

Sherman, Chris, and Gary Price. *The Invisible Web: Uncovering Information Sources Search Engines Can't See.* Medford, NJ.: Cyberage books, 2001.

Want, Robert S. *How to Search the Web: A Quick Reference Guide to Finding Things on the World Wide Web.* 3rd ed. New York: Want Pub., 2000.

Williams, Martha E. *Gale Directory of Databases.* Farmington Hills, Mi.: Gale group. Annual, 2 volumes.

# 10

# Literature and Criticism

## Objectives

After studying this chapter the student shall be able to

- locate poems, short stories and other forms of literature published in anthologies and periodicals
- find critical analyses of plays, poems, short stories, novels and speeches
- identify and record the indexes of literary forms owned by the library
- locate plot summaries

## General Information

Literary forms include plays, poems, short stories, novels and speeches. Obviously, there are many items that one might want to retrieve. Finding one poem may be difficult or impossible if one only uses the catalog. Students will find the task less demanding if they consult a special catalog, anthology or index. Poems, short stories and essays are usually published in collections called anthologies or in subject-specific periodicals. Anthologies may include the works of one or multiple authors. The scope is determined by the editor. With practice the student will find anthologies by using the catalog. Correct subject headings are essential to seeking materials. The subject heading books (see Chapter 4) provide alternate headings useful in this task. For example, to locate a particular play, the correct heading is drama, not plays. With some practice one will learn key subject headings and no longer need to consult the book each time a subject heading is needed. Besides using anthologies, the student will use alternative research sources, such as indexes, catalogs, abstracts and the internet.

## Indexes and Catalogs

The *Short Story Index* (Figure 10.1), published by the H. W. Wilson Company, is a guide to locating short stories that have been published in collections. The index lists the stories by author's name, title and subject, and all entries are in one alphabet. Also it identifies the book or periodi-

cal title in which the story appeared. For example, Mark Twain's story "Cannibalism in the cars" is in the collection *The Arbor House Celebrity Book of Horror Stories* edited by C.G. Waugh and M.H. Greenberg. The format is typical "Wilson" format (see Chapter 8). This index is extremely comprehensive and should be sufficient for most purposes.

*Short Story Criticism* is an introduction to major short story writers of all eras and nationalities. The editors have chosen the most important published criticism. Each volume includes 8–10 authors and each entry reflects the amount of critical attention the author has received. The chosen criticisms are from English language publications or foreign critics in translation. Each entry includes bio-

Paperbacks may be shelved in special racks for convenient browsing.

**TURKEY, PROVINCIAL AND RURAL**
Baykurt, F. Freckles
Baykurt, F. A report from Kuloba
Nesin, A. Dog tails
The **turkey** season. Munro, A.

**TURKEYS**
Barr, J. G. How Tom Croghan carved the turkey
The Lunatic and his turkey
Munro, A. The turkey season

**TURKISH BATHS**
Trollope, A. The Turkish bath
The **Turkman.** Olesha, Y.

**TURKS IN GERMANY**
Baykurt, F. Monica
The **turn** of the screw. James, H.
The **turn** of the tide. Forester, C. S.
**Turnabout.** Knudtsen, I.
**Turned.** Gilman, C. P.

**Turner, Brian**
Selected letters from Panickers' travels
Pioneer letters: the letter as literature
**Turner, George**
A pursuit of miracles
Universe 12
**Turner, Harry**
Shwartz
Hoki, H. ed. Thrillers, chillers & killers
**Turner, Robert**
Christmas gift
Alfred Hitchcock's Death-reach
The **turner's** wife. Reynolds, J.
**Turning.** Dillon, E.
The **turning** point. Cameron, E.
The **turning** point. Hodgson, S.

**TURNIPS**
Brown, F. Blood
Bulychev, K. Tale of the turnip
**Tursun, Sattor**
Maker of dombras
Soviet Lit no 5:97-107 '81

**TURTLES**
Anaya, R. A. Salomon's story
Dahl, R. The boy who talked with animals
Deagon, A. A natural history
Deagon, A. The second and final vision of Mrs Fuquay
Highsmith, P. The terrapin

**TUSCALOOSA.** See Alabama—Tuscaloosa

**TUTORS**
Andersen, B. The break
Auchincloss, L. Charade
Desai, A. Private tuition by Mr Bose
Hogan, D. Thoughts
Malamud, B. The German refugee
Stewart, J. I. M. Tea with Mr Montacute
**Tuttle, Anthony**
Person to person
McCalls 110:100-01 Jl '83
**Tuttle, Lisa**
Need
Shadows 4

Sun city
Waugh, C. G. and Greenberg, M. H. eds. The Arbor House Celebrity book of horror stories
Where the stones grow
McCauley, K. ed. Dark forces
Wives
The Best from Fantasy & Science Fiction; 24th ser.
**Twain, Mark**
Cannibalism in the cars
Waugh, C. G. and Greenberg, M. H. eds. The Arbor House Celebrity book of horror stories
The celebrated jumping frog of Calaveras County
Blakey, G. G. ed. The gambler's companion
Litz, A. W. ed. Major American short stories
The Oxford Book of short stories
Same as: The notorious jumping frog of Calaveras County
How to tell a story
Litz, A. W. ed. Major American short stories
The £ 1,000,000 bank-note
Sullivan, N. comp. The treasury of American short stories
Science v. luck
Blakey, G. G. ed. The gambler's companion
Sold to Satan
Silverberg, R. and Greenberg, M. H. comps. The Arbor House Treasury of science fiction masterpieces
The stolen white elephant
Pronzini, B.; Malzberg, B. N. and Greenberg, M. H. comps. The Arbor House Treasury of mystery and suspense
The story of the good little boy
Grey, M. C. ed. Angels and awakenings
*For other stories by this author* see Clemens, Samuel Langhorne

**Parodies, travesties, etc.**

Baber, A. How I got screwed and almost tattooed, by Huck Finn
The **twelfth** statue. Ellin, S.
The **twelve** figures of the world. Borges, J. L. and Bioy-Casares, A.
The **twelve** healers and other remedies. Mairowitz, D. Z.
**Twelve** years old. Asimov, I.
The **twentieth** century murder case. Malzberg, B. N.
**28** hours in an open boat by Stephen Crane. Baker, L.
The **twenty**-fourth voyage. Lem, S.
**Twenty**-nine pens of Simon Englehart. Bernstein, L. S.
**Twenty**-one good men and true. Francis, D.
**21** Main Street No. Jeromm, Z. Z.
The **23** brown paper bags. Ritchie, J.
**Twenty**-three, please. Hall, L. S.
**Twenty**-two cents a day. Ritchie, J.
**Twenty** years late. Tendriakov, V. F.

Figure 10.1

graphical and critical introduction; a list of principal works in chronological order; criticism; bibliographical citations and additional readings. Cumulative index for authors, titles and nationalities is included in each volume.

*The Essay and General Literature Index* is a guide to essays and short articles published in books rather than periodicals. For information about an author, one looks under the author's name. There are also subject headings to provide access to items when an author's name is unknown to the student. Figure 10.2 is a typical entry. The author's name, Twain, heads the entry. In the center of the column, the term "about" shows that the items under this heading are articles about Mark Twain — biographical information, but not articles written by him. The first item is by D. Levin, titled "Innocents Abroad: From Mark Twain and Henry James to Bellow, Malamud and Baldwin" in a collection by D. Levin, *Forms of Uncertainty: essays in historical criticism* on pages 289–310. Further down the column the heading appears in the center, "About individual works." Under this heading are articles about *The Adventures of Huckleberry Finn,* etc. For complete information about anthologies indexed in *Essay and General Literature Index,* see the back of each volume. *Essay and General Literature Index* is also available on WilsonWeb (updated daily) and WilsonDisc (updated quarterly). Figure 10.3 for a WilsonWeb search for Mark Twain.

Speeches and plays are indexed in respective volumes. *The Speech Index,* edited by Roberta Sutton, has been enlarged several times and is comprehensive. The *Play Index,* another Wilson index, is arranged in the typical format with the plays arranged by subject, author and title in one alphabet. The entries include information such as the number of acts, the number of male and female roles, the number of scenes, and in which collection the plays appear. The electronic edition of *Play Index* (WilsonWeb) includes more than 44,000 plays published since 1949. Wilson plans to add links from *Play Index* to the full text of plays available on the internet.

The *Fiction Catalog* (Figure 10.4) is also published by Wilson. It is one of the few sources that provide an index to novels by subject. If a novel about the Revolutionary War is needed, a check of the *Fiction Catalog* would provide a list of novels by authors and titles about the Revolutionary War. The *Fiction Catalog* gives book reviews for many novels listed. There are additional catalogs to "fictions by special subject," such as science fiction or mysteries.

*Grangers Index to Poetry* is a selective index to poems that appear in generally accessible collections. There are several editions that include many anthologies published over the years. A poem may be located by

LITERATURE AND CRITICISM    115

NERAL LITERATURE INDEX

Twain, Mark, 1835-1910
**About**
Levin, D. Innocents abroad: from Mark Twain and Henry James to Bellow, Malamud, and Baldwin. (In Levin, D. Forms of uncertainty: essays in historical criticism p289-310)
Subryan, C. Mark Twain and the black challenge. (In Satire or evasion?; ed. by J. S. Leonard, T. A. Tenney, and T. M. Davis p91-102)
**About individual works**
*The adventures of Huckleberry Finn*
Barksdale, R. History, slavery, and thematic irony in Huckleberry Finn. (In Satire or evasion?; ed. by J. S. Leonard, T. A. Tenney, and T. M. Davis p49-55)
Bell, B. W. Twain's "nigger" Jim: the tragic face behind the minstrel mask. (In Satire or evasion?; ed. by J. S. Leonard, T. A. Tenney, and T. M. Davis p124-40)
Davis, M. K. The veil rent in Twain: degradation and revelation in Adventures of Huckleberry Finn. (In Satire or evasion?; ed. by J. S. Leonard, T. A. Tenney, and T. M. Davis p77-90)
Henry, P. The struggle for tolerance: race and censorship in Huckleberry Finn. (In Satire or evasion?; ed. by J. S. Leonard, T. A. Tenney, and T. M. Davis p25-48)
Jones, B. H. Huck and Jim: a reconsideration. (In Satire or evasion?; ed. by J. S. Leonard, T. A. Tenney, and T. M. Davis p154-72)
Jones, R. S. Nigger and knowledge: white double-consciousness in Adventures of Huckleberry Finn. (In Satire or evasion?; ed. by J. S. Leonard, T. A. Tenney, and T. M. Davis p173-94)
Lester, J. Morality and Adventures of Huckleberry Finn. (In Satire or evasion?; ed. by J. S. Leonard, T. A. Tenney, and T. M. Davis p199-207)
Miller, J. H. Three problems of fictional form: first-person narration in David Copperfield and Huckleberry Finn. (In Miller, J. H. Victorian subjects p91-107)
Nichols, C. H. "A true book—with wome stretchers": Huck Finn today. (In Satire or evasion?; ed. by J. S. Leonard, T. A. Tenney, and T. M. Davis p208-15)
Nilon, C. H. The ending of Huckleberry Finn: "freeing the free Negro". (In Satire or evasion?; ed. by J. S. Leonard, T. A. Tenney, and T. M. Davis p62-76)
Rampersad, A. Adventures of Huckleberry Finn and Afro-American literature. (In Satire or evasion?; ed. by J. S. Leonard, T. A. Tenney, and T. M. Davis p216-27)
Smith, D. L. Huck, Jim, and American racial discourse. (In Satire or evasion?; ed. by J. S. Leonard, T. A. Tenney, and T. M. Davis p103-20)
Wallace, J. H. The case against Huck Finn. (In Satire or evasion?; ed. by J. S. Leonard, T. A. Tenney, and T. M. Davis p16-24)
Williams, K. J. Adventures of Huckleberry Finn; or, Mark Twain's racial ambiguity. (In Satire or evasion?; ed. by J. S. Leonard, T. A. Tenney, and T. M. Davis p228-37)

1992 ANNUAL

Twain, Mark, 1835-1910—About individual works — The adventures of Huckleberry Finn—*Continued*
Woodard, F., and MacCann, D. Minstrel shackles and nineteenth-century "liberality" in Huckleberry Finn. (In Satire or evasion?; ed. by J. S. Leonard, T. A. Tenney, and T. M. Davis p141-53)
*Pudd'nhead Wilson*
Sundquist, E. J. Mark Twain and Homer Plessy. (In The New American studies: essays from Representations; ed. by P. Fisher p112-38)
**Bibliography**
Sattelmeyer, R. Mark Twain. (In American literary scholarship, 1990 p93-106)
**Political and social views**
Williams, K. J. Adventures of Huckleberry Finn; or, Mark Twain's racial ambiguity. (In Satire or evasion?; ed. by J. S. Leonard, T. A. Tenney, and T. M. Davis p228-37)
Tweedsmuir, John Buchan, Baron See Buchan, John, 1875-1940
**Twentieth century**
Arnheim, R. In the company of the century. (In Arnheim, R. To the rescue of art: twenty-six essays p236-43)
Twersky, David
Israel and Zionism. (In The Schocken guide to Jewish books; ed. by B. W. Holtz p149-63)
Twin Peaks (Television program)
Denzin, N. K. Wild about Lynch: beyond Blue velvet. (In Denzin, N. K. Images of postmodern society p65-81)
Twining, William L.
Maine and legal education: a comment. (In The Victorian achievement of Sir Henry Maine; ed. by A. Diamond p209-16)
Tyler, Royall, 1757-1826
"The path of my mountain": Buddhism in Nō. (In Flowing traces; ed. by J. H. Sanford, W. R. Lafleur, and M. Nagatomi p149-79)
Tyler's Insurrection, 1381
Crane, S. The writing lesson of 1381. (In Chaucer's England; ed. by B. A. Hanawalt p201-21)
Green, R. F. John Ball's letters: literary history and historical literature. (In Chaucer's England; ed. by B. A. Hanawalt p176-200)
Typography See Printing
Typology (Theology)
Smolinski, R. Jehovah's peculium: the New Jerusalem and the Jews in Puritan eschatology. (In Early American literature and culture; ed. by K. Z. Derounian-Stodola p84-108)
Tyranny See Despotism
Tyrrell, Ian R.
Women and temperance in international perspective: the world's WCTU, 1880s-1920s. (In Drinking: behavior and belief in modern history; ed. by S. Barrows and R. Room p217-40)
Tyson, Sue
(jt. auth) See Halle, Randall; Sokeland, Sherri, and Tyson, Sue

Tytler, Harriet

Suleri, S. Th
Suleri, S. Th
p75-110)
Tzahou-Alexand
A vase-painte
Acropolis: a
Acropolis 606.
Greek art; ed.
214)

UAW See Unite
Agricultural In
Umansky, Eller
Spiritual exp
gious lives in
States. (In J
perspective; e
Umphlett, Wile
Bibliography
American spo
Umphlett pl9
Formulaic s
fiction traditi
mance in juv
Achievement
ed. by W. L
Unamuno, Mig
A

Quinones,
Quinones, R.
81)
Unani medicin
Roman
Uncertainty
Broome, J.
principle. (I
ed. by J. G
Meeks, J. C
of decision
the investme
nomic man;
Uncle Tom's
Staiger, J.
intertextualit
and receptio
preting film
Undefinability
Undergraduate
Underground
Underground
1945) See
Underground
Tischler, E
and the Gl
the sixties;
Underground
Unger, Richa
Marine pa
building. (I
ed. by D. F

**Figure 10.2**

using the author index, the subject index, or the title or first line index. The preface of the *Poetry Index Annual* declares that it "has been developed to provide access to the preponderance of anthologized poetry which is not indexed anywhere." It also claims to be the "only work to systematically index *all* anthologies as they are published." The dictionary format provides entries by author, title and subject.

Current Search: (twain, mark) <in> ALL
Records: 309
In: Essay & General Lit
Link To:    Ⓢ S·F·X LINCCWeb SFX

| | | |
|---|---|---|
| 80% ⌐ 1 Ⓢ S·F·X | | Lewis, G. The legacy of Huckleberry Finn. In: Splendor in the short grass. University of Texas Press, 2005 |

80% ⌐ 1    Lewis, G. The legacy of Huckleberry Finn. In: Splendor in the short grass. University of Texas
Ⓢ S·F·X    Press, 2005

80% ⌐ 2    Barash, D. P., et. al., On the complaints of Portnoy, Caulfield, Huck Finn, and the Brothers
Ⓢ S·F·X    Karamazov everywhere: parent-offspring conflict. In: Madame Bovary's ovaries. Delacourt Press,
2005

80% ⌐ 3    Cohen, R. *Mark Twain* and William Dean Howells. In: Cohen, Rachel. A chance meeting.
Ⓢ S·F·X    Random House, 2004

80% ⌐ 4    Folks, J. J. *Twain* and the garden of the world: cultural consolidation on the American frontier. In:
Ⓢ S·F·X    In a time of disorder. Lang, P., 2004

80% ⌐ 5    Tenn, W. An innocent in time: *Mark Twain* in King Arthur's court. In: Dancing naked. NESFA
Ⓢ S·F·X    Press, 2004

80% ⌐ 6    Kucich, J. J. The politics of heaven: the Ghost Dance, The gates ajar, and Captain Stormfield. In:
Ⓢ S·F·X    Spectral America. University of Wisconsin PressPopular Press, 2004

80% ⌐ 7    Cohen, R. Willa Cather and *Mark Twain*. In: Cohen, Rachel. A chance meeting. Random House,
Ⓢ S·F·X    2004

80% ⌐ 8    Wonham, H. B. "I want a real coon": *Twain* and ethnic caricature. In: Wonham, Henry B.. Playing
Ⓢ S·F·X    the races. Oxford University Press, 2004

80% ⌐ 9    Cohen, R. *Mark Twain* and Ulysses S. Grant. In: Cohen, Rachel. A chance meeting. Random
Ⓢ S·F·X    House, 2004

80% ⌐ 10    Kazin, A. Creatures of circumstance: *Mark Twain*. In: Kazin, Alfred. Alfred Kazin's America.
Ⓢ S·F·X    HarperCollins, 2003

**Figure 10.3**

## *Criticism and Interpretation*

Articles concerning literary works may be found by using the catalog, periodical indexes and explicators. When using the catalog look for the subheadings Criticism and Interpretation. For example, Stevenson, Robert Louis 1859–1895 — Criticism and Interpretation.

An explicator is a bibliography of articles about a literary work. Most explicators are specific, e.g. the poetry explication. There are guides, histories and dictionaries available for forms of literature. Concordances are also available for many authors and for specific works, such as the Bible. A concordance lists and locates all uses of specific words by an author in either his or her entire output or just in one or more works. There are also many books that can be consulted to help identify a quotation, such as

FICTION CATALOG
FOURTEENTH EDITION

**Trollope, Joanna**—*Continued*
Frances, her quiet, devoted twin, finds love with the sexy, supportive, but married—and foreign—Luis. This British author excels at setting up the stuff of female fantasy and, from those worn materials, making something that draws you in and slams you with a thud of emotion so authentic it becomes your own." New Yorker

**Truman, Margaret, 1924-**
Murder at the Library of Congress. Random House 1999 322p $25
ISBN 0-375-50068-5         LC 99-14953
Also available large print edition $25 (ISBN 0-375-40865-7)
"Pre-Columbian art expert Annabel Smith has been asked to write an article on a second diary of Columbus' voyage—if such an artifact really exists. Her research takes her into the inner workings of LC and leads to the discovery of illicit payoffs and the solutions to a pair of murders, one old, one new." Booklist

Murder at the National Cathedral. Random House 1990 293p o.p.
        LC 89-43433
Sleuth Mackensie Smith "and his lover, Annabel Reed, have just been married. Then the Episcopal priest who performed the service is murdered, and criminal law professor Smith launches his investigation. . . . Links between a world peace organization, federal and international spy networks, scorned lovers, activist priests, and distraught choir boys are . . . interwoven into the plot." Booklist

Murder at the Watergate; a novel. Random House 1998 333p $25
ISBN 0-679-43535-2         LC 98-3725
Vice President Joseph Aprile, "is determined to stake out a position on Mexico different from his president's as he prepares to seek the Oval Office in the next election. Mackensie Smith, law professor at George Washington University and a friend of Aprile's is in an ideal position to help, since he is already scheduled to be in Mexico as a U.N. election observer. When Mackensie accepts a clandestine assignment to meet with a Mexican rebel leader on Aprile's behalf, he is launched into a dangerous and deadly game involving diplomats and assassins, politicians and traitors, aristocrats and rebels." Publ Wkly

Murder in the White House; a novel. Arbor House 1980 235p o.p.
        LC 79-54004
"When Secretary of State Blaine is murdered in the Lincoln Sitting Room of the White House, President Webster orders Special Counsel Fairchild to coordinate efforts to solve the case with the authorities. The lawyer turned detective begins investigating everyone with access to the White House, including Webster, the First Lady and her daughter Lynne." Publ Wkly

Murder on Capitol Hill; a novel. Arbor House 1981 255p o.p.
        LC 80-70223
"Lawyer Lydia James agrees to the request of Veronica Caldwell to act as counsel for the senatorial committee investigating the killing of her husband, Senate Majority leader Cale Caldwell. He has been stabbed at a reception honoring him, where his black-sheep son Mark,

member of a fanatical cult, is among the 200 or more guests. Mark is arrested for the murder, and also on suspicion of having killed Jimmye, Veronica's niece, years earlier, an unsolved crime. His mother and brother, Cale Jr., sorrowfully agree that Mark is guilty, but Lydia believes the charges are trumped up. She gets herself into dicey situations, chasing clues." Publ Wkly

**Trumbo, Dalton, 1905-1976**
Johnny got his gun. Lippincott 1939 309p o.p.
"Far more than an antiwar polemic, this compassionate description of the effects of war on one soldier is a poignant tribute to the human instinct to survive. Badly mutilated, blind, and deaf, Johnny fights to communicate with an uncomprehending medical world debating his fate." Shapiro. Fic for Youth. 3d edition

**Truscott, Lucian K., 1947-**
Dress gray; [by] Lucian K. Truscott IV. Doubleday 1979 c1978 489p o.p.
        LC 78-1250
A West Point "plebe is found drowned; information, quickly suppressed, indicates he was murdered; a cadet, one Rysam Parker Slaight III, gets wind of the coverup and finds himself in trouble with the coverup authorities, a group of West Point officers and some powerful cronies at the Pentagon." New Yorker
Followed by Full dress gray

Full dress gray; [by] Lucian K. Truscott IV. Morrow 1998 384p $25
ISBN 0-688-15993-1         LC 98-4320
In this sequel to Dress gray, Ry Slaight "returns to West Point 30 years later as its newly appointed superintendent. His daughter Jacey is a company commander in the cadet corps. When one of her plebes dies during dress parade, Jacey sets out to find the cause of her death. Not even a brutal assault by fellow cadets stops her in her quest. The investigation leads to the army's highest circles and uncovers a conspiracy to subvert the cadets' treasured Honor Code. The result is a thoroughly satisfying mystery story with an uncommon setting." Libr J

Heart of war. Dutton 1997 370p o.p.
        LC 96-29876
The protagonist of this thriller is "Maj. Kara Guldry, a lawyer and West Point graduate who is assigned to investigate the murder of a Lt. Sheila Worthy. Kara soon discovers that the young woman's lover was none other than General Beckwith, the base commander. After her friend, Lannie Love, another Beckwith mistress, is stabbed in a similar manner, Kara is convinced that Beckwith is the key to the murders." Libr J
"Despite some occasionally breathy prose, Truscott's novel provides a fascinating peek behind the olive drab curtain, blending a solid plot with a piercing critique of hypocrisy, power politics and sexual misconduct in today's armed forces." N Y Times Book Rev

**Tryon, Thomas**
In the fire of spring. Knopf 1991 609p o.p.
        LC 91-414
In this sequel to The wings of the morning "a runaway slave, Rose Mills, is helped to safety by the abolitionist Appleton Talcott and two of his daughters as they return

Figure 10.4

*Bartlett's Familiar Quotations*. Most of these have subject and keyword indexes besides author indexes.

To locate reviews of movies, plays, television shows or other performances, follow the same general procedure used for finding book reviews. Reviews are most likely to be found in newspapers, periodicals and the internet and the subject headings should name the type of performance: Moving Pictures — Reviews. Libraries have not gotten around to using the simpler terms Films or Movies. To find plot summaries, use the catalog or check to see if the library owns some Magill sets, such as *Masterplots*. These sets include the characters in the story plus a short summary of the plot. They are not adequate substitutes for reading the work but may help to refresh the memory.

Remember, before using an unfamiliar index, guide, bibliography or other reference tool, read the introductory information to figure out the organization of the work, included or excluded materials, and scope or other limitations of the work being consulted.

## Online Sources

Are you a fiction buff? Does your major include a study of fiction? *NoveList*, available in some libraries, provides access to more than 125,000 titles. Among the searchable area are: author read-alikes; book discussion guides, annotated booklists and reviews. Boolean searching is available as is browsing by category, genre, theme, etc. This database is updated monthly and adds approximately 9,000 titles annually.

*LitFinder* (formerly *Poemfinder.com*) is a service from Thomson-Gale. It currently includes poems, stories, essays, plays and speeches. The full text of 125,000+ poems: 850,000 poem citations: thousands of full text stories: more than 1,000 full text plays and the best known speeches of 2,500 years are included in this database. Basic, advanced and expert searching levels are available. The database uses stop words and Boolean searching is included.

## Exercises for Chapter 10

1. Using the catalog, identify and record the indexes of various literary forms owned by your library.
2. Using the general information in this chapter and using what you have

learned in earlier chapters, answer the following questions. List the sources used to answer the questions.

(A)    Where can you find a copy of the poem "Birches" by Robert Frost.

(B)    Find the titles and locations of three short stories written by Anton Chekhov.

(C)    Find two book reviews of *The Five People You Meet in Heaven* by Mitch Albom.

(D)    Locate two reviews of the movie *The Five People You Meet in Heaven.*

(E)    Find three plays written by Neil Simon including productions for stage, radio and television. Locate the reviews for one of them.

(F)    Find an analysis or criticism of two works by Mark Twain.

(G)    Find a plot summary of a novel by James Fennimore Cooper.

## Important Terms in Chapter 10

concordance
*explicator*
*anthology*

## Important Books for Chapter 10

Adamson, Lynda. *World Historical Fiction: An Annotated Guide to Novels for Adults and Young Adults.* Phoenix, Ariz.: Oryx Press, 1999.

*American Poetry Index: An Author and Title Index to Poetry by Americans in Single Author Collections.* V. 1– , 1981–82, ed. by Editorial Board, Granger Book Co. Great Neck, NY: Granger, 1988.

Bartlett, John, and Justin Kaplan. *Familiar Quotations: A Collection of Passages, Phrases, and Proverbs Traced to Their Sources in Ancient and Modern Literature.* 17th edition, Boston: Little Brown, 2002.

Carruth, Gorton, and Eugene Ehrlich. *The Harper Book of American Quotations.* New York: Harper & Row, 1988.

*Contemporary Literary Criticism: Excerpts from Criticism of the Works of Today's Novelists, Poets, Playwrights, Short Story Writers, Scriptwriters, and Other Creative Writers.* Detroit: Gale Research. 1973–. Cumulative indexes included.

*Essay and General Literature Index, 1900–1933: An Index to About 40,000 Essays and Articles in 2144 Volumes of Collections of Essays and Miscellaneous Works.* Edited by Minnie Earl Sears and Marion Shaw. New York: H. W. Wilson, 1934. (Kept up-to-date with supplements for 1934–1940, 1941–1947, 1948–1954, 1955–1959, 1960–1964, 1965–1969, 1970–1974, 1975–1979, 1980–1984, 1985–1989,1990–1994, 1995–1999, 2000–2004, with annual, biennial or triennial cumulations. Also available on WilsonWeb.

*Fiction Catalog.* 14th ed. New York: H. W. Wilson, 2000. Supplements, 2001–.

Harner, James L. *Literary Research Guide: A Guide to Reference Sources for the Study of Literatures in English and Related Topics.* 4th ed. New York: Moden Language Association of America, 2002.

Keller, Dean Howard. *Index to Plays in Periodicals.* Rev. and enl. ed. Metuchen, NJ: Scarecrow, 1979. *Index to Plays in periodicals, 1977–1987.* Metuchen, NJ, Scarecrow Press, 1990.

Serafin, Steven. *Encyclopedia of World Literature in the 20th Century.* 3rd ed. Detroit: St. James Press, 1999.

Kale, Tessa and Edith Granger. *The Columbia Granger's Index to Poetry in Anthologies.* 12th ed. New York, Columbia University press, 2002.

King, Neil and Sarah King. *Dictionary of Literature in English.* Chicago, Ill: Fitzroy Dearborn Publishers, 2002.

Kuntz, Joseph Marshall. *Poetry Explication: A Check List of Interpretation Since 1925 of British and American Poems Past and Present.* 3rd ed. Boston: G. K. Hall, 1980.

Magill, Frank N. *Masterpieces of World Literature.* New York: Harper and Row, 1989.

*Masterplots.* 2nd revised edition, ed. by Frank Magill. Englewood Cliffs, NJ: Salem Press, 1996. (Available series include: European Fiction, British and Commonwealth Fiction, American Fiction, Short Stories, World Fiction, Women's Literature, Nonfiction, Poetry, Juvenile and Young Adult Literature, and Drama.)

*Masterplots II. American Fiction Series.* Edited by Steven G. Kellerman. Rev. ed. Pasadena, Ca: Salem Press, 2000. 6 vols.

*Masterplots II. Poetry Series.* Edited by Philip K. Jason. Rev. ed. Pasadena, Ca: Salem Press, 2002. 8 vols.

*Masterplots II. Drama Series.* Edited by Christian Hollis Moe. Rev. Ed. Pasadena, Ca: Salem Press, 2004. 4 vols.

*Masterplots II. Short Story Series.* Edited by Charles E. May. Rev. ed. Pasadena, Ca: Salem Press, 2004. 8 vols.

*Masterplots Annual Volume, 1954–.* Edited by Frank Magill. New York: Salem, 1955–.

Modern Language Association of America. *MLA International Bibliography of Books and Articles on the Modern Language and Literatures, 1921–*. Published as a supplement to PMLA Journal). Also available on CR-ROM.

Moss, Joyce and George Wilson. *Literature and Its Time: Profiles of 300 Notable Literary Works and the Historical Events That Influenced Them*. Detroit: Gale Research, 1997. (5 volumes). Supplement 1, 2 vols. 2003.

Moulton, Charles Wells. *The Library of Literary Criticism of English and American* Authors. Buffalo, NY: Moulton, 1901–05. Eight vols. Reprinted by Peter Smith, 1959.

Newton, Keith. *The Columbia Granger's Index to Poetry in Collected and Selected Works*. 2nd ed. New York: Columbia University Press, 2004.

*Play Index*, 1949–1952, 1953–1960, 1961–1967, 1968–1972, 1973–1977, 1978–1982, 1983–1987, 1988–1992, 1993–1997. New York: H. W. Wilson, 1949–.

*Poetry Index Annual*. Great Neck, NY: Granger, 1982–1993. Ceased publication.

Ruppert, James and John R. Leo. *Guide to American Poetry Explication*. Bostom, Mass.: G.K. Hall, 1989. 2 vols.

*Short Story Criticism: Excerpts from Criticism of the Works of Short Fiction Writers*. Edited by Janet Witalec. Detroit: Gale Research, 1988–. (v. 61 published in early 2003.)

*Short Story Index*. New York: H. W. Wilson, 1953–.

Sutton, Roberta. *Speech Index: An Index to 259 Collections of World Famous Orations and Speeches for Various Occasions*. 4th ed. Metuchen, NJ: Scarecrow, 1966. Supplements 1966–1970 by Sutton and Charity Mitchell (1972); supplement, 1971–1975 by Charity Mitchell (1977); supplement, 1966–1980 by Charity Mitchell (1982).

*Teachers & Writers Handbook of Poetry Forms*. Edited by Ron Padgett. New York: Teachers & Writers Collaborative, 1987.

Trudeau, Lawrence J. *Poetry Criticism: v. 61, excerpts from criticisms of the works of the most significant and widely studied poets of world literature*. Detroit, Thomson Gale, 2005.

Williams, Robert Coleman, ed. A *Concordance to the Collected Poems of Dylan Thomas*. Lincoln: University of Nebraska Press, 1966.

# 11

# E-Books

## Objectives

After studying this chapter the student shall be able to

- define e-books
- determine if e-books are available through the library catalog
- find e-books via the internet

## General Information

Electronic books (e-books) have been available for more than 30 years but recent advances in digital technology have made them more available and easier to obtain and read. Basically, e-books are digital versions of books already in print format. Some newer titles may actually be published in both print and digital format at the same time.

Project Gutenberg began in 1971 at the University of Illinois and was one of the first to transfer books to digital format. Book titles in the public domain (titles where the copyright had expired) were the first titles to be transferred to digital format and offered free via the internet. Hardware and software are required for accessing e-books. There are several readers designed especially for use with e-books. To view (read) e-books with a computer, it is generally necessary to have access to Adobe software. Some sites allow e-books to be downloaded to a personal computer or a palm.

The Library of Congress has been involved with digitizing documents since the early 1990s. Preservation of documents that were too fragile to be handled was important. Congress has funded a national digital preservation program involving many universities, foundations and organizations.

Many reference books and periodicals are available in e-format. The library either subscribes (as with a printed copy of a periodical — see chapter 8) or purchases documents in e-format. For reference books such as encyclopedias, dictionaries or Books in Print access is only available if the library purchases (or subscribes) from the publisher. These types of sources are generally not available free via the internet. Not all libraries subscribe to the same e-books. Descriptions of a few of the most popular ebook suppliers follow.

## Project Gutenberg

According to their web site (*www.gutenberg.org*) as of November 1, 2005, Project Gutenberg, with more than 16,000 titles, is the largest free collection of e-books. Their mission statement is "To encourage the creation and distribution of eBooks." The Project Gutenberg website provides simple directions for use. The catalog can be searched by author, title, language, words in the full text or recently posted titles. The site is updated daily with full text search updated weekly. The site lists the languages in which more than 50 books are available along with categories, such as audio books, recorded music, sheet music, pictures, etc.

## NetLibrary

NetLibrary is a division of OCLC (see chapter 15) and is available from subscribing libraries. The collection includes literature, fiction, reference works, scholarly works and publicly accessible titles. Not all libraries subscribe to the entire NetLibrary collection which includes in excess of 18,000 e-books. Some libraries permit access only from the library but some may permit access from outside the library. A valid library card is generally required for access to the NetLibrary collection. If your library subscribes to NetLibrary you will need to check with one of the librarians for procedures on accessing NetLibrary from outside the library. The site is generally available 24/7.

# *ebrary*

ebrary was founded in 1999 and its collection exceeds 60,000 titles. Access is easily gained via Google or other search engines and is available "anytime/anywhere" according to their home page (*www.ebrary.com*). Libraries or institutions can subscribe to one of several plans. Their mission statement as stated on their web page is "To become the global standard for secure distribution, acquisition and management of valuable authoritative documents over computer networks." This site allows multiple simultaneous users. Access to ebrary Reader or its Isaac (in development in 2005) are required to use the collection.

## *Other Sites*

Searching the internet with Google or other search engines will proved access to other suppliers of e-books. Many are associated with universities, public libraries or government agencies. An example of a university based site with free access to e-books is at the University of Pennsylvania. Check out their web site *www.digital.library.upenn.edu*. The University of Michigan has a directory of e-texts at The Internet Public Library at *www.ipl.org*.

## *Exercises for Chapter 11*

1. Does your library subscribe to e-books? If so, how are the accessed from
   a. within the library?
   b. outside the library?
2. Access Project Gutenberg and search for your favorite author. What did you find?
3. Using Google, Yahoo or other search engine and locate at least two sites/sources of e-books. Log on to each site and
   a. Search for your favorite author or a subject
   b. Compare the types of searches available
   c. Compare the ease and speed of the searches
   d. Make a list of the websites you found most useful for future reference

## Important Terms for Chapter 11

*e-books*
*public domain*

## Important Books for Chapter 11

Curtis, Richard, and William Thomas Quick. *How to Get Your E-Book Published: An Insider's Guide to the World of Electronic Publishing.* Cincinnati, Ohio: Writer's Digest Books, 2002.

Kleper, Michael L. *The Handbook of Digital Publishing.* 2 vols. Upper Saddle River, NJ: Prentice Hall PTR, 2001.

Van Buren, Chris, and Jeff Cogswell. *Poor Richard's Creating E-Books: How Authors, Publishers and Corporations Get into Digital Print.* Lakewood, Co.: Top Floor Publishing, 2001.

# 12

# Governmental Information and Government Documents

## Objectives

After studying this chapter the student shall be able to

- find names and addresses of congressmen and state officials in any district in any state
- find the name, address and organizational history of any federal agency
- find information about function and membership of any congressional committee
- use sources to locate data on local governments
- use the *Congressional Record* to find information on congressional proceedings
- find documents using indexes and bibliographies
- use the *Monthly Catalog* (paper or online) to find specific documents
- recognize the indexes and guides for documents located in the library
- determine the type of information available in indexes and directories of depositories

## Governments—Local, State, Federal

This section deals with finding information about municipal, county, state or federal governments and their officials. There are many directories and guides that provide this kind of information and some examples are described in this chapter. If the library does not have these specific titles it will have similar ones. If the student is unable to locate the texts (check the H and J section in the reference section) then they should ask the librarian for assistance.

The *Municipal Year Book*, published by the International City Management Association, provides a variety of information about cities, including profiles, population statistics, types of government, salaries of employees, services provided and the names of officials (e.g., mayor, police chief and fire chief). It also includes discussions of the state regulations that affect municipalities. The volume has both textual descriptions and comparative charts. Another useful source of information on municipal and county governments is the *County and City Data Book*, which is published by the U.S. Bureau of the Census as a supplement to the *Statistical Abstracts of the United States.*

There are several other sources of information about state governments and elected officials. Many states publish a handbook describing the organization of the state government. For example, New York State publishes the *Manual for the Use of the Legislature of the State of New York* (commonly referred to as the "blue book"). This annual volume provides a copy of the state's constitution, a short history of the state, names of elected officials, biographies and photographs of the highest ranking members of the executive department and state legislature, and a complete organizational description of all departments of state government. These descriptions include names of department heads, office addresses and discussions of each department's responsibilities. They also include some political information, such as the names and addresses of state and county major party officeholders.

The federal government publishes another item, the *United States Government Manual* (formally the *United States Government Organization Manual*), annually and it is invaluable in untangling the mysteries of locating agencies within particular departments, what their functions are, where they are located (including regional offices) and who is in charge. The manual includes organizational charts that help in determining the hierarchical structure of each agency. The inclusion of regional offices with the names, addresses and phone numbers is also useful. Finally, the manual includes a comprehensive subject index that can be used to decide which agency or agencies are involved with specific tasks.

The Government Printing Office (GPO) issues the *Congressional Directory* that has a brief biography of every member of Congress. Besides

Government Document collections are often shelved separately from the rest of the collection.

the biographies, it includes the district numbers and the counties within each district. Also included are all committee assignments, statistical information about Congress, floor plans of the Capitol building, names of members of the executive branch, diplomats and consular officers in the United States, and members of the press who are entitled to admission to Congress, as well as other esoteric but useful bits of information about Congress. The *Congressional Staff Directory* contains the names of members of Congress, but its most functional feature is the listing of all the staff members who work for members of Congress and on congressional committees. The directory also lists 9,900 cities with a population of more than 1,500 along with the names of members of congress who represent the city. The key personnel aides to the executive branch are recorded with the office addresses, titles and phone numbers.

The *Congressional Quarterly Almanac*, published annually, is particularly valuable in providing information on actions taken by Congress during a particular year. It also encompasses other information such as roll call votes, lobbyists and presidential messages to Congress. The summaries of legislation, background and reports of action taken provide beginning information for researching congressional action in any area.

The *Congressional Record* is issued daily and contains the complete text of presidential messages, debates and congressional speeches. It also contains votes on all bills, although the texts of the bills are not included. The GPO publishes the *Record* only when Congress is in session. Indexes are published after the session ends. Members may add to the *Record* and this additional information, "extension of remarks," may be included as an appendix but may be omitted from the final edition of the *Record*.

The format, order of information and indexing have varied since the *Record* began in 1873, so one should read the introductory remarks before using the *Record* or its indexes. For materials before 1873 the following titles should be consulted: *Debates and Proceedings, Annals of Congress* (1789–1824); *Register of Debates* (1824–1837); and *Congressional Globe* (1833–1873). They are published in both microfilm and paper copy.

## Government Documents

Governments at all levels publish many documents. The United States government documents are usually easier to identify and locate than those of small municipalities or county governments. Most state governments publish checklists of their publications which simply identify publications.

Libraries designated as "depositories," receive documents free of charge from municipal, county, state or federal governments.

The scope and quality of holdings in a library depend on a variety of factors, such as the date of institution and how heavily the public uses the holdings. Theft, damage and misplacement cause document loss. Some depositories do not receive all documents. These libraries are designated as selective depositories, since they choose only those documents they wish to receive. Libraries have indexes and guides to documents and directories of depository libraries. Federal documents and those reports produced by federal contracts are not copyrighted and the public is free to use them.

## Federal Depository Library System

The first depository libraries were created in 1813. Congress created the Federal Depository Library System (FDLP) by enactment in 1857 and 1858. In 1869 the position of superintendent of documents was created. The Printing Act of 1895 consolidated many previous laws and departments which dealt with aspects of preparation, printing and distribution of public documents. This act also established a "systematic program for bibliographic control" with the creation of *Monthly Catalog* and the *Document Catalog*. This act also expanded the number of depositories and created "by law" depositories which included state libraries, governmental agency libraries and West Point and Annapolis. This system was relatively unchanged until 1962 when the Depository Act of 1962 was passed.

There are 53 regional depositories which receive all items designated for depositories. Each state has a regional depository and some states have two regional depositories. "Over 1,300 public, academic, state and law libraries serve as an information link with the Federal Government by maintaining collections of Government publications" (Monthly Catalog PRELIM.11, December 2003). Each congressional district is entitled to have two depositories although with changes in district boundaries over the years some districts have more than two. Executive departments of the federal government, accredited law schools, service academies and independent government agencies can request to be depositories.

Depository libraries are subject to rules concerning free access to the collection by the general public, the retaining and discarding of documents and inspection of the collection by staff from the superintendent of documents office. Regional depositories are responsible for providing free access, interlibrary loans and reference services in their region. To locate the nearest depository library check *www.gpoaccess.gov/libraries.html*.

Some depository items are published only in paper format, others only in microform or magnetic format and others are available in either paper, microform format (in which case the depository library can choose which format it prefers) or via the internet.

## SuDoc Classification System

Government documents are not harder to use or find, they are just organized differently. Unlike the Dewey Decimal or Library of Congress classification systems which arrange materials by subject, the SuDoc system is a provenance (or hierarchy) system. This system arranges material by the issuing agency and its various departments. The documents are arranged in a hierarchy order for each agency. They are specified as follows: parent agency, sub agency, series or generic type, individual publication and date. See Figure 12.1 from the *Monthly Catalog* and note that the departments' names are in the center of the column. The SuDoc number is also in heavy black type. It begins with one or two letters to identify the agency (see Figure 12.1). The D is for the Defense Department. The number after the letter(s) and before the decimal indicate the level, e.g. 1 for cabinet level document. The number after the decimal indicates the type of document, e.g. directive, report, newsletter, etc. As with the Dewey and LC systems there are charts noting the numbers used for departmental levels and types of documents. The numbers and letter after the colon provide information about the update of publication and the format of the document, e.g. 990 means published in 1990. Formats can be paper, microform, magnetic tape, etc. Each format has a specific number. The frequent reorganization within the federal government sometimes causes disorder with this system. See Figure 12.2 for the sample explanations printed at the beginning of each issue of the *Monthly Catalog*.

Figure 12.3 is the beginning of the entries for Military History (Defense Department) as found on the internet via *www.gpoaccess.gov*. Searching can be done by selecting from menus or by typing in terms to be searched. Note that the entries appear very different in format from the entries in the print edition of the *Monthly Catalog*. Also note that those items available for purchase include the price and an order can be placed by adding the item to your cart. Look at the second entry in Figure 12.3 for the book titled *Cedar Creek*. Note that the SuDoc number comes at the end of the entry. The SuDoc number still begins with a **D** (D 114.2:C 32)

Energy  Department

### ARMY ELECTRONICS RESEARCH AND DEVELOPMENT COMMAND
Defense Dept.
Fort Monmouth, NJ 07703

**2003-19708**          D 111.14:(V.NO.&NOS.)A

Army communicator .
  (PB)   ●Item 0343-C-02 (online)
  I.   Purl:   http://purl.access.gpo.gov/GPO/LPS1510   OCLC
44763570

### MILITARY HISTORY CENTER
Defense Dept.
Washington, DC 20315

**2003-19709**          D 114.2:SO 5/2

United States forces, Somalia . — 2003.
  v, 276 p. :   ●Item 0344
  OCLC 53017662

**2003-19710**          D 114.19:C 76

Soldier-statesmen of the Constitution . — 1987.
  xiii, 298 p. :   ●Item 344-G   ●Item 344-G (online)   S/N 008-
029-00153-5
  I.   Purl:   http://purl.access.gpo.gov/GPO/LPS36445   OCLC
15549460

**2003-19711**          D 114.20:(NOS.)A

Army history .
  v. : (PB / US Army)   ●Item 0345-B (MF)
  OCLC 21546174

### CHEMICAL CORPS
Defense Dept.
Fort McClellan, AL 36205-5020

**2003-19712**          D 116.17:(DATE)A

CML Army chemical review .
  v. : (PB)   ●Item 0346-A (MF)   S/N 708-067-00000-8
  OCLC 26201542

### NAVY DEPARTMENT
Defense Dept.
Washington, DC 20350

**2003-19713**          D 201.2:SD-34

Effects of directed energy weapons . — [1994]
  ●Item 03070 (online)
  I.   Purl:   http://purl.access.gpo.gov/GPO/LPS36040   OCLC
52995356

### NAVAL EDUCATION AND TRAINING COMMAND
Defense Dept.
Pensacola, FL 32508

**2003-19714**          D 207.208/2:P45/9

Military requirements for petty officers third and second class. —
[2001 ed.]. — 2001.
  1 v. (various pagings) :   Shipping list no.: 2003-0261-P.   ●Item
0404
  OCLC 53017726

Page  22

### AIR FORCE DEPARTMENT
Defense Dept.
Washington, DC 20330

**2003-19715**          D 301 26/2:(DATE)

AUL index to military periodicals (AULIMP) . — [1989]-
  ●Item 0424-I (online)
  I.   Purl:   http://purl.access.gpo.gov/GPO/LPS3260   OCLC
52995105

**2003-19716**          D 301.26/2:(V.NO.&NOS.)

Air University Library index to military periodicals .
  v. ;   ●Item 0424-I (MF)   ●Item 0424-I (online)
  I.   Purl:   http://purl.access.gpo.gov/GPO/LPS3260   OCLC
25394637

**2003-19717**          D 301.45/19-13:(DATE)A

Research highlights .
  ●Item 0422-B-04 (online)
  I.   Purl:   http://purl.access.gpo.gov/GPO/LPS21718   OCLC
50507271

### AIR FORCE ACADEMY
Defense Dept.
Air Force Academy, CO 80840

**2003-19718**          D 305.6/5:(DATE)A

Cadet handbook .
  v. :   ●Item 0425-A-16
  OCLC 45095113

### ENERGY DEPARTMENT
Washington, DC 20585

**2003-19719**          E 1.2:AC 7/(DATE)

Acquisition & assistance digest .
  v. ;   ●Item 0429-A (MF)
  I.   Purl:   Electronic   version:   http://purl.access.gpo.gov/GPO/
LPS36662   OCLC 36901672

**2003-19720**          E 1.2:G 29/5/(DATE)

Geothermal today .
  v. :   ●Item 0429-A (MF)
  OCLC 50036329

**2003-19721**          E 1.23:(NOS.)

Materials & components in fossil energy applications .
  ●Item 0474-A-04 (online)
  I.   Purl:   http://purl.access.gpo.gov/GPO/LPS11933   OCLC
46940806

**2003-19722**          E 1.23:(NOS.)A

Materials & components in fossil energy applications .
  v. ;   ●Item 0474-A-04 (MF)
  I.   Purl:   http://purl.access.gpo.gov/GPO/LPS11933   OCLC
26000057

**2003-19723**          E 1.38/5:(DATE)

Wind power today .
  v. :   ●Item 0429-P-09 (MF)
  I. Purl:   PDF version: http://purl.access.gpo.gov/GPO/LPS36582
OCLC 44712421

**2003-19724**          E 1.68/2:(NOS.)

Site characterization progress report. Yucca Mountain, Nevada .
  v. ;   ●Item 0474-B-07 (MF)
  OCLC 53007911

**2003-19725**          E 1.90/3:(DATE)

Environmental management .
  v. :   ●Item 0474-B-06

**Figure 12.1**

## Catalog Arrangement/Sample Entry

This catalog contains brief descriptions of U.S. Government publications arranged in Superintendent of Documents (SuDocs) classification number order and may be accessed by title keyword index (alphabetical list of truncated titles, arranged by important words selected from publications titles). These brief records are based on full bibliographic records available in the online version of the Monthly Catalog which is cumulated from 1994, available as the Catalog of U.S. Government Publications (**CGP**) on the GPO Access internet site at **http://www.gpoaccess.gov/cgp/index.html** The following sample entry is a composite designed to illustrate the major features of a brief Monthly Catalog citation.

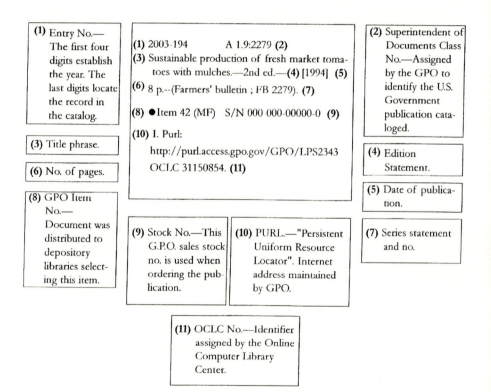

**(1)** Entry No.—The first four digits establish the year. The last digits locate the record in the catalog.

**(3)** Title phrase.

**(6)** No. of pages.

**(8)** GPO Item No.—Document was distributed to depository libraries selecting this item.

**(1)** 2003-194          A 1.9:2279 **(2)**
**(3)** Sustainable production of fresh market tomatoes with mulches.—2nd ed.—**(4)** [1994] **(5)**
**(6)** 8 p.--(Farmers' bulletin ; FB 2279). **(7)**
**(8)** ●Item 42 (MF)   S/N 000 000-00000-0 **(9)**
**(10)** I. Purl:
       http://purl.access.gpo.gov/GPO/LPS2343
       OCLC 31150854. **(11)**

**(2)** Superintendent of Documents Class No.—Assigned by the GPO to identify the U.S. Government publication cataloged.

**(4)** Edition Statement.

**(5)** Date of publication.

**(7)** Series statement and no.

**(9)** Stock No.—This G.P.O. sales stock no. is used when ordering the publication.

**(10)** PURL.—"Persistent Uniform Resource Locator". Internet address maintained by GPO.

**(11)** OCLC No.—Identifier assigned by the Online Computer Library Center.

**Figure 12.2**

for the Defense Department. There is also a notation that this document is out of print and thus not available for purchase.

Government Printing Office (GPO) database is also available via OCLC's FirstSearch. Figure 12.4 is a basic keyword search for documents about military history. Figure 12.5 is the OCLC entry for one item retrieved

# Subject Bibliography

## Military History (098)

Civil War | Korean Conflict | Persian Gulf Conflict | Revolutionary War | Vietnam War
World War I | World War II | General History

**New Titles** Sign up to receive e-mail notification when new
**by Topic** titles become available for this category through the
**E-mail Alert Service** New Titles By Topic E-mail Alert Service.

## CIVIL WAR

### Battle of ... Self-Guided Tour:

**Ball's Bluff.** BOOK. 2001. Discusses a battle which took place in Virginia on October 20, 1861. The disastrous defeat of the Union forces resulted in the death of a United States Senator, the arrest of a Union general, and the creation of a Congressional oversight committee that would keep senior Union commanders looking over their shoulders for the remainder of the war. Includes Selected Biographical Sketches. 92 p.; ill. 0-16-066557-4

S/N 008-029-00372-4 – $7.50  **Add to Cart** In Stock - Warehouse and Retail (Priced)

**Cedar Creek.** BOOK. 1992. Discusses a battle which took place in Virginia on October 19, 1864 and was won by Union forces. Describes 12 sites which were important to the battle and which may be explored through self-guided automobile tours. Includes maps and sepia photographs. 54 p.; ill. 0-16-026854-0
D 114.2:C 32

S/N 008-029-00214-1 – $3.50 Out of Print - GPO

**New Market.** BOOK. 1988. Discusses a Civil War battle which was fought in 1864 in Virginia and won by the Confederate forces. Describes 12 sites which were important to the battle and which may be explored at the site through guided tours. Includes maps and sepia photographs. 60 p.; ill. 0-16-001989-3
D 114.2:B 32/2

S/N 008-029-00187-0 – $3.50  **Add to Cart** In Stock - Warehouse and Retail (Priced)

**Second Manassas.** BOOK. 1990. Third in a series of booklets on American battlefields intended to help soldiers use the past to enhance their understanding of the United States Army's future. Examines the Battle of Second Manassas in the form of a tour which goes to 12 locations important to aspects of the battle. Stops on the tour have been selected to help the visitor see the battle developing. 76 p.; ill. D 114.2:M 31

Figure 12.3

in the search in Figure 12.4. Note that the search retrieved 736 documents and the search strategy is included (keyword Military AND keyword history). The entry looks similar to book entries found in OCLC's World-Cat. (see Chapter 15 ). Look for the descriptor **Class Descriptors:** to find GPO and the SuDoc number. The SuDoc number begins with a **D** indicating that this document was issued from the Defense Department. Find the descriptor **Access:** and note the reference to *http://purl.access.gpo.gov.* Compare the formats of Figure 12.1, 12.3 and 12.5 and note the differences.

## *Government Printing Office (GPO)*

The Printing Act of 1860 created the GPO and it opened on March 4, 1861. The GPO is officially an agency of the legislative branch but the president appoints the public printer with the consent of Congress. The public printer and the GPO are accountable to that body. The Public Printer is the individual who oversees the Government Printing Office. The position was created by Congress. A message from the public printer (2005) indicated that the GPO is at the "epicenter of technological changes as it embraces its historic mission while looking to the digital future."

The office of superintendent of documents was established on March 3, 1869, as a part of the Department of the Interior and transferred to the GPO in 1895. The Congressional Joint Committee on Printing (JCP) is a sort of board of directors for the GPO.

The GPO is the largest publisher in the United States and perhaps in the world. It acts like other publishers and also prints many items. Due to the large volume of material to be printed, the GPO contracts out many of the printing jobs to small printing companies. It coordinates the operations from the Washington, D.C., offices. There are also 13 regional printing offices as well as the Consumer Information Office in Pueblo, Colorado, which acts as a distributor. The GPO also operates some bookstores which sell government documents. Some bookstore chains also stock some government documents. Documents may also be ordered online. Go to *www.gpoaccess.gov* to access the online bookstore.

The 1895 law allows the superintendent of documents to sell documents and the GPO selects titles to include in the sales program. Currently there is a formula for determining the sale price: cost + 50 percent. This sales program generates revenue for the GPO and allows the agency to support the documents sent free to depository libraries and those documents distributed to the general public free of charge (many through the

## GPO Basic Search

- Enter search terms in one or more boxes and click on **Search**.

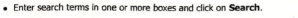

**Home     Databases     Searching     Results**     Staff View | My Account | Options | Comments
                                                                      | **Exit** | Hide tips

Basic Search   Advanced Search   Expert Search   Previous Searches   Go to page

**Intro   News   Help**                    Current database: **GPO**

Search   Clear

**Search in database:**   GPO
                          U.S. government publications                    (Updated: 2005-05-11)

**Keyword**   military history

**Title**

**Author**

Search   Clear

Figure 12.4

center in Pueblo). Recently the GPO made some changes in its system of payment and now accepts major credit cards besides prepayment and deposit accounts. The GPO sells many documents to commercial publishers which then may be reprinted and sold or used in other ways. For example, the census material, in magnetic format, is sold to many types of corporations that can manipulate the data for their own use. All these sales operations generate revenue that makes the GPO a self-sustaining operation, requiring little or no taxpayer funds. Due to cutbacks in the Reagan administration, fewer documents (titles) were published and print runs were smaller thus curtailing the public's access to some information.

# Government Printing Office on the Internet

GPO Access is the free electronic access service provided by the Government Printing Office at www.access.gpo.gov. All information that is provided through this site is the official published version and can be used without restriction unless specifically noted. The *GPO Services* section includes **A-Z Resources List; Locate a Federal Depository; U.S. Government online Bookstore** and **Ben's Guide to the U.S. Government.** The

## GPO Monthly Catalog Detailed Record

• Click on a checkbox to mark a record to be e-mailed or printed in Marked Records.

**Home**    **Databases**    **Searching**    **Results**    Staff View | My Account | Options | Comments
| **Exit** | Hide tips

**List of Records**    **Detailed Record**    **Marked Records**    **Saved Records**    Go to page

---

**Libraries  E-mail  Print  Export  Help**    **GPO Monthly Catalog** results for: **kw: military and kw: history.**
Record **1** of **736.**

◀ 1    ▶    **Mark:** ☐
Prev       Next

**GET THIS ITEM**

**Availability:** **Check the catalogs in your library.**
• Libraries worldwide that own item: 79
• ⊞ Search the catalog at your library

**FIND RELATED**

**More Like This:** Advanced options ...

**Title:** **Field artillery in military operations other than war
an overview of the US experience.**

**Corp Author(s):** U.S. Army Command and General Staff College.; Combat Studies Institute.

**Publication:** Fort Leavenworth, Kan. : Combat Studies Institute Press,

**Year:** 2005

**Language:** English

**Series:** Global war on terrorism occasional paper ;; 4;

**Access:** 🌐 http://purl.access.gpo.gov/GPO/LPS59560

**SUBJECT(S)**

**Descriptor:** Armed Forces -- Operations other than war.
Artillery, Field and mountain -- United States -- History.
War on Terrorism, 2001

**Note(s):** Title from title screen (viewed on April 5, 2005)./ Includes bibliographical references.

**System Info:** Mode of access: Internet from the Combined Arms Research Library, Command &
General Staff College web site. Address as of 4/5/05:
http://www.cgsc.army.mil/carl/download/csipubs/GWOT%5F4.pdf; current access is
available via PURL.

**Class Descriptors:** **GPO No:** D 110.2:F 45; **GovDoc:** D 110.2:F 45; **GPO Item No:** 0359-C (online)

**Document Type:** Book

**Accession No:** **OCLC:** 58803425

**Database:** GPO

Figure 12.5

*GPO Access Resources by Branch* lists the three branches of government
with many subdivisions (links) for searching. The *GPO Access Resources
by Topics* provides a drop down menu to begin the searching process. The
*Federal-Wide Resources* section also provides a drop down menu for accessing many databases. Featured Items may include items of current interest and items from the archives. A link to *Get assistance from a Federal
Depository librarian* (a pilot project in 2005) provided online chats providing assistance in locating and using federal documents.

User support is available Monday–Friday from 7:00 A.M. and 9:00 P.M. (except Federal holidays) EST or by phone (1-866-512-1800) or by FAX at 1-202-512-2104. This comprehensive service is funded by the Federal Depository Program (Public Law 10340 the Government Printing Office Electronic Information Enhancement Act, 1993).

# National Technical Information Service (NTIS)

The NTIS in the Commerce Department was established on September 2, 1970. Its "primary purpose is to assist U.S. industries to accelerate the development of new products and processes as well as helping the U.S. maintain a leading worldwide economic competitive position." (*www.ntis. gov* May 2005). Much of the material available from NTIS may not be available from depository libraries. Not all unclassified documents are designated as depository items. More than three million products are available for purchase from the NTIS. Of these, more than 600,000 are searchable from their website, *www.ntis.gov*. The database includes more than 350 subject areas from over 200 federal agencies. Some records include links to free full-text publications or downloaded directly from the NTIS archival copy for a nominal charge. The website indicates that thousands of items are added weekly. These materials are in various formats including online, paper copy, multimedia, electronic CD-ROM and microfiche. The NTIS is required by law to recover its costs from the sale of its documents so it is more expensive to purchase from NTIS than from the GPO. Sometimes, especially with reports of research done on government contracts, documents are available sooner from NTIS than from the GPO. Some of the reports available from NTIS are prepared and published by individuals, corporations, universities, etc., that have done research using federal funds.

# Federal Documents

Most documents sought by library users are United States government publications. The federal documents, most of which are published by the GPO, are indexed and identified in several publications. One can identify early dated documents by using a *Descriptive Catalogue of Government Publications of the United States, September 5, 1774–March 4, 1881,* compiled by Perley Poore, 1885. The *Comprehensive Index to Publications of the United States, 1881–1894* by John G. Ames, 1905, identifies documents in the years following. The current index, *Monthly Catalog of Government Publications (Monthly Cat* for short) first appeared in 1895 and is still published monthly. Collections also contain specific checklists and catalogs of federal documents that deal with subjects such as forestry or are records of agencies or departments, such as congressional hearings.

Before using the *Monthly Cat*, one should examine the instructions at the beginning of the volume because the format and indexing have changed from time to time. Each monthly issue is arranged alphabetically by agency issuing the document. Each document is given a number similar to an abstract number, called the *Monthly Cat* number. This number appears in the left margin for each document or column of each page. Early volumes of the *Monthly Cat* had only an annual subject index, but since 1975 additional indexes such as title and report indexes have been added. In Figure 12.1 after the department headings (in the center of the entry) you will find a number in bold type that starts with a year a dash and another number. See the first entry under **Military History Center** and find the number **2003-19709**. This is the *Monthly Cat* or entry number. On the same line is the SuDoc number, in this entry **D 114.2:SO 5/2**. This is the "SuDoc" number, assigned by the superintendent of documents who is in charge of the GPO and other government printing operations. Depository libraries usually do not catalog their documents but file them by the SuDoc number, which in a sense is the "call" number. The other symbols in the entry show additional information such as where to purchase a copy of the document and its depository status.

The large black dot shows depository items. The last line of each entry is an OCLC number. The OCLC system will be discussed in Chapter 15. Since 1976 when the *Monthly Cat* changed its format it has been available on magnetic tape. Some large libraries that also have large depository collections like the New York State Library have loaded the tape for the monthly catalog into their Online Public Catalog (OPAC). This ensures that users have access to all the information in the *Monthly Cat* since 1976 by using the OPAC only. Easier access to government documents is thus made possible as well as making more individuals aware of the variety of information available from documents. Since documents are not usually in the catalog, many students and faculty forget that they are a valuable source of information. The *Monthly Cat* is also available in some libraries on CDs and via FirstSearch (see Figures 12.4 and 12.5), adding ways of searching for documents.

The *Index to U.S. Government Periodicals* is published commercially and is an index to 185 selected periodicals published by the U.S. government. The index is published quarterly with annual accumulations. Its format is similar to that used by the Wilson indexes discussed in Chapter 8.

The Congressional Information Services (CIS) publishes a variety of reference books about government and indexes to documents, including the *American Statistics Index, CIS/Index* and *CIS Serials Set Index*. CIS publications all include lengthy explanations and examples of entries and this introductory material should be read before the student uses any CIS publication for the first time. As its title suggests, *American Statistics Index* presents statistics published by the federal government. Many departments and agencies besides the Census Bureau publish statistics. The *CIS/Index* has several sections: Legislative Histories of U.S. Public Laws, Index to Congressional Publications and Public Laws, and Abstracts of Congressional Publications. This index is published monthly with an annual accumulation, the *CIS/Annual*. Multi-year indexes are available for the index volumes, but not the abstract volumes. The *U.S. Serial Set* has been known by various names and has changed in format and content. Generally the set consists of congressional publications; reports and documents of both the house and senate, treaty documents and senate executive reports. This set is a primary source for locating the texts of reports, treaties, bill, special reports, etc. The numbering system in the *U.S. Serial Set* has changed from time to time so it is important to consult the introductory material. Since 1970 CIS has provided full-text microfiche for all publications covered in CIS indexes. Many libraries (not necessarily depositories) have purchased these microfiche. CIS uses its own numbering system for its microfiche edition of the *U.S. Serial Set* and those numbers will also appear in the CIS indexes.

# Educational Resources
# Information Center (ERIC)

The collecting, abstracting, indexing, distribution, etc., of significant education related reports and journal articles is the mission of ERIC, the national system of clearinghouses located at universities and or professional organizations. *Resources in Education* (RIE) a GPO publication, is an abstracting journal providing bibliographic information and identification of the reports, published and unpublished. Libraries may subscribe

## ERIC List of Records

- Click on a title to see the detailed record.
- Click on a checkbox to mark a record to be e-mailed or printed in Marked Records.
- **Refine your search results: 3,111  (Show me how)**

Staff View | My Account | Options | Comments

**Home    Databases    Searching    Results**    | **Exit** | Hide tips

List of Records    Detailed Record    Marked Records    Saved Records    Go to page

ERIC results for: **kw: college and kw: students and kw: library. (Save Search)**

Related Subjects    Related Authors    Limit    E-mail    Print    Export    Help

Records found: **3,111**

Find related:    Books etc. (WorldCat)    Articles (ArticleFirst)    Journal Articles (ECO)    Reference Resources (WorldAlmanac)    Previous Searches

◀ 1 ▶
Prev    Next

☐ 1. **Problem-Based Learning in Science. ERIC Digest.**
Access ERIC: ● FullText **Author:** Sonmez, Duygu; Lee, Hyonyong **Publication:** U.S. Ohio **No. of Pages:** 4 **Accession No:** ED482724  ● See more details for locating this item

☐ 2. **Financial Activity & Condition Taxpayer Summary (FACTS), 2002.**
Access ERIC: ● FullText **Author:** Piotrowski, Craig; Moore, Anne **Publication:** U.S. Wisconsin **No. of Pages:** 29 **Accession No:** ED482593  ● See more details for locating this item

☐ 3. **The Improving Literacy through School Libraries Program of "No Child Left Behind": Tips for Writing a Winning Grant Proposal. ERIC Digest.**
Access ERIC: ● FullText **Author:** Mardis, Marcia A. **Publication:** U.S. New York **No. of Pages:** 4 **Accession No:** ED482561  ● See more details for locating this item

☐ 4. **Career Development of Older Adults. ERIC Digest.**
Access ERIC: ● FullText **Author:** Imel, Susan **Publication:** U.S. Ohio **No. of Pages:** 4 **Accession No:** ED482538  ● See more details for locating this item

☐ 5. **A Study of Library Anxiety in History and Physical Education Majors.**
Access ERIC: ● FullText **Author:** Brannan, Joyce A. **Publication:** U.S. Mississippi **No. of Pages:** 72 **Accession No:** ED482508  ● See more details for locating this item

☐ 6. **Generation 1.5 Students and College Writing. ERIC Digest.**
Access ERIC: ● FullText **Author:** Harklau, Linda **Publication:** U.S. District of Columbia **No. of Pages:** 4 **Accession No:** ED482491  ● See more details for locating this item

☐ 7. **Austin Community College Benchmarking Update.**
Access ERIC: ● FullText **Publication:** U.S. Texas **No. of Pages:** 81 **Accession No:** ED482169
● See more details for locating this item

☐ 8. **To Inform Their Discretion: Designing an Integrated Learning Community Focusing on Civic Engagement.**
Access ERIC: ● FullText **Author:** Moore, Jonelle; Dille, Brian J. **Publication:** U.S. Arizona **No. of Pages:** 9 **Accession No:** ED481943  ● See more details for locating this item

Figure 12.6

to ERIC and receive copies of the reports in microfiche format. The fiche are usually filed by the number found at the beginning of each entry in RIE, the ERIC document number. See figure 12.7 for an ERIC citation retrieved via FirstSearch. Find the descriptor **Accession No:** and you will find the ERIC number. For the document in Figure 12.7 the ERIC number is **ED482491**. Figure 12.6 was a keyword search *college* AND *students*

| | |
|---|---|
| **Availability:** | • 🔵 Connect to the catalog at your library |
| | FIND RELATED |
| **More Like This:** | Advanced options ... |
| **Accession No:** | ED482491 |
| **Title:** | **Generation 1.5 Students and College Writing. ERIC Digest.** |
| **Access ERIC:** | 🟢 FullText |
| **Author(s):** | Harklau, Linda |
| **Corp Author(s):** | ERIC Clearinghouse on Languages and Linguistics, Washington, DC. |
| **Publication:** | U.S.; District of Columbia; 2003-10-00 |
| **Description:** | 4 p. |
| **Language:** | English |
| **Report No:** | EDO-FL-03-05 |
| **Abstract:** | An increasing number of U.S. high school graduates enter college while still in the process of learning English. Referred to as generation 1.5 students because they share characteristics of both first- and second-generation immigrants, they do not fit into any of the traditional categories of nonnative English speakers enrolled in college writing courses, nor have they been the focus of much research on students learning to write in English as a second language. Familiar with U.S. culture and schooling, generation 1.5 students have different learning needs from other English language learners, such as immigrants with limited English proficiency and international students who travel to the United States for the express purpose of earning an American college degree. This digest discusses some of the special needs of generation 1.5 students in the area of writing instruction and explores issues faced by English-as-a-Second-Language (ESL) and college writing programs in providing these students with appropriate writing instruction at the college level. (Author/VWL) |
| | **SUBJECT(S)** |
| **Descriptor:** | **(Major):** English (Second Language)<br>Student Placement<br>Writing (Composition)<br>Writing Instruction<br>**(Minor):** High Schools<br>Higher Education<br>Second Language Instruction<br>Second Language Learning<br>Student Needs |
| **Identifier:** | ERIC Digests |
| **Note(s):** | **Funding:** Office of Educational Research and Improvement (ED), Washington, DC. ED-99-CO-0008/ **Report:** EDO-FL-03-05 |
| **Announcement:** | RIEJUL2004 |
| **Document Type:** | Document (RIE) |
| **Record Type:** | 071 Information Analyses--ERIC IAPs; 073 Eric Digest in Full Text |
| **Clearinghouse:** | FL027927 |
| **Availability:** | **Level:** 1<br>**Alternate:** ERIC Clearinghouse on Languages and Linguistics, 4646 40th Street NW, Washington, DC 20016. Tel: 800-276-9834 (Toll Free). For full text: http://www.cal.org/ericcll/DIGEST. |
| **ERIC Digest:** | An increasing number of U.S. high school graduates enter college while still in the process of learning English. Referred to as generation 1.5 students because they share characteristics of both first- and second-generation immigrants (Rumbaut & Ima, 1988), |

**Figure 12.7**

AND *library*. The search found 3,111 entries. Item number 6 from the search is shown in Figure 12.7. When viewing this citation online the entire document will be displayed as indicated by the short description found for item 6 in figure 12.6. The numbering system is similar to but not identical to the system used in the *Monthly Cat*.

*Current Index to Journals in Education* published by Oryx Press is the second index providing access to materials collected by ERIC. This publication indexes approximately 750 journals/serials, and issues monthly and semi-annual accumulations. The information included in each entry is typical of other abstracting services discussed in Chapter 8 with the addition of a list of descriptors.

Students also may identify ERIC documents by searching the indexes via online vendors, such as DIALOG, or on CDs available in many libraries. To help in searching the ERIC files online or via CDs it is useful to consult the *Thesaurus of ERIC Descriptors* .

## *Exercises for Chapter 12*

1. Using the catalog, list the indexes and guides to documents in your library. Record call numbers for future reference.
2. Using the *Monthly Catalog*, answer the following questions.
    (A)   Check the subject index for 1980, 1985, 1995 and 2005 for documents issued each year on Biological Warfare.
        1. Compare the number of documents issued each year.
        2. What agency issued the most documents?
        3. Are most of the documents found in depository libraries?
    (B)   Using an online access to GPO publications search for documents about prisoner abuse in the Iraq war.
        1. What agencies issued the documents?
        2. Is the full text available online?
3. Choose one U.S. senator from your home state and locate the following information:
    (A)   Washington address
    (B)   committee assignments
    (C)   names of chief aides
4. Find the following information:
    (A)   The name of the vice president under Harry Truman.
    (B)   The location of the Federal Reserve Banks.
    (C)   The name of the chief judge in your state.

5. Find the population of your home county. List all the sources in your library which provide this information. You should include all sources discussed in previous chapters.

## Important Terms in Chapter 12

Monthly Catalog number
*SuDoc number*
*Superintendent of Documents*
*NTIS*
*depository library*
*GPO*
*municipality*
*ERIC*

## Important Books for Chapter 12

### GUIDES

Cheney, Debora (Debora Lee). *The Complete Guide to Citing Government Information Sources: A Manual for Social Science & Business Research.* 3rd ed. Rev. Bethesda, MD.: LexisNexis; Congressional Information Service, 2002.

*Directory of Government Document Collections and Librarians* 7th ed. Government Documents Roundtable, American Library Association, ed. by Barbara Kile and Audrey Taylor. Washington, DC: Congressional Information Service, 1997.

*Government Assistance Almanac.* Washington, D.C.: Foggy Bottom Publications, 1985–. Annual. "The guide to all federal programs available to the American public."

*Government Phone Book USA.* Detroit, MI.: Omnigraphics, Inc., 1997–. Annual. Continues *Government Directory of Addresses and Telephone Numbers.*

*Government Reference Books.* Edited by LeRoy Schwarzkopf. Littleton, CO: Libraries Unlimited, 1970–. (Biennial guide to U.S. government publications.)

Hardy, Gayle J., and Judith Schiek Robinson. *Subject Guide to U.S. Government Reference Sources.* 2nd ed. Englewood, CO: Libraries Unlimited, 1996.

Herman, Edward. *Locating United States Government Information: A Guide to Sources.* Buffalo, NY: W. S. Hein, 1997. Also available is an Internet supplement.

Hoffmann, Frank W. *Guide to Popular U.S. Government Publications.* 5th ed. Englewood, CO: Libraries Unlimited, 1998.

Houston, James E. ed. *Thesaurus of ERIC Descriptors.* 14th ed., Phoenix, AZ: Oryx, 2001.

*Librarian's Guide to Public Records.* Tempe, AZ.: BRB Publications, 1995–.

Maxwell, Bruce. *Washington Online: How to Access the Federal Government on the Internet* 1998. Washington, DC: Congressional Quarterly, 1997.

Morehead, Joe. *Introduction to United States Public Documents.* 5th ed. Littleton, CO: Libraries Unlimited, 1996.

*Public Records Online: The National Guide to Private and Public Government Online Sources of Public Records.* Tempe, AZ: Facts on Demand Press, 1997. Annual.

Ross, John M. *How to Use Major Indexes to U.S. Government Publications.* Chicago, IL: American Library Association, 1989.

*State Information Directory.* Washington, D.C.: CQ Press, 2000–.

*Tapping State Government Information Sources.* Lori L. Smith, et al. Westport. Conn.: Greenwood Press, 2003.

*United States Government Internet Manual.* Lanham, MD.: Bernan Press, 2003–. Annual. Replaced *Government information on the internet.*

*Washington Information Directory.* Washington, D.C.: Congressional Quarterly, Inc. 1976/76–. Annual

## U.S. PUBLICATIONS — INDEXES

*American Statistics Index. V.* 1–, 1973–. Washington, DC: Congressional Information Service, 1973–. Part 1 Index. Part 2 Abstracts. A comprehensive guide and index to the statistical publications of the U.S. government.

Ames, John G. *Comprehensive Index to the Publications of the United States Government, 1881–1893.* Washington, DC: GOP, 1976.

*CIS/Index. V.* 1–, 1970–. Bethesda, MD: Congressional Information Service, 1970–.

*Congressional Record: Containing the Proceedings and Debates of the 43rd Congress — March 4, 1987–.* Washington, DC: GOP, 1973–. V. 1–. (Issued daily while Congress is in session. Revised, bound form issued at the end of each session.)

*Current Index to Journals in Education.* Phoenix, AZ: Oryx, 1969–2001. Ceased publication in 2001.

*Government Reports Announcements & Index. V.* 75–, 1975–. Springfield,

VA: U.S. Department of Commerce, NTIS, 1975–. Earlier volumes have various titles.

*Index to Annals of the Congress of the United States, 1st Congress Through 18th Congress, 1789–1824.* Washington, DC: U.S. Historical Documents Institution, 1970 (reprint ed.).

*Index to the Register of Debates in Congress. Containing Indexes to the Appendices, 18th Congress, 1st Session, 1824–1837.* Washington, DC: Gales & Seaton, 1976. Compiled from authentic materials (reprint ed.).

*Index to U.S. Government Periodicals, 1970–.* Chicago: Infodata International, 1970–.

*Indexes to the Congressional Globe, 23rd Congress to the 42nd Congress, Dec. 2, 1833–March 3, 1873.* Washington, DC: Office of the Congressional Globe, 1970. (Reprint of 1834–73 ed.)

Poore, Benjamin Perley. *A Descriptive Catalogue of the Government Publications of the United States, Sept. 5, 1774–March 4, 1881.* Comp. by order of Congress. Washington, D.C.: GOP, 1885.

*Resources in Education.* Phoenix, AZ: Oryx, 1980–.

Scientific & Technical Aerospace Reports. National Aeronautics & Space Administration. *STAR, and Abstract Journal.* V. 1–, 1963–. Washington, D.C.: GOP, 1963–. Also available online beginning Feb 13, 2001. Biweekly. No longer distributed to depository libraries in physical form. System requires Adobe Acrobat Reader.

## UNITED NATIONS PUBLICATION

*A Comprehensive Handbook of the United Nations: A Documentary Presentation in Two Volumes.* Compiled and edited by Minchuan Ku. New York: Monarch Press, 1978.

Gordenker, Leon. *The UN Secretary-General and Secretariat.* Abingdon, Oxon: New York, NY.: Routledge, 2005.

United Nations and Dag Hammerskjold Library. *Checklist of United Nations Documents, 1946–1949.* New York, 1949–1953.

_____ and _____. *United Nations Documents Index.* New York, pub. Monthly beginning with 1950.

_____ and _____. Secretary-General. *Public Papers of the Secretaries-General of the United Nations.* Andrew W. Cordier, Wilder Foote, and Max Harrelson, eds. New York: Columbia University Press, 1969–1977 (8 vols.).

*United Nations Document Series Symbols, 1946–1996.* Dag Hammarskjold Library, United Nations, 1998.

*United Nations Documentation: List of Basic References Sources.* Dag Hammarskjold Library, 1995.

*United Nations Secretaries General: A Bibliography with Indexes.* Huntington, NY.: Nova Science Publishers, 1999.

*UN Secretary-General: A Bibliography.* New York: United Nations. Dag Hammarskjold Library, 1996. Access via World Wide Web. "This bibliography is a comprehensive listing of books and journal articles concerning in whole, or in part, with the office and powers of the secretary-general of the United Nations..." (Preface).

## GUIDES TO GOVERNMENT AND ELECTED OFFICIALS

*Congressional Quarterly Almanac, a Service for Editors and Commentators.* V. 1–, 1945–. Washington, D.C.: Congressional Quarterly, 1945–.

*Congressional Quarterly's Politics in America.* Washington, C.C.: CQ Press, 1989–. Biennial. Has a companion publication, *Who's Who in Congress.*

*Congressional Directory.* Lexington, KY.: The Council of State Governments, 1998–. Annual. Includes elective officials, legislative leadership, committees and staff and administrative officials. Also available on CD-ROM.

*The Florida Handbook.* Tallahassee: Peninsular Pub. Co., 1947/48–. Annual. Includes explanations of departments, names, addresses and phone numbers of departments, photos, list of state legislators, discussions on important topics, some state history, etc. Many states publish similar handbooks, usually annually.

*Municipal Year Book: An Authoritative Resume of Activities and Statistical Data of American Cities.* Washington, D.C.: International City Management Association, 1934–.

*Official Congressional Directory.* Washington, D.C.: GOP, 1900–.

*State Blue Books, Legislative Manuals and Reference Publications: A Selective Bibliography.* Edited by Lynn Hellebust. Topeka, KS: Government Research Service, 1990.

United States Bureau of the Census. *County and City Data Book.* 1949–. Washington, D.C.: GOP, 1949–.

*United States Manual 1973–.* Federal Register, Washington, D.C.: GOP, 1973–. (Earlier title, United States Government Organization Manual.)

# 13

# Biography

## *Objectives*

After studying this chapter the student shall be able to

- list the biographical sources the library holds
- figure out what each source contains
- locate biographical information for specific individuals
- use the Internet and online sources to locate biographical information

## *General Information*

Students often think of biographies as book-length histories of individuals, but there are many sources that provide brief biographical information. Often the only bit of information needed is a current address, date of birth, place of employment or current occupation. To find the sources of biography in the library, one checks the catalog under the subject Biography. There is an extensive list of entries under the broad heading Biography and entries with subheadings such as Biography — Dictionaries. The student should take a brief cursory look through all the entries. To find a book-length biography of a specific person, look in the catalog under the individual's name as a subject, e.g., Lincoln, Abraham. Those which are subject entries refer to books with biographical information. When looking through the entries under the subject heading Biography one will find some biographical indexes, some for biographical dictionaries and some for biographical encyclopedias. Each of these sources includes many individuals. A few examples of biographical sources available in many libraries are listed below.

# Indexes

*Biography Index* (Figure 13.1), published by H. W. Wilson Company, is a quarterly index to biographical information in books and periodicals. Multi-year volumes replace quarterly and annual volumes. They are arranged alphabetically by the name of the biographee, and at the back of the volume is a list of the biographees arranged by profession and occupation. The format on the print index is the same as other Wilson indexes discussed in earlier chapters. In Figure 13.1 find the entry for Joan, of Arc, Saint, 1412–1431. Note the subheadings; Bibliography; Juvenile Fiction and Juvenile Literature for a total of 3 different titles. *Biography Index* on WilsonWeb includes a retrospective index covering 1946 to present. According to H.W. Wilson Company, this retrospective index has nearly a million citations. Figure 13.2 is a WilsonWeb entry from a search of *Biography Index*. Compare the format of the entry with the one in Figure 13.1, the print edition of **Biography Index**.

The *Biography and Genealogy Master Index* is an index to biographies in more than 250 biographical dictionaries and Who's Whos. The base set was published in 1981 and there are five-year cumulations, for 1981 to 1985, 1986 to 1990, 1991–1995, plus annual volumes. This set was preceded by the *Biographical Dictionaries Master Index* published in 1975 and 1976. This set of indexes saves time and eliminates guessing which biographical dictionaries should be consulted.

# Marquis Publications

Most of the biographical dictionaries with a title beginning with "Who's Who in..." are published by Marquis. They publish an index to all their biographical publications, *Marquis Who's Who Publications, Index to Who's Who Book*. The 1990 edition includes over 253,500 individuals listed in the latest edition of 13 different Who's Who titles. Not all books in the Who's Who series are published annually. Perhaps the most familiar in the Who's Who series is *Who's Who in America* (Figure 13.3). The volumes in this series include brief biographical information about notable living

**Jiménez, Francisco, 1943-, author and critic**
Meier, Matt S. Mexican American biographies; a historical dictionary, 1836-1987. Greenwood Press 1988 p111-12 bibl
**Jiménez, Juan Ramón, Spanish poet**
Historical dictionary of modern Spain, 1700-1988; Robert W. Kern, editor-in-chief; Meredith D. Dodge, associate editor. Greenwood Press 1990 p280-2 bibl maps
**Jiménez, Luis, 1940-, sculptor**
Meier, Matt S. Mexican American biographies; a historical dictionary, 1836-1987. Greenwood Press 1988 p112 bibl
**Jiménez, Marcos Pérez** *See* Pérez Jiménez, Marcos, 1914-
**Jiménez, Mario Echandi** *See* Echandi Jiménez, Mario, 1915-
**Jiménez de Cisneros, Francisco, 1436?-1517, Spanish cardinal and statesman**
Fernández-Armesto, F. Humanist, inquisitor, mystic: Cardinal Jimenez de Cisneros. il *Hist Today* 38:33-40 O '88
**Jiménez Oreamuno, Ricardo, 1859-1945, Costa Rican president**
Biographical dictionary of Latin American and Caribbean political leaders; edited by Robert J. Alexander. Greenwood Press 1988 p232 bibl
**Jimmy the Greek, television sports commentator**
Jimmy the Greek's bizarre excursion into racial history costs him his job at CBS. il por *People Wkly* 29:35 F 1 '88
Lupica, M. The Greek in purgatory. il *Esquire* 111:43-4+ Ja '89
**Jin, Sungho, Korean metallurgist**
Smith, E. T. The dogged push to overcome resistance. por *Bus Week* Sp Issue:84 '89 Innovation in America
**Jinga** *See* Nzinga, Queen of Matamba, 1582-1663
**Jinnah, Mohamed Ali, 1876-1948, Islamic leader**
Ahmad, Riaz. Quaid-i-Azam Mohammad Ali Jinnah: the formative years, 1892-1920. National Institute of Historical and Cultural research 1986 254p bibl
Beg, Aziz. Jinnah and his times; a biography. Babur & Amer Publs. 1986 949p bibl il pors
Jinnah, Fatima, and Mujahid, Sharif. My brother. Quaid-e-Azam Acad. 1987 112p il pors
**Jiranek, Leo, d. 1990, interior and furniture designer**
Obituary
*N Y Times* pB-6 Ja 30 '90
*N Y Times Biogr Serv* 21:117 Ja '90
**Jitkoff, Andrew, d. 1989, investment manager**
Obituary
*N Y Times* pB-14 Je 8 '89
**Jñānadeva, fl. 1290, Indian poet**
Abhayananda, Swami. Jnaneshvar; the life and works of the celebrated thirteenth century Indian mystic-poet. Atma Bks. 1989 260p bibl
**Joan, of Arc, Saint, 1412-1431**
Paine, Albert Bigelow. The girl in white armor; the story of Joan of Arc [condensation] (In Reader's digest great biographies, v7. Reader's Digest Assn. 1989 p148-260) il
**Juvenile literature**
Banfield, Susan. Joan of Arc. Chelsea House 1988 111p bibl il
Nottridge, Harold. Joan of Arc. Bookwright Press 1988 32p il
**Joanna I, Queen of Naples, 1327?-1382**
Opfell, Olga S. Queens, empresses, grand duchesses, and regents; women rulers of Europe, A.D. 1328-1989. McFarland & Co. 1989 p6-13 bibl il pors
**Joanna II, Queen of Naples, 1371-1435**
Opfell, Olga S. Queens, empresses, grand duchesses, and regents; women rulers of Europe, A.D. 1328-1989. McFarland & Co. 1989 p31-5 bibl il pors
**Jobes, Nancy, comatose patient**
Colen, B. D. The extraordinary case of the woman who couldn't die. il por *Redbook* 172:126-9+ Mr '89
**Jobim, Antonio Carlos, Brazilian singer and songwriter**
Holston, M. Bossa nova: Jobim's beat goes on. il pors *Américas* 40:2-7 N/D '88
**Jobs, Steven, computer executive**
A conversation with Steve Jobs [interview] por *Commun ACM* 32:436-43 Ap '89
Gendron, G. and Burlingham, B. The entrepreneur of the decade: an interview with Steve Jobs. pors *Inc* 11:114-16+ Ap '89 Tenth Anniversary special issue
Meyer, Michael R. The Alexander complex; the dreams that drive the great businessmen. Times Bks. 1989 p15-51
Patton, P. Steve Jobs: out for revenge. por *N Y Times Biogr Serv* 20:750-3 Ag '89
Patton, P. Steve Jobs: out for revenge. por *N Y Times Mag* p22-3+ Ag 6 '89
Schwartz, J. Steve Jobs comes back. il pors *Newsweek* 112:46-9+ O 24 '88
Second coming for Steven Jobs. por *Macleans* 101:24 Ja 25 '88
**Juvenile literature**
Contemporary heroes and heroines; Ray B. Browne, editor; in association with Glenn J. Browne and Kevin O. Browne. Gale Res. 1990 p217-20 bibl il pors
**Jobson, Edward R., d. 1988, publishing executive**
Obituary
*N Y Times Biogr Serv* 19:585 My '88
**Jocelin, Elizabeth, 1596-1622, English author**
British women writers; a critical reference guide; edited by Janet Todd. Continuum 1989 p367-8 bibl
An Encyclopedia of British women writers; edited by Paul Schlueter, June Schlueter. Garland 1988 p258 bibl
**Jodl, Alfred, 1890-1946, German general**
Encyclopedia of the Holocaust; Israel Gutman, editor in chief; [pub. in assn. with] Yad Vashem, Sifriat Poalim Publishing House. Macmillan 1990 p751-2 bibl il pors maps facsims
**Joe, Oreland, sculptor and painter**
Morgan, P. J. Oreland Joe: spirits of stone. il por *Southwest Art* 17:66-70 Ja '88
**Joelson, Edith Weisskopf-** *See* Weisskopf-Joelson, Edith, 1910-1983
**Joffe, Irwin, d. 1989, clothing executive**
Obituary
*N Y Times* pA-20 Ag 3 '89
**Joffé, Roland, English director**
Dialogue on film: Roland Joffé [interview] il *Am Film* 13:9-11 D '87
**Joffrey, Robert, dancer, choreographer and director**
Current biography yearbook, 1988; editor, Charles Moritz; associate editors, Henry Sloan [et al.]; assistant editor, Irene C. Park. Wilson, H.W. 1988 p644 bibl pors
Kisselgoff, A. Robert Joffrey and his great American dream. por *N Y Times Biogr Serv* 19:381-3 Ap '88
Obituary
*Dance Mag* il pors 62:52-6, 56-7 Je '88
*N Y Times Biogr Serv* por 19:346-7 Mr '88
*Natl Rev* 40:18 Ap 29 '88
Zide-Booth, R. Dancing for Joffrey. il *Dance Chron* 12 no1:48-104 '89
**Johansen, David, singer**
Dougherty, M. David Johansen used to bare it with the Dolls, but alter ego Buster Poindexter is a bigger grin. il pors *People Wkly* 29:90-1 Ja 25 '88
Goldman, D. Buster Poindexter (aka David Johansen). il por *Sch Update* 120:28 Ap 8 '88
Murphy, E. Buster Poindexter: a personality crisis resolved. il por *Roll Stone* p26 F 11 '88
**Johanson, Donald C., anthropologist**
Johanson, Donald C., and Shreeve, James. Lucy's child; the discovery of a human ancestor. Morrow 1989 318p bibl il pors maps
**Johansson, Ingemar, Swedish boxer**
Ladson, W. Didn't you used to be . . . pors *Sport* 80:78 Jl '89
**John XXIII, Pope, 1881-1963**
Wynn, Wilton. Keepers of the keys; John XXIII, Paul VI and John Paul II: three who changed the Church. Random House 1988 278p
**John, Brynmor, 1934-1988, British cabinet member**
Obituary
*N Y Times* pD-26 D 15 '88
**John, Elton, English singer and songwriter**
Elton John won't go breaking estranged wife Renate's heart—he's a 'Single man' again, but friendly. pors *People Wkly* 30:85 D 5 '88
**John, Grace Spaulding, 1890-1972, painter**
Sussmann, M. H. Grace Spaulding John. il por *Southwest Art* 18:74-8 Je '88
**John, Joyce, illustrator**
Something about the author, v59; facts and pictures about authors and illustrators of books for young people; edited by Anne Commire. Gale Res. 1990 p104-5 bibl il pors
**John, Patrick Roland, 1937-, Dominica prime minister**
Biographical dictionary of Latin American and Caribbean political leaders; edited by Robert J. Alexander. Greenwood Press 1988 p232-4 bibl
**John, Tommy, baseball player**
Kelly, Robert E. Baseball's best; Hall of Fame pretenders active in the eighties. McFarland & Co. 1988 p173-5 bibl
**John Paul I, Pope, 1912-1978**
Cornwell, John. A thief in the night; the mysterious death of Pope John I. Simon & Schuster 1989 366p il

Figure 13.1

Current Search: (joan, of arc,saint) <in> ALL

    Records: 47

      In: Biography Index

    Limit To: 🔲 Peer Reviewed              Link To: ⑤ S·F·X LINCCWeb SFX

80%  ⎡ 1 of 1       ⎡     Biography Index   ⎤

⑤ S·F·X

                          Title: *Joan of Arc* and the Hundred Years War

            Personal Author: Fraioli, Deborah A.

          Biography Name: *Joan of Arc, Saint*, 1412-1431

            Responsibility: Deborah A. Fraioli

                  Publisher: Greenwood Press

            Publication Year: 2005

                      Pages: 185

    Physical Description: Annotated bibliography

  Language of Document: English

                      ISBN: 0-313-32458-1 (alk. paper)

                    Series: Greenwood guides to historic events *of* the medieval world

              Subject(s): Saints; *Joan of Arc, Saint*, 1412-1431

          Document Type: Books; Individual biographies

      LC Classification: DC103

     LC Control Number: 2004-22531

            Update Code: 20050404

    Accession Number: 200541012557000

**Figure 13.2**

Americans. Other Marquis Who's Who volumes are limited in one way or another: regional areas (*Who's Who in the East*) for instance; professions (*Who's Who in Finance and Industry*); or special categories (*Who's Who of American Women*). Marquis also publishes historical volumes as companions to *Who's Who in America*. These volumes, entitled *Who Was Who in America*, began coverage (of notable Americans) with the year 1607.

## *Authors*

There are several sources of biographical information that deal specifically with authors. The Gale Research Company publishes the *Author Biographies Master Index*, which is similar to the *Biography and Genealogy Master Index* discussed above. Another useful Gale publication is *Contemporary Authors* which includes authors of nontechnical works, living

BIOGRAPHY 153

**UPSON, STUART BARNARD,** advertising agency executive; b. Cin., Apr. 14, 1925; s. Mark and Alice (Barnard) U.; m. Barbara Jussen, Nov. 2, 1946; children: Marguerite Nichols, Anne Marcus, Stuart Barnard. BS, Yale U., 1945. With Dancer, Fitzgerald, Sample, Inc., N.Y.C., 1946-86, sr. v.p., 1963-66, exec. v.p., 1966-67, pres., 1967-74, chmn., 1974-86, DFS-Dorland, N.Y.C., 1986-87; dir. Saatchi & Saatchi Inc., N.Y.C., 1987—. Bd. dirs. Fresh Air Fund, N.Y., Advt. Coun. With USNR, 1943-46. Mem. St. Elmo Soc. Clubs: Wee Burn Country (Darien); Sky (N.Y.C.); Blind Brook, Pine Valley Golf, Ocean Forest Golf. Home: 16 Wrenfield Ln Darien CT 06820-2201 Office: Saatchi & Saatchi Inc 375 Hudson St New York NY 10014-3658

**UPSON, THOMAS FISHER,** judge, former state senator, lawyer; b. Waterbury, Conn., Sept. 30, 1941; s. J. Warren and Grace (Fisher) U.; m. Barbara Secor (div. Jan. 1979); children: Secor, Chauncey Julius; m. Katherine Wolff, June 1, 1996. BA in History, Washington and Jefferson Coll., 1963; LLB, U. Conn., 1968; postgrad., Trinity Coll., 1969—72, Georgetown U., 1971—72. Bar: Conn., 1969, U.S. Dist. Ct. (2d dist.) 1969, U.S. Supreme Ct. 1973. Lawyer Upson & Secor, Waterbury, 1969—70, 1974—76; lawyer, spl. asst. U.S. Dept. Commerce, Washington, 1970—72; lawyer, spl. asst. to adminstr. GSA, Washington, 1973—74; dir. admissions St. Margaret's McTernan Sch., Waterbury, 1977—78; with divsn. spl. revenue State of Conn., Hartford, 1978—82; assoc. Moynahan & Ruskin, Waterbury, 1979—81; ptnr. Upson & Daly, Waterbury, 1981—2001; mem. Conn. Senate, Hartford, 1985—2001, chmn. gen. law com., vice-chmn. jud. com., majority whip, 1985—86, asst. minority leader, 1987-88, 89-90, minority leader protempore, 1991-92, dep. minority leader, 1993-94, dep. majority leader, chmn. jud. com., 1995-96, dep., then asst. minority leader, ranking mem. jud. com., 1997-2000; judge Superior Ct. State of Conn., Hartford, 2001—. Moderator 1st Congl. Ch., Waterbury, 1986-91; bd. dirs. Easter Seals-United Way, Waterbury, 1984-88; Rep. candidate for Congress, 6th Dist. Conn., 1976; mem. Conn. Rep. Ctrl. com., 1983-91; mem. Waterbury Rep. Town Com., 1980-85; dir. Mattatuck Mus., 1993-2003; former dir. Waterbury Symphony Orch.; former sec. and dir. First Ch. Housing, Inc.; pres. Naugatuck Valley Devel. Corp., 1975-76. Mem. ABA, Conn. Bar Assn., Waterbury Bar Assn., SAR, Soc. Colonial Wars, Soc. of the Founders of the Hartford, Phi Gamma Delta, Univ. Club (Waterbury). Lodges: Kiwanis (former pres., lt. gov. SW New Eng. dist.), Elks. Republican. Congregationalist. Avocations: hiking, music, history. Home: 210 Southwest Rd Waterbury CT 06708-3214 Office: Ansonia/Milford Jud Dist 14 W River St Milford CT 06460-3396

**UPTIGROVE, KENNETH R.** library administrator; b. Flint, Mich., Oct. 6, 1943; s. Kenneth R. and Ilah L. (Horton) U.; m. Suzanne C. Glass, Apr. 6, 1968; children: Chad K., Kathy S. BA, U. Mich., 1967, MLS, 1969. Br. rsch. libr. Genesee County Libr., Flint, 1963-69; sch. libr. Kearsley Community Schs., Flint, 1969-70; dir. Owosso (Mich.) Pub. Libr., 1970—94, Shiawassee Dist. Libr., Owosso, 1994—. Contbr. articles to mags. Mem. ALA, Mich. Library Assn. (Pub. library div. sec.-treas. 1981-82, chmn. coop. caucus 1986-87, mgmt. and adminstrn. caucus, sec.-treas. 1988-89), Flint Area Library Assn. (pres. 1970), Ruffed Grouse Soc. (pres. Lansing chpt. 1979-81, treas. Mich. coun. 1983-89, pres. 1989—), Owosso Circulators (pres. 1987-88), Kiwanis (Chmn. coms. 1980—, pres. 1999-2000, sec. 2001-02). Congregationalist. Office: Shiawassee Dist Libr 502 W Main St Owosso MI 48867-2687

**UPTON, ARTHUR CANFIELD,** experimental pathologist, educator; b. Ann Arbor, Mich., Feb. 27, 1923; s. Herbert Hawkes and Ellen (Canfield) Upton; m. Elizabeth Bache Perry, Mar. 1, 1946; children: Rebecca A., Melissa P., Bradley C. Grad., Phillips Acad., Andover, Mass., 1941; BA, U. Mich., 1944, MD, 1946. Intern Univ. Hosp., Ann Arbor, 1947, resident, 1948—49; instr. pathology U. Mich. Med. Sch., 1950—51; pathologist Oak Ridge (Tenn.) Nat. Lab., 1951—54, chief pathology-physiology sect., 1954—69; prof. pathology SUNY Med. Sch. at Stony Brook, 1969—77, chmn. dept. pathology, 1969—70, dean Sch. Basic Health Scis., 1970—75; dir. Nat. Cancer Inst., Bethesda, Md., 1977—79; prof., chmn. dept. environ. medicine NYU Med. Sch., N.Y.C., 1980—92, prof. emeritus, 1993—; clin. prof. radiology U. N.Mex. Sch. Medicine, 1993—95, clin. prof. pathology, 1992—95; clin. prof. environ. and cmty. medicine U. Medicine and Dentistry N.J.-Robert Wood Johnson Med. Sch., 1995—. Attending pathologist Brookhaven Nat. Lab., 1969—77; dir. Inst. Environ. Medicine, Med. Sch., NYU, 1980—92; mem. various coms. nat. and internat. orgns.; lectr. in field; mem. adv. bd. GM Cancer Rsch. Found. Assoc. editor Cancer Rsch., mem. editl. bd. Internat. Union Against Cancer. Served with U.S. Army, 1943—46. Named nat. lectr., Sigma Xi, 1989—91; recipient Ernest Orlando Lawrence award for atomic field, 1965, Claude M. Fuess award, 1980, Sarah L. Poilley award for pub. health, 1983, CHUMS Physician of Yr. award, 1985, Basic Cell Rsch. in Cytology Lectureship award, 1985, Fred W. Stewart award, 1986, Ramazzini award, 1986, Lovelace Med. Found. award, 1993. Fellow: N.Y. Acad. Sci., Soc. Risk Analysis (Outstanding Achievement award 1997); mem.: AAAS, Ramazzini Inst. (pres. 1992—2003), Assn. Univ. Environ. Health Sci. Ctrs. (pres. 1982—90), Internat. Assn. Radiation Rsch., N.Y. State Health Rsch. Coun. (chmn. 1982—90), Soc. Exptl. Biology and Medicine, Sci. Rsch. Soc. Am., Gerontol. Soc., Peruvian Oncology Soc. (hon.), Japan Cancer Assn. (hon.), Am. Soc. Exptl. Pathology (pres. 1967—68), Am. Assn. Cancer Rsch. (pres. 1963—64), Internat. Assn. Radiation Rsch. (pres. 1983—87, 1983—87), Radiation Rsch. Soc. (councilor 1963—64, pres. 1965—66), Inst. Medicine of NAS (Comfort-Crookshank award for cancer rsch. 1979), Internat. Acad. Pathology, Am. Assn. Pathologists and Bacteriologists, Sigma Xi, Nu Sigma Nu, Alpha Omega Alpha, Phi Gamma Delta, Phi Beta Kappa. Achievements include research in on pathology of radiation injury and endocrine glands, on cancer, on carcinogenesis, on experimental leukemia on aging. Office: Robert Wood Johnson Med Sch Rm N-112 675 Hoe's Ln Piscataway NJ 08854 Home: 250 E Alameda Apt 636 Santa Fe NM 87501 Office Phone: 732-235-3460. Business E-Mail: acupton@eohsi.rutgers.edu.

**UPTON, RICHARD THOMAS,** artist; b. Hartford, Conn., May 27, 1931; s. Ray Granville and Helen Marie (Colla) U.; 1 son, Richard Thomas, II. BFA, U. Conn., 1960; MFA, Ind. U., 1963. Artist-in-residence Artists for the Environ., Del. Water Gap, 1972, UGA Program Abroad, Cortona, Italy, 1982-85. Numerous exhibns. including most recently, exhibitions include Condeso/Lawler Gallery, N.Y.C., 1995, Nat. Acad. of Design, 1996, The Language of Landscape, 1997, Sordoni Art Gallery, 1997, The Drawings of Richard Upton: Ireland & Italy, List Art Gallery, Swarthmore, Ben Shahn Art Galleries, 1998, Landscape and Memory, The Paintings and Drawings of Richard Upton, 1982-1999, Houghton Gallery, The Cooper Union for the Advancement of Sci. and Art, N.Y.C., 1999, Represented in permanent collections Zimmerli Art Mus., Nat. Mus. of Am. Art, Smithsonian Instn., Mus. Modern Art, N.Y.C., Victoria and Albert Mus., London, Bibliot Nat., Paris, Montreal Mus. Fine Arts, Rose Art Mus. Brandeis, Mus. Fine Art, Houston, Nat. Acad. Design, N.Y.C., Met. Mus. Art, The Tang Tchg. Mus. and Art Gallery, Skidmore Coll.; artist (commns. include) Eros Thanatos Suite (German poem and woodcuts), Interlaken Corp., Providence, 1967, Salamovka Poster, Okla. Art Ctr., 1974, artist (with poems by Stanley Kunitz) River Road Suite, 1976, suite of drawing Robert Lowell at 66, 1977, suite of drawings Salmagundi mag. for humanities, The Anxious Landscape, paintings, drawings Bellarmine Coll., Louisville, 1989. With USNR, 1950-54. Recipient designer award Interlaken Corp., 1967; subject of monographs: Richard Upton and the Rhetoric of Landscape, Paul Hayes Tucker, U. Mass., U. Wash. Press, 1991, The Tuscan Landscapes of Richard Upton, Stanley C. Grand, Sordoni Art Gallery & Fred Licht, curator, Collezione Peggy Guggenheim, Venice, Wilkes U., 1997, The Drawings of Richard Upton, David Shapiro, Salmagundi, Skidmore Coll., 1997, Landscape & Memory: The Paintings & Drawings of Richard Upton, 1982-98, The Irwin S. Chanin Sch. Architecture of Cooper Union, 1999, A Table of Green Fields: Richard Upton's Cortona Landscapes, Richard Howard, 1999, List Gallery, Ben Shahn Galleries About Painting; Tang Teaching Mus. Art Gallery, 2004; fellow Fulbright Found., 1964, Ballinglen Arts Found., Ireland, 1994; grantee Nat. Endowment for Arts/Artists for Environ., 1972, Richard Florsheim Fund, 1992; elected to Nat. Acad. of Design, 1995, Tang Teaching Mus. and Art Gallery, 2004. Home: 1 North Ln Saratoga Springs NY 12866-4369

**UPTON PUCCINELLI, NANCY MARIE,** education educator, researcher; b. Walnut Creek, Calif., Apr. 27, 1971; d. Eugene Frank and Helen Louise Puccinelli; m. David Mark Upton, July 27, 2002. BA, U. of Calif., 1993; MA, Harvard Grad. Sch. of Arts and Scis., 2000; PhD, Harvard Grad. Sch. of Arts and Scis., Mass., 2000. Intern Am. Heart Assn., West Covina, Calif., 1993; tchg. asst. Harvard Grad. Sch. of Arts and Scis., Cambridge, 1995—99, rsch. asst., 1996—99; post-doctoral fellow Harvard Bus. Sch., Boston, 1999—2001; lectr. Boston U. Grad. Sch. of Mgmt., 2000; asst. prof. Emerson Coll., Boston, 2001—03; asst. prof. Sawyer Sch. of Mgmt. Suffolk Univ., 2003—; post-doctoral fellowship Harvard Bus. Sch. Cons. Coca-Cola, Germany, 2000, Procter & Gamble, Cin., 2000, Mind of the Market Lab, Harvard Bus. Sch., Boston, 2000—01. Author: (journal article) Jour. of Nonverbal Behavior, Occupl. Therapy Jour. of Rsch., (conf. paper) Easter Psychol. Assn., Assn. of Consumer Rsch., Am. Psychol. Soc. (Am. Psychol. Soc. Student Rsch. Caucus Student Rsch. Competition, 1996), (conf. special session) Soc. for Consumer Psychology, Harvard Bus. Sch. Case, (conf. paper) Soc. for Consumer Psychology. Nominee Outstanding Tchg. award, Melaine and Stanley Miller; fellow Grad. Fellowship, Kappa Kappa Gamma Found., 1995—98; grantee U. Honors Program Rsch. Grant, Am. Honda Found., 1992, Mini-Grant, U. of Calif. Riverside, 1992, Elsie Hopestill Stimson Meml. Fund, Harvard U., 1994—95, Rsch. Travel Grant, Harvard Grad. Student Coun., 1996, Barbara Ditmars Bequest, Harvard U., 1997, John B. Knox Bequest, 1997, Maria E. McMaster Bequest, 1997, Grant, Am. Psychol. Soc. Student Caucus, 1997, Faculty Advancement Fund Grant, Emerson Coll., 2001, 2002, Summer Rsch. Grant, 2002, Travel Grant, 2002, 2003. Mem.: Soc. for Consumer Psychology, Assn. of Consumer Rsch. Avocation: internat. travel. Office: Suffolk Univ 8 Ashburton Pl Boston MA 02108-2770 Personal E-mail: nancy@upton.com.

**URAHN, SUSAN K.** foundation administrator; BA in Sociology, D of Policy & Adminstrn., U. Minn. With rsch. dept. Minn. Ho. Reps.; dir. planning & evaluation Pew Charitable Trusts, Phila., 1994—. Rschr. in field. Contbr. tech. reports to profl. pubs. Office: Pew Charitable Trusts 2005 Market St Ste 1700 Philadelphia PA 19103-7017

**URAKAMI, AKIO,** manufacturing company executive; b. Tokyo, Apr. 17, 1942; came to U.S., 1991; s. Yutaka and Tomiko (Nagai) U.; m. Keiko Tanaka, Feb. 7, 1971; children: Yuji, Masako, Kota. BS, Tokyo Inst. Tech., 1965; MS, Northwestern U., 1967, PhD, 1970. Rsch. engr. Ryobi Ltd., Hiroshima, Japan, 1970-72, corp. planning mgr., 1972-76, v.p. internat., 1976-84, exec. v.p., 1984-91; chmn., pres. Ryobi N.Am., Inc., Easly Anderson, S.C., 1991—. Mem. pres.'s adv. coun. Clemson (S.C.) u., 1992—. Trustee The Urakami Found., Hiroshima, 1978—; bd. dirs. Japan Am. Assn. of We. S.C., Greenville, 1992—. Mem. Keizai Doyu Kai. Office: Ryobi NAm Inc PO Box 1207 Anderson SC 29622-1207

**URAL, ERDEM A.** engineering executive, educator; PhD, U. Mich. Pres. Loss Prevention Sci. and Technologies, Inc., Stoughton, Mass., 2001—; adj. prof. fire protection engring. Worcester (Mass.) Poly. Inst., 2001—. Mem. Aviation Rulemaking Adv. Com. Fuel Tank Inerting Harmonization Working Group. Contbr. articles to profl. publs., chpt. to handbook. Safety and health divsn. AIChE, New York, NY, 2002—; pres. adv. bd. Literacy Volunteers of Am., MML, Norwood, Mass., 2001. Recipient Outstanding Achievement award, FM Global; fellow, NATO, 1976—79, Rackham Sch. Grad. Studies, U.S. Dept. Energy. Mem.: NFPA (mem. phys. and chm. data consistency adv. bd. 2002—), AIChE (mem. editl. bd. Process Savety Progress), ASTM (chmn. com. 1999). Tau Beta Pi. Achievements include research in gas and dust explosions; fire/explosion protection and incident investigations; quantification of thermal environments produced by fire, heat and smoke detection; smoke transport-aging-deposition processes. Office: Loss Prevention Sci and Tech 659 Pearl St Stoughton MA 02072

Figure 13.3

or deceased. Starting with v. 187 coverage expanded to include international authors. A cumulative index is published twice annually. This set has several series and numbers in the hundreds of volumes. Other author biographical dictionaries are *European Authors, 1000–1900*, edited by Stanley J. Kunitz and Vineta Colby; *Twentieth Century Authors* (with supplements), edited by Stanley J. Kuntz and Howard Haycraft; and *World Authors, 1950–70* (supplement to previous title), edited by John Wakeman.

## Additional Information

There are more specific biographical dictionaries published. Some include only living persons, some only deceased, some are combined lists, some are by profession and some by country or geographical region. Some examples include: *American Men and Women of Science*, *Dictionary of American Biography*, and *Current Biography* (Figure 13.4). *Current Biography* is another Wilson publication and appears monthly. Most entries are several pages in length and often include a photograph. The *Current Biography Yearbook* (Figure 13.5) is a multiyear index to the print edition. *Current Biography* is also available on WilsonWeb and is updated monthly. For more information about biographical dictionaries in the library consult one or more of the guides to references sources discussed earlier. *Guide to Reference Books*, edited by Balay, includes many biographical dictionaries with descriptions (see its section AH pp. 281–317, 11th edition).

Other sources of biographical information in all libraries have been discussed in previous chapters. Encyclopedias, both general and subject (see Chapter 7), have biographies. Biographical information, including obituaries, is available in newspapers. Consult the index to the newspaper. Look under "Deaths" to find obituaries. The *New York Times* has published a volume indexing all obituaries that appeared from 1858 to 1968, a supplement for 1969 to 1978 and supplements to 1996. The *Personal Name Index to the New York Times* is the best source for finding personal names (and thus biographical information) that appeared in the *New York Times*. The main set includes all names that appeared until 1974. A supplement brings the set up to 2001. The *New York Times* does not publish or approve of the *Personal Name Index*. Another useful source of biographical information is the *Essay and General Literature Index* (see Chapter 9). Also many periodicals include biographical information. To locate biographical articles, use the periodical indexes (see Chapter 8). Biographies also may be located by using bibliographies (see Chapter 5).

# Current Biography®

APRIL 2000

A naturalized American citizen who was born in Czechoslovakia and came to the United States at age 11, Madeleine Korbel Albright served as the country's permanent representative to the United Nations for four years before becoming the 64th U.S. secretary of state, in 1997. During her tenure at the U.N., Albright acted not merely as a spokesperson for the executive arm of the U.S. government but as a key behind-the-scenes strategist and policy-maker. Now, as the first woman to be appointed secretary of state and the highest-ranking woman in government in U.S. history, Albright has broken into one of the nation's last male bastions of power. Though staunchly Democratic in ideology, she has won nearly unanimous support from all political corners, because of her strong pro-American stance toward foreign policy and her direct, almost confrontational style. Her conviction, clear perspectives, and common touch have helped to make American foreign policy relevant again to U.S. citizens.

Courtesy of the U.S. State Department

### Albright, Madeleine Korbel

(AHL-brite, MAD-eh-lin KOR-bel)

NOTE: An earlier article on Madeleine Albright appeared in *Current Biography* in 1995.

*May 15, 1937– United States Secretary of State*

*Address: c/o U.S. State Department, 2201 C St. N.W., Washington, DC 20520*

The daughter of Josef Korbel, a Czechoslovakian diplomat, and the former Anna Spiegelová, Albright was born on May 15, 1937 in Prague. She has a younger sister, Anna Katherine Korbel Silva, and a younger brother, John Joseph Korbel. At birth she was named Marie Jana Körbelová; the name "Madeleine" evolved from "Madlenka," a childhood nickname. A loyal member of the Czech government as well as a secular Jew, Josef Korbel was forced to flee his native land with his family after the dismemberment and occupation of Czechoslovakia by Germany in 1939. They lived for two weeks in Belgrade, Yugoslavia, and then settled in London, where Madeleine became fluent in English. After World War II ended, in 1945, Korbel worked briefly in Prague before accepting a three-year assignment in Belgrade as ambassador to Yugoslavia. Being uprooted time and again apparently did not faze young Madeleine. "I made friends very easily," she told Molly Sinclair for the *Washington Post* (January 6, 1991). "I think it has to do with the fact that I lived in a lot of different countries, went to a lot of different schools, and was always being put into situations where I had to relate to the people around me." Beginning when she was seven or eight, she was tutored by governesses for a year or two, because her father, who staunchly opposed totalitarianism, wanted to avoid exposing her to the influence of communism in Yugoslavian schools. At age 10 she

**Figure 13.4**

Hughes, Edward James *see* Hughes, Ted
Hughes, Harold E. obit Jan 97
Hughes, John Sep 91
Hughes, Richard J. obit Feb 93
Hughes, Ted obit Jan 99
Hughley, D.L. Mar 2000
Huizenga, H. Wayne Jan 95
Hull, Brett Feb 92
Humphry, Derek Mar 95
Hunt, Helen Nov 96
Hunt, James B., Jr. Jun 93
Hunt, John obit Jan 99
Hunter, Catfish obit Nov 99
Hunter, Holly Jul 94
Hunter, Jim *see* Hunter, Catfish
Hunter, Ross obit May 96
Husak, Gustav obit Jan 92
Hussein, King of Jordan obit Apr 99
Husseini, Faisal al- Jan 98
Hutchison, Kay Bailey Sep 97
Hutton, Lauren Jul 94
Hynde, Chrissie Apr 93

Ice Cube Aug 95
Ice-T Sep 94
Idei, Nobuyuki Mar 97
Idol, Billy Jan 94
Iglesias, Enrique Apr 99
Il Sung, Kim *see* Kim Il Sung
Iman Jun 95
Imus, Don Feb 96
Indigo Girls *see* Ray, Amy, and Saliers, Emily
Ingalls, Jeremy obit Jul 2000
Ingalls, Mildred Dodge Jeremy *see* Ingalls, Jeremy obit
Ionesco, Eugène obit Jun 94
Ireland, Patricia Jun 92
Irvan, Ernie Jul 98
Irwin, Margaret obit Yrbk 91
Irwin, Robert Jan 93
Irwin, Steve Aug 2000
Isaacs, Susan Oct 93
Isaak, Chris May 93
Itami, Juzo obit Mar 98
Ives, Burl obit Jun 95
Ivey, Artis *see* Coolio
Ivey, John E., Jr. obit Aug 92
Ivey, Judith Jun 93
Ivins, Molly Jun 2000
Izetbegović, Alija Aug 93

Jabbar, Kareem Abdul *see* Abdul-Jabbar, Kareem
Jack, Homer A. obit Oct 93
Jackson, Bo Jun 91
Jackson, Janet Jun 91

Jackson, Jesse L., Jr. May 98
Jackson, Joe Feb 96
Jackson, O'Shea *see* Ice Cube
Jackson, Phil Jul 92
Jackson, Samuel L. Nov 96
Jackson, Shirley Ann Jul 99
Jacobs, Amos *see* Thomas, Danny
Jacobs, Marc Feb 98
Jacobson, Leon obit Feb 93
Jaffe, Harold W. Sep 92
Jaffe, Susan Sep 97
Jagan, Cheddi obit May 97
Jagr, Jaromir Apr 97
Jakobovits, Immanuel obit Feb 2000
Jamali, Mohd F. obit Aug 97
Janeway, Eliot obit Apr 93
Jansen, Dan Sep 94
Jarreau, Al Oct 92
Järvi, Neeme Nov 93
Jay, Ricky May 94
Jayewardene, J. R. obit Jan 97
Jefferson, Margo L. Jun 99
Jemison, Mae C. Jul 93
Jenkins, Lew obit Yrbk 91
Jerusalem, Siegfried Sep 92
Jett, Joan Sep 93
Jiang Qing *see* Chiang Ch'ing
Jiang Qing obit Jan 92
Jiang Zemin May 95
Jillette, Penn *see* Penn & Teller
Jingsheng, Wei *see* Wei Jingsheng
Jobim, Antonio Carlos Jul 91 obit Feb 95
Jobs, Steven Sep 98
John, John Pico obit Sep 93
John Paul II Mar 2000
Johnson, Bernice *see* Reagon, Bernice Johnson
Johnson, Betsey Jan 94
Johnson, Beverly Sep 94
Johnson, Charles Sep 91
Johnson, Clarence L. obit Mar 91
Johnson, Davey Sep 99
Johnson, Dwayne "The Rock" Jul 2000
Johnson, Frank M. obit Oct 99
Johnson, Jimmy Jul 94
Johnson, Joseph E. obit Jan 91
Johnson, Kathie Lee *see* Gifford, Kathie Lee
Johnson, Keyshawn Oct 99
Johnson, Marguerite Annie *see* Angelou, Maya
Johnson, Michael Jul 96
Johnson, Paul Sep 94
Johnson, Philip C. Nov 91
Johnson, Randy Sep 2000
Johnson, Robert L. Apr 94

Johnson, U. Alexis obit Jun 97
Johnston, Lynn Feb 98
Jolie, Angelina Oct 2000
Jones, Bill T. Jul 93
Jones, Cherry May 08
Jones, Chuck May 96
Jones, David Robert *see* Bowie, David
Jones, George Feb 95
Jones, James Earl Nov 94
Jones, Jerry May 96
Jones, Kimberly Denise *see* Lil' Kim
Jones, Marion Oct 98
Jones, Roger W. obit Aug 93
Jones, Roy Jr. Feb 99
Jones, Sam Houston obit Yrbk 91
Jones, Tommy Lee Oct 95
Jong, Erica Apr 97
Jonsson, John Erik obit Nov 95
Jordan, Barbara C. Apr 93 obit Apr 96
Jordan, I. King Jan 91
Jordan, Michael Feb 97
Jordan, Michael H. Feb 98
Jordan, Neil Aug 93
Jordan, Vernon E., Jr. Aug 93
Joseph, Keith obit Feb 95
Joseph, Lord *see* Joseph, Keith
Jospin, Lionel Robert Jun 2000
Joxe, Louis obit Jun 91
Juan Carlos, Count of Barcelona obit Jun 93
Judd, Ashley Feb 2000
Judd, Walter H. obit Apr 94
Judd, Wynonna *see* Wynonna
Judge Judy *see* Sheindlin, Judith
Judge, Mike May 97
Julia, Raul obit Jan 95
Julia y Araelay, Raul Rafael Carlos *see* Julia, Raul
Jung, Andrea May 2000

Kabakov, Ilya Apr 98
Kadare, Ismail Feb 92
Kaganovich, Lazar M. obit Sep 91
Kahane, Meir obit Jan 91
Kahn, Madeline obit Mar 2000
Kahn, Roger Jun 2000
Kamali, Norma Nov 98
Kaminski, Janusz Mar 2000
Kamprad, Ingvar Jun 98
Kanin, Garson obit Jun 99
Kanter, Rosabeth Moss Jun 96

Figure 13.5

## *Internet Sources*

Some of the print sources listed earlier in this chapter are also available online, either through services such as FirstSearch or through other commercial databases. For example, many items that appear in the *New York Times* are available in full text versions if you search for an individual's name on the internet. Searching for biographical information via the internet may result in finding full text information from newspapers and periodicals. Some sources such as FirstSearch or Biography Resource Center must be searched through a library catalog unless you have an account with the database owner. The Biography Resource Center provides options such as thumbnail biographies, magazine citations or narrative biographies. A link to websites or Marquis publications is provided. The Biography Resource Center also provides a list of "Biographical facts Search" with searches based on facts such as nationality, occupation or gender. The advanced search feature provides searches for the full text, by keyword, source or date. Some search engines such as Google and Yahoo are also useful in finding biographical information. In June 2005 both were searched for biographical information on Stephen King. Both provided thousands of results. However the first 20 or so sites on Google provided better links for actual biographical information.

## *Exercises for Chapter 13*

1. List the biographical indexes owned by your library. Include the call numbers.
2. Using biographical indexes, biographical dictionaries and other sources owned by your library, look up the biographies of the individuals listed below. Look in at least two sources for each. Record the sources where you found the information. If the individual is not located in the first two sources, check at least three more sources. Be sure to record the name of the individual checked.
   (A)   Your congressman
   (B)   Your favorite author
   (C)   Pope John Paul II
   (D)   Dan Rather
   (E)   Bill O'Reilly
3. Find the name of a pianist and then locate a biography for that person.

# Important Term in Chapter 13

*obituaries*

# Important Books for Chapter 13

*American Men and Women of Science*, 21st ed. New York: R. R. Bowker Database Publishing Group, 2003.

*Author Biographies Master Index*: a consolidated index of more than 1,140,000 biographical sketches concerning authors living and dead as they appear in a selection of the principal biographical dictionaries devoted to authors, poets, journalists, and other literary figures. Ed. by Dennis La Beau. 5th ed. Detroit: Gale Research, 1997. Ceased publication with 5th edition.

*Biographical Dictionaries Master Index*. Ed. 1, 1975–76. Detroit: Gale Research, 1975. Supplements.

*Biography and Genealogy Master Index*. Gale Research, 1981–. Base volumes published in 1981. Five year cumulations for 1981 to 1985, 1986 to 1990 and 1991–1995, annual volumes. Annual updates. Covers more than 250 biographical dictionaries and Who's Whos. Also available on CD.

*Biography Index: A Cumulative Index to Biographical Materials in Books and Magazines*. New York: H. W. Wilson, 1947–. Available online via OCLC's FirstSearch and WilsonWeb.

*Contemporary Authors: A Bio-Bibliographical Guide to Current Authors and Their Works*. Detroit: Gale Research, 1962–. Available online via Infotrac.

*Current Biography*. V. 1–, 1940–. New York: H. W. Wilson, 1940–(monthly except August). Available on CD-ROM and WilsonWeb.

*Dictionary of American Biography*. Published under the auspices of the American Council of Learned Societies. New York: Scribner's; London: Milford, 1928–37. 20 vols. plus index. As of 1998 there are 10 supplementary volumes plus an index to the supplements. Also available in microfiche format.

*Dictionary of National Biography*. Edited by Sir Leslie Stephen and Sir Sidney Lee. London: Smith Elder, 1908. 22 vols. Reprinted, 1938. Supplements and cumulative indexes to various supplements.

*Encyclopedia of World Biography*. 2nd edition. Detroit: Gale Research, 1998–2004. 24 volumes.

Kunitz, Stanley Jasspon, and Vineta Colby. *European Authors, 1000–1900:*

*A Biographical Dictionary of European Literature.* New York: H. W. Wilson, 1967.

_____, and Howard Haycroft. *Twentieth Century Authors: A Biographical Dictionary of Modern Literature.* New York: H. W. Wilson, 1942.

*Marquis Who's Who Publications, Index to Who's Who Books, 1974–.* Chicago, Marquis, 1975–.

*New York Times Obituary Index, 1858–1968.* New York: New York Times, 1970. Supplement 1969–1978, pub. 1980. Supplement 1975–1996, pub. 1998.

Wakeman, John. *World Authors, 1950–1970; A Companion Volume to "Twentieth Century Authors."* New York: H. W. Wilson, 1975.

*Who Was Who in America: A Companion Biographical Reference Work to "Who's Who in America."* Chicago: Marquis. 1963–(V. 9 is 1985–1989 published in 1989). Index 1607–1989.

*Who's Who in America: A Biographical Dictionary of Notable Living Men and Women.* Chicago: Marquis, 1899– (biennial). (59th ed. is 2005).

*Who's Who in Finance and Industry, 1936–.* Chicago: Marquis, 1936–.

*Who's Who in the East: A Biographical Dictionary of Leading Men and Women in the Eastern United States.* V. 1–, 1942/43. Chicago: Marquis, 1943–.

*Who's Who in the Socialists Countries of Europe: A Biographical Encyclopedia of More Than 12,600 Leading Personalities in Albania, Bulgaria, Czechoslovakia, German Democratic Republic, Hungary, Poland, Romania, Yugoslavia.* New York: K. G. Saur, 1989.

*Who's Who of American Women: A Biographical Dictionary of Notable Living American Women.* Ed. 1–, 1958–9. Chicago: Marquis, 1958–.

# 14

# Business, Career and Consumer Information

## Objectives

After studying this chapter the student shall be able to

- locate firms manufacturing specific products
- locate names and addresses of companies and business organizations
- locate information about specific business, industries and organizations
- use consumer-advocate publications to find information about products
- locate information about careers and occupations

## General Information

This chapter deals with the location of information about manufacturers, retail stores, consumer-orientated organizations and other types of businesses. Finding and using this information is useful in job hunting, purchasing and consumer complaining. This chapter focuses on some specific reference books for business and consumer information. Besides the new sources introduced in this chapter, one also may wish to consult sources discussed in earlier chapters, for example the yellow pages of the telephone directory and the ads in newspapers.

161

# *Business*

*Thomas' Register of American Manufacturers* 2005 (100th anniversary edition with 16 volumes) has several sections. The first section (volumes 1 through 14 of the 2005 edition) is a list of products and services available from the various companies by type of company. For example, if the names of knitting mills in an area are needed, one should look in *Thomas' Register* under "knit goods," where there is a listing by states of the names and addresses of knitting mills. The next section, company profiles (volumes 15 and 16), is an alphabetical listing of companies including addresses; phone and FAX numbers; URL addresses, asset ratings; email addresses and company officials. Older editions have a third, and last, section (the "Thom Cat") that contains the catalogs of about 10 percent of the included companies. If one desires a new valve for a water heater and there is no local distributor for that manufacturer, the catalog contains the address and phone number of the manufacturer. Many manufacturers' catalogs include diagrams, pictures and part numbers. The *Register* also may be useful in providing the names, addresses and phone numbers of firms involved in a specific type of business. This kind of listing is helpful to individuals looking for a job in a specific industry.

Dun & Bradstreet, an agency supplying credit information and credit ratings, publishes several useful directories. For example, their *Million Dollar Directory* lists corporations with a net worth of $1,000,000 or more. The directory lists businesses alphabetically and gives the following information for each business: the address, the phone number, the number of employees, the annual sales, the type of business and names (with titles) of the executives. There are a variety of indexes enabling the user to identify businesses by type, geographical area and executives' names. These indexes make it easy to locate firms of certain types in specific geographical areas; for example, all the photographic suppliers in New England.

The Moody's manuals, covering a dozen topics such as public utilities, transportation and banks and finance, give lengthy reports about the businesses included. The articles include a corporate history, information on stocks, financial status and statements, management and other information. Moody's manuals are published by Dun & Bradstreet.

*The Standard & Poor's Register of Corporations, Directors and Executives* is a directory to American and Canadian businesses and generally gives the same type of information found in the Dun & Bradstreet directories. The *Standard & Poor's 500 Guide* tracks 500 companies. Each entry

Microform readers are often also printers. They are usually located in a separate room with the cabinets of film and fiche.

includes highlights, business summary, charts and tables dealing with earnings, revenue and other company financial information.

Hoover's handbooks have many volumes including *American Business* which profiles 750 major U.S. companies. The information included is supplied by the company. If companies fail to supply information then reliable third party sources are used. Entries include general information about the company; a brief history; a list of executives; locations; products/operations; competitors and historical financial information. Other volumes of Hoover's handbook series include *World Business* (profiles of major global enterprises); *Private Companies* (profiles of major U.S. private enterprises) and *Emerging Companies* (profiles of America's most exciting growth enterprises). The volume on Emerging Companies includes a master index to all the Hoover's handbooks for that year. Hoover's company information is also available on the internet at *www.hoovers.com*.

Many libraries subscribe to **ReferenceUSA**, an internet-based services for locating businesses and information about them. In 2005 their home page claims they include more than 12 million U.S. businesses and 1 million Canadian businesses; 102 million U.S. residents and 11 million Canadian residents; and 683,000 U.S. health care providers. The information is compiled from telephone directories, corporate reports (such as 10-Ks), newspapers and millions of phone calls made annually. They claim to contact businesses with more than 100 employees twice a year. Their definition of businesses is rather broad. They include churches, schools and government organizations as well a large and small businesses. It's a handy way to locate the nearest branch of a big business or a local pizza delivery service.

## *Organizations—Profit, Nonprofit, etc.*

*The Encyclopedia of Associations* issues a new edition approximately every other year. Volume 1 (which has several physical volumes) is the *National Organizations of the United States.* It is arranged by subject (a classified list) and includes a keyword index to the organization's name. Volume 2 is *Geographic and Executive Indexes. The* geographic index section lists all organizations in volume 1 alphabetically by state and city. The executive index is a list of executives listed in volume one, arranged alphabetically by surnames. Volume 3 is *New Associations and Projects* and is a supplement to volume 1. Volume 4 is *International Organizations.* There is a seven volume guide to regional, state and local organizations. Entries

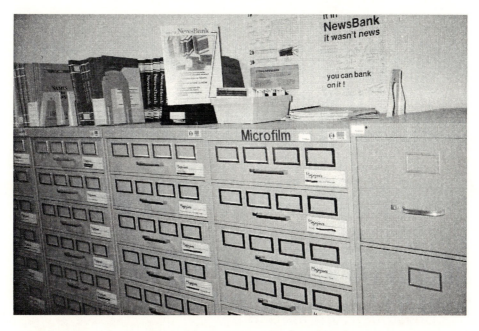

**Microfiche and microfilm cabinets are usually found in the same room as the readers.**

in volumes 1, 3 and 4 provide the full name of the association, the address and phone number, the name of the director and a description of the association. The description may include the following types of information: date founded, number of members, number of staff, publications, committees, annual meetings and conventions, and a brief history of the organization. The keyword index enables the user to identify the organization even if only one word of the organization's name is known. The classified format provides a means of locating all organizations of a similar type without knowing the names of any specific organizations.

The *National Trade and Professional Associations of the United States* is a directory that lists more than "7,600 active trade associations, professional societies, technical organizations and labor unions" (*National Trade and Professional Associations of the United States,* 2004 ed. P. 11). This directory has numerous indexes. Among the more unusual indexes are those for budget; acronyms; meetings and management firms. Entries include date the organization was founded; number of members; number of staff; budgets; names of directors; historical information; meetings and publications.

## Career Information

Most libraries have at least a few sources of information about careers. Most public libraries will have a special section with career information. Some of these sources circulate but in general they are for library use only. The U.S. Department of Labor Statistics, *Occupational Outlook Handbook* provides descriptions of occupations, professional and non-professional. Descriptions include nature of the work; working conditions; employment; training, other qualifications and advancement; job outlook; earnings; related occupations; and sources of additional information. Career sections may also include information on internships, directories of job hotlines, and handbooks with practice civil service or military tests. For examples of specific titles, see the list at the end of this chapter. For career information on the internet try the following sites: www.ajb.dni.us (America's job Bank) and www.monster.com.

## Consumer Information

Government agencies at several levels publish information guides. Some publications deal with specific products or industries, while others are directories of sources of information. Some useful directories and other reports are published by groups not associated with any government, such as groups coordinated by Ralph Nader. For examples of specific books see the bibliography at the end of this chapter.

There are also several journals devoted to the consumer. The most widely known is *Consumer Reports,* a monthly magazine reporting on all sorts of products. This magazine lacks association with any company or governmental agency and contains tests and reports on consumer products. *Consumer Reports* also publishes an annual buyer's guide. Independent publications of this type provide useful, unbiased information on consumer goods. Smart consumers research before making major purchases such as a car, television or major appliance. Wise consumers also know that they can complain and that they have rights when products are defective. Using reference sources such as those discussed or listed in the bibliography helps the consumer in locating information when it is needed, e.g., names, addresses and phone numbers of corporations, governmental agencies or private groups that can answer questions or provide assistance. In researching business or consumer information, periodicals and newspapers (Chapter 8) and government documents (Chapter 12) also provide information. The indexes to periodicals *(Business Periodicals Index)*, the *Monthly Catalog* (for federal documents, especially the Consumer Protection Agency, see Chapter 12) and newspaper indexes (e.g., those of the *New York Times* and the *Wall Street Journal)* are also useful sources.

## Exercises for Chapter 14

1. Find the names and addresses of firms manufacturing tennis equipment.
2. Locate at least one industry study and one consumer organization study on the use of air bags in automobiles.
3. Locate and record the name, address and phone number of the consumer protection group nearest to your home.
4. Locate the corporate headquarters of Verizon and the name of the chief executive.

## Important Books for Chapter 14

### Business

*American Big Business Directory.* Omaha, NB: American Business Directories, 2004. 2 vols. Available in paper, magnetic tape, PC diskettes or CD-ROM. It includes over 62,000 organizations with 250 or more employees. Vol. 1 is alphabetical listing a–r, Vol. 2 is s–z, and S.I.C. code; alphabetical list of executives; and market planning statistics. Annual

*The Blackwell Encyclopedia of Management. Business Ethics.* Edited by patricia Hogue Werhane and R. Edward Freeman.Malden, MA: Blackwell Pub., 2005.

Botto, Francis. *Dictionary of E-Business.* 2nd ed. Chichester, England; Hoboken, NJ: Wiley, 2003.

*Business Periodicals Index.* New York: H. W. Wilson, 1958–, v. 1 (monthly). A cumulative subject index to periodicals in the field of accounting, advertising, banking and finance, general business insurance, labor and management, marketing and purchasing, public administration, taxation, specific businesses, industries and trades. Also available via FirstSearch or WilsonLine in some libraries.

Colin, P. H. *Dictionary of Business.* 4th ed. London: Bloomsbury, 2004.

*Consultants and Consulting Organizations Directory: A Reference Guide to More Than 24,000 Concerns and Individuals Engaged in Consultation for Business, Industry and Government,* 27th ed. Detroit: Gale Research, 2004. (2 vols.)

Daniells, Lorna M., et al. *How to Find Information About Companies.* 8th ed. Washington, D.C.: Washington Researchers 1997. (3 vols)

*Encyclopedia of Associations.* 41st ed. Edited by Katherine Gruber. Detroit: Gale Research, 2004.

*Encyclopedia of Business Information Sources.* 19th ed. Detroit: Gale Research, 2004.

*Hoover's Handbook of American Business.* Austin, Tx: Sycamore productions, Inc. 2005.

*Million Dollar Directory,* 1959–. New York: Dun & Bradstreet, Inc., 1959– (annual).

*The New Palgrave: A Dictionary of Economics.* London: Macmillan, 2002. (4 vols.) This is the successor to the *Dictionary of Political Economy.*

*National Trade and Professional Associations of the United States.* 39th ed. Washington, D.C.: Columbia Books, Inc., 2004. Annual

*Standard & Poor's 500 Guide.* New York: McGraw-Hill, 1994–. Annual

*Standard & Poor's Register of Corporations, Directors and Executives, United States and Canada, 1928–* (annual). 2005 edition is 2 vols.

Moss, Rita and Diane Wheeler Strauss. *Strauss's Handbook of Business Information: a guide for librarians, students, and researchers.* 2nd ed. Westport, CT: Libraries Unlimited, 2004.

*Thomas' Register of American Manufacturers.* New York: Thomas' Publishing, 190?– (2004 edition has 16 volumes.)

*U.S. Industrial Directory: The Direct Link to Industrial Products and Suppliers.* New Providence, NJ: Reed International/Cahners, 1997. (3 vols.)

Wechman, Robert L. *Dictionary of Economics and Business: A Thousand Key Terms and People.* Champaign: Stipes Publishing, 1997.

*World Chamber of Commerce Directory.* Loveland, OH: Worldwide Chamber of Commerce Directory, 1989– (annual).

## CONSUMERS

Cline, Elizabeth. *The Bargain Buyer's Guide 2004.* Lowell Miller. Bearsville, NY: The Print Project, 2004. Formerly *Wholesale by Mail & Online.*

*Consumer Protection Handbook.* Chicago, ILL: American Bar Association. Section of Antitrust Law, 2004.

*Consumer Reports,* May 1936–. Mt. Vernon, NY: Consumer's Union of the United States, 1936– (monthly). *Buyer's Guide* is the December issue.

*Consumer Reports Best Buys for Your Home.* Yonkers, NY: Consumers Union of United States, Inc., 2003.

*Consumer Reports Digital Buying Guide.* Yonkers, NY: Consumer Reports, 2004.

*Consumer Sourcebook: a subject guide to over 23,000 federal, state and local government agencies and offices, national...* 17th ed. Detroit: Gale Group, 2005.

*Consumer's Index to Product Evaluation and Information Sources.* V. 1, no. 1–, Winter 1974– (quarterly with annual cumulations).

*Consumer's Resource Handbook.* Washington, DC: U.S. Office of Consumer Affairs, 1997.

Gillis, Jack. *The Used Car Book 2002–2003.* 15th ed. New York: Harper-Resource, 2002.

Jasper, Margaret C. *What If the Product Doesn't Work: Warranties and Guarantees.* Dobbs Ferry, NY: Oceana Publications, 2003.

Kalin, Stanley R., and Susan A. Longacre. *Product Safety Handbook: Manufacturers Guide to Legal Requirements & Management Strategies.* Rockville, MD: Government Institutes, 2001.

Lesko, Matthew, with Mary Ann Martello. *Gobs and Gobs of Free Stuff.* 3rd ed. Kensington, MD: Information USA, Inc., 2002.

Miller, Michael. *Bargin Hunter's Secrets to Online $hopping.* Indianapolis, IN: Que Publishing, 2004.

Williams, Sheila and George M Basharis. *Bankruptcy Abuse Prevention & Consumer Protection Act of 2005: Law and Explanation.* Chicago: Aspen Publishers, 2005.

## CAREER

*America's Top 300 Jobs: A Complete Career Handbook.* 9th ed. Indianapolis, IN: JIST Publishing, Inc., 2004. Based on information in the *Occupational Outlook Handbook.*

Bobrow, Jerry, et. al. *Barron's Civil Service Clerical Exams...* 5th ed., Hauppauge, NY: Barron's, 2005.

*Career Discovery Encyclopedia.* Edited by Carol J. Summerfield. 5th ed. Chicago: J. G. Ferguson Publishing Company, 1993. 8 volumes.

*Civil Service Handbook.* 15th ed. Arco Publishing. Lawrenceville, NJ: Thomson/Peterson's, 2005. Alternate title, *Arco Civil Service Handbook.*

Copeland, Joyce Hadley. *Where the Jobs Are: The Hottest Careers for the 21st Century.* 3rd ed. Franklin Lakes, NJ: The Career Press, 2000.

*Encyclopedia of Career and Vocational Guidance.* Edited by William E. Hopke. 11th ed. Chicago: J. G. Ferguson Publishing Company, 2000. (4 vols.)

Farr, Michael, and LaVerne L. Ludden. *200 Best Jobs for College Graduates.* 2nd ed. Indianapolis, IN: JIST Publishing, Inc., 2003. Previous titled *Best Jobs for the 21st Century.*

Fisher, Helen S. *American Salaries and Wages Survey.* 7th ed. Detroit: Gale Research Inc., 2003.

Krannich, Ronald L. and Wendy S. Enelow. *Best Resumes and CV's for International Jobs: Your Passport to the Global Job Market.* Manassas Park, VA: Impact Publications, 2002.

*Occupational Outlook Handbook.* U. S. Department of Labor, 22nd ed., 1996–1997. Bureau of Labor Statistics, Washington, DC: U.S.G.P.O. 1947– (Biennial).

*Peterson's Internships, 2005.* 25th ed. Lawrenceville, NJ: Thomson Learning, 2005. Includees about 50,000 paid and unpaid internships.

# 15

# Nonprint Materials
# and Special Services

## Objectives

After studying this chapter the student shall be able to

- recognize the formats of microfilm and microfiche and explain how they may be used
- use interlibrary loans to access remote materials
- use the OCLC system to locate materials
- request computer searches when needed

## Nonprint Materials

Most libraries lump many things under the term *nonprint*. Often the term includes everything that is not a book or a periodical (that is, not printed on paper). The term then includes a variety of microprint formats; also records, audiotapes, videotapes, DVDs, CDs, films and slides. Some libraries even lend the equipment needed for using these nonprint materials, such as microprint readers and cassette players.

The materials in microprint (reduced size) come in several formats. Microfilm is 16mm or 35mm and on reels. Microfiche is usually a 4 × 6 transparent card. The size of print on both microfilm and microform is usually reduced 24 times. Some microfiche is reduced 48 times. Ultrafiche is similar to microfiche, but the size of the card may be 3 × 5 or 4 × 6 and the print is reduced 98 times. An ultrafiche (3 × 5) can contain up to 1,000 pages. Microcards can be 3 × 5, 4 × 6 or 5 × 8 in size but are opaque rather than transparent and may have printing on both sides of the card. Mechanical readers are needed to use all microforms. Some readers can be used with more than one format. Others are printers. They can be used to make "hard" or paper copy from the microform. The type of microform (negative or positive) and the type of copier will decide the format of the hard copy. Most microforms are positive, black letters on a white background. Some copiers use a dry photographic process so that the hard copy will be the opposite of what is seen on the screen. Positive film produces a negative image (white letters on a black background) hard copy. Some companies have designed reader/printers that are similar to photocopying machines and the hard copy is identical with what is seen on the screen. One brand of machine also senses if the microform is negative or positive and always produces a positive hard copy. These machines use plain paper which produces more permanent and readable copy.

Most readers have pictures or diagrams showing how to use the reader. If the directions are unclear or any doubt exists about the operation of the equipment, the user should request assistance from a member of the library staff. Improper use of equipment or the use of the wrong equipment can result in damage to the microform or the reader.

## Special Library Services

Libraries provide services besides housing information. They provide reserve, reference and interlibrary loans. Reserves may range from holding a book that has been out in circulation to setting aside many books for a class. Reference services help users find the answers to questions. The help may vary from using the catalog to doing computer searches of databases. Most such searches available are of databases used to produce periodical indexes. These searches are generally faster and more complete than manual searches. Libraries may charge a fee for this type of service. One database in widespread use is PsycLIT (online version of *Psychological Abstracts*). From it one can obtain a computer generated list of summaries of all the journal articles on a particular topic. To obtain this information the searcher must provide key terms — descriptors — that are entered into the computer. The method is progressive in that the topic must be narrowed until the precise information can be processed. Usually librarians will provide professional help to do these searches, since it requires

**Public libraries have large video/DVD collections.**

some experience to handle the terminal and to choose and enter appropriate descriptors. Some libraries have computer terminals available for student use. For more information, see chapters 9 and 16 on CD-ROM, databases and computers in libraries.

Interlibrary loan (ILL) is a procedure for borrowing books, periodicals and other materials from other libraries. It is extremely helpful in obtaining information not available locally. Each library has its own rules for interlibrary loans and it is probably necessary to ask at the reference or interlibrary loan librarian's desk for the forms and procedures to use. Some libraries charge for interlibrary loan service and others do not.

To speed up the processing of requests for ILL the student or faculty member should provide complete information. If for example, a book is being requested, provide the author's complete name, the title of the book, publisher and date of publication. A request for a book by Jones, no first name or initial, even if the title, publisher and date are provided probably will be returned to the requester with a statement that there is insufficient information to process the request. If the needed material is a journal article, the requester must provide complete information: the full title of the journal with the volume number, date and pages, and the author's name and the title of the article. If the information is incomplete, the librarian is likely to return the request for additional information. Many librarians ask for a *verification*. The verification denotes where the user found the citation. Some libraries will not even begin to process on ILL request if the verification is not supplied. A valid verification would be any type of reference source discussed in this book.

If the request is for a book, the book will be sent. But, if the request is for a journal article, a photocopy will be sent. The time from presentation of the request to the ILL desk until the material arrives will be determined by the system(s) used by the borrowing library. For regional loans, local delivery systems are frequently used and the elapsed time probably will be short. If the requested materials must come from a distant library, the lending library will be shipping the materials either by the U.S. Postal Service or United Parcel Service. Library materials shipped in either of these ways usually takes longer to arrive at the borrowing library. For fast service, some libraries will fax a copy of journal articles. This service frequently carries a charge. Students should plan ahead.

## OCLC

OCLC, is an international online database of the holdings of more than 53,000 libraries in 96 countries. The OCLC headquarters and computers are located in Dublin, Ohio. The member libraries include the Library of Congress, the National Library of Medicine, the National Library of Canada and the British Lending Library. They provide cataloging information that is available then to all members. The system recorded its one billionth holding on August 11, 2005. As of November 1, 2005, there were more than one billion 10 million records with new records added about every four seconds. To watch the holdings grow, log on to OCLC's website (*www.oclc.org*) and choose news and events. Holding records are for all types of library materials: books, periodicals, pamphlets, records, audio tapes, videotapes, government documents, etc. OCLC numbers are assigned as new items are cataloged. The OCLC database may be searched in about 30 different ways, including: by author's name, title, author-title, series title, keyword, access method, material type, genre/form, musical composition, OCLC number, SuDoc number, ISBN number, ISSN number, LC card number, CODEN and others. ISBN is the international standard book number, and ISSN is the international standard serial number. CODEN is a code assigned to serials by indexing services such as *Biological Abstracts* and *Chemical Abstracts*.

**Browsing the AV collection (music CDs, videos and DVDs).**

Each record in the OCLC database has a holding's list attached to it. Thus every member library that has a copy of *War and Peace* will have its symbol attached to the record. If a library does not own a copy of *War and Peace* it can call up the record and see which libraries own a copy. Each edition, translation, etc., of *War and Peace* will have its own record and holding's list. Besides cataloging information the system simplifies transmitting interlibrary loan requests between member libraries. As of April 2005, 128 million ILL's had been processed. It also checks in periodicals, produces union lists of serials by regions or other specific areas and searches other databases from which periodical indexes are produced. One of OCLC's most popular services is FirstSearch. It is available in more than 20,000 libraries in 96 countries and in early 2005 had more than 75 different databases available. WorldCat is the database most frequently searched. It is OCLC's main database with more than 58 million records. The subscribing libraries can subscribe to a few or all of the databases available on FirstSearch. Pricing options also allow individuals to search FirstSearch by subscription or by per-search. The holdings symbols for all libraries holding the item (book or periodical) may be displayed by clicking on *Libraries Worldwide*. Many databases available via OCLC are also accessible from DIALOG and other vendors. A library or individual can buy searches for FirstSearch at a fixed rate per search, there are no connect times or per item charges. OCLC charges for all services provided. Members of OCLC may participate in different components of the program.

## Exercises for Chapter 15

1. Make a note of the ILL procedures and regulations in your library. Be sure to check on charges and the average length of time before requested materials arrive.
2. Ask the reference librarian if your library is a member of OCLC. If yes, ask about the scope of your library's participation in OCLC services.

## Important Terms in Chapter 15

database
*OCLC*
*interlibrary loan (ILL)*
*ultrafiche*
*microcards*
*nonprint*
*microfiche*
*microfilm*
*verification*
*readers*

## Important Books for Chapter 15

Boucher, Virginia. *Interlibrary Loan Practices Handbook*. 2nd ed. Chicago: American Library Association, 1997.

Burwell, Helen P., and Carolyn N. Hills. *Directory of Fee-Based Information Services*. Houston, TX: Burwell Enterprises, 1984– (annual).

*Guide to Microforms in Print*. Westport, CT: Meckler, 1961– (annual). Author-title vol., subject volume and supplements.

Morris, Leslie R., and Sandra Chass Morris. *Interlibrary Loan Policies Directory*. 7th ed. New York: Neal-Schuman Publishers, 2002. Each entry lists policies, charges, address, phone numbers, FAX numbers, etc. for over 2,000 libraries. Directory is arranged by states.

# 16

# Online Computer Use in Libraries and Schools

## Objectives

After studying this chapter the student shall be able to

- identify where computers are used in the library
- identify available computer services in the library
- locate books and journals on computers
- recognize how databases are used

## Definitions

Below are listed several terms commonly used in the discussion of computers.

**Compact Disc** — is a type of optically read computer memory. It was invented in 1980 by Philips Electronics N.V. and the Sony Corporation. It generally is used to store data files.

**DVD** — is the abbreviation for a digital videodisc. It has the same dimensions as a CD but stores video files rather than data files.

**Floppy Disk (Diskette)** — a flat circular plate with a magnetic surface, usually enclosed plastic case. Data (information) may be stored on one or both sides.

**Hardware** — the physical equipment: the computer, monitor, keyboard, etc.

Librarians often teach classes in the use of all aspects of the library, its collections, and resources.

Keyboard—device for entering information into a computer by depressing keys. Computer keyboards are similar to typewriter keyboards.

Modem—a device used to transmit computer signals over communication (usually telephone or cable) facilities.

Monitor—a screen for observing, viewing or controlling the operation of the computer. Most look very much like a TV screen. They may be colored or monochromatic (one color, usually green or amber).

Password—a secret word or symbol to be typed into a computer that allows the operator access to the system and prevents unauthorized access.

Peripherals—any device outside the central processing unit (disk drives, printers, monitors, etc.).

Printer—a device that prints information from the computer; used to produce a "hard" (paper) copy of the desired data.

Program—instructions to the computer enabling the computer to perform desired tasks.

Software—programs for the computer.

## *General Information*

Most libraries use computers for a variety of tasks. A few libraries restrict computers use to staff only but most libraries have many computers available for public use. Those libraries having computers for public use provide a wide range of assistance, including general instruction, formal classes and instruction sheets at each terminal. The kind and number of computer resources available and regulations regarding use vary from library to library. Many school libraries use Apple computers and most public, college and university libraries use PCs.

Regulations on the use of computers differ, as do the types of software owned by the library. Most public libraries do not allow sign-up for computer searching (usually Internet or e-mail) for more than a day in advance and usually limit access to less than one hour. These services are very popular and resources are limited.

Computers have been in common use for many years and most people have some computer literacy. For those who are "computer challenged" library staff will provide individual assistance.

Database searching is available in many libraries. It will probably be via the Internet. It might also include some of the commercial vendors such as DIALOG (which charge by the minute). Using the Internet to access some services such as OCLC's FirstSearch or DIALOG will usually eliminates the cost of a long distance phone call. For more information about the Internet and FirstSearch refer back to parts of chapters 2, 3, 8, 9, 11, 12 and 14. If a commercial source such as DIALOG is searched, generally the librarian does the searching since the system is complex and costly if the search is not properly formulated. Searches from commercial vendors can be printed while online or printed off-line and mailed to the library. The off-line printing tends to be much less expensive and the few days delay in viewing the results is acceptable to most users. In school media centers there is often a charge for printing results from an online search or a search of a CD-ROM on site. Many public libraries and some college and university libraries also charge for printing. The reasons vary but generally include discouraging the printing of non-required information, the cost of paper and cartridges for the printer. With proper equipment and a willingness to pay the bill, searching can be done from home.

The catalog should be consulted for books on computers. For libraries using the Library of Congress system, most books will be in the QA76s; in Dewey libraries, books will be in the 004–005s and the 510s. These are not the only locations, so the catalog should be checked. Libraries may have journals on computers and computing. The periodicals list contains the items the library subscribes to that deal with computers. Popular computer magazines include: *Computer World; Personal Computing; PC World; PC Magazine; Smart Computing; Macworld; Linux User, Wired, PC Today; Family PC;* and *Computer Shopper.*

## Exercises for Chapter 16

1. Determine where your library computers are located. What kind are they?
2. Who is allowed to use the equipment?
3. List the rules for software use in your library.
4. List the rules for using the computers in your library.
5. To what computer periodicals does your library subscribe?

## Important Terms in Chapter 16

database
*software*
*vendor*
*terminal*
*monitor*
*modem*
*password*
*hardware*
*microcomputer*
*peripherals*
*printer*
*floppy disk (diskette)*
*keyboard*
*CD*
*DVD*

## Important Books for Chapter 16

Barrett, Daniel J. *Net Research: Finding Information Online.* Sebastopol, CA: Songline Studies: O'Reilly and Associates, 1997.

*Books and Periodicals Online: A Directory of Online Publications.* 2 volumes. Washington, DC: Library Technology Alliance, 1997.

Connors, Martin. *Online Database Search Services Directory*, 2nd edition. Detroit: Gale Research, 1984-. Two volumes, published semiannually.

*Directory of Periodicals Online.* New York, NY: Library technology Alliance, 2005 — (serial. Three sections: Humanities and Religion; Medical and Pharmaceutical; and Science and Technology).

Downing, Douglas A.; Michael A. Covington and Melody Mauldin Covington. *Dictionary of Computer and Internet Terms.* 8th edition. Hauppauge, NY: Barron's Educational Series, Inc. 2003.

Hahn, Harley. *Harley Hahn's The Internet Yellow Pages.* Berkeley: Osborne McGraw-Hill, 2002–. Serial published annually.

Hartman, Karen. *Searching and researching on the Internet and the World Wide Web.* 4th ed. Wilsonville, OR: Franklin, Beedle, 2004.

# 17

# Hints for Writing Papers

## Objectives

After studying this chapter the student shall be able to

- use note cards as an adjunct to library research
- use a database to take notes
- label cards for retrieval and bibliography writing
- be aware of the various uses of word processors in footnoting, outlining, indexing and composing papers
- find an appropriate method for citing other authors
- distinguish between primary and secondary sources and know the advantage of using primary sources
- define and avoid plagiarism
- understand copyright and the rules governing the photocopying of material

## General Information

Writing term papers and reports can be a laborious process, particularly is the writer does not use efficient methods of data collection and retrieval. Thus, it is important to develop techniques that will enable one to avoid unnecessary work. The following discussion is not meant as a comprehensive discourse on how to write term papers since there are many excellent term paper manuals that may be consulted for this purpose. Rather, hints that the author has found useful in writing papers are presented.

## *Taking Notes with Note Cards*

The first step to writing the paper is to conceptualize the topic. Research in the library follows. How to find materials has been discussed extensively in the prior chapters. Gathering and transcribing data in a useful form so that it may be retrieved later must be done efficiently. One extremely useful way of saving data is by using lined index cards. Each piece of data should be abstracted and transcribed to cards, preferably the 4 × 6 or the 5 × 8 cards. This may sound simple minded and one may ask why notebook paper is not equally good. Using cards has several advantages. First, a card or set of cards can be easily sorted by topics later and then resorted using other categories; this is more difficult with notebook paper. Second, more materials on the same topic or from the same source may be added more easily later by just adding cards. Third, when writing an outline cards may be sorted by subheadings.

For writing note cards, the following hints will be helpful. Include on the first card for each source the information that will be needed in the footnote and the bibliography. On each subsequent card for the source show the author and the date of the work at the top. This will save all the accumulated work that has already been done in case the cards get dropped or mixed up. Frequently when doing research reviews, one may find several articles by the same author written at different times. When the paper is written it is difficult to recall from which articles that piece of information derives, thus the need for the author and date on each card.

## *Taking Notes with a Database*

Using a database for note taking can be an invaluable aid to the student. Databases allow information to be stored in records and fields. Each record contains all the information about a particular source, magazine article, book or reference citation. Within each record, many fields may be designated to contain selected information about that record. Thus, for each source, there is a record with multiple fields.

As the student finds additional articles, he can enter the information about the article into the database by record. A typical record might look like the following:

**Record #1**
*Field Name*

| | |
|---|---|
| Author | Mills, Frederick A. |
| Title | "Databasing for Fun and Profit" |
| Journal | *Popular Databasing* |
| Date | July 1985 |
| Volume # | 7:12 |
| Pages | 35–43 |
| Content | This article contains information about the newest databases available; with emphasis on their application at home. |
| Subject | Databases |

Other fields may be added as needed. The better databases allow 20 or more fields for each record. Once the information has been entered (this can be done a little at a time) it can be selected in a variety of ways for later use by sorting by any of the fields. Sorting the above record by author will give the bibliographic references necessary for the report.

Another sort by subject provides clusters of records that form sections of chapters to be written. Another sorting by date would be helpful in writing in a time or historic framework. Instead of carrying around many individual index cards, the student can store all the information necessary for writing the paper on a single diskette or CD.

The fields and records may be output to a printer in any way the user desires. For example, a printed list with just the authors' names, or just the names of the journal articles, could be printed out. Furthermore, the format is flexible so that the spacing and line setups can be determined by the author. As more entries are added to the database the information is automatically added, and revised copies of the lists can be printed out in a matter of minutes. This feature alone could save hours of sorting and typing.

The writer must learn to use the database. But this time is well spent. No special knowledge of the computer is necessary to begin working with a database. Anyone can sit at the computer, follow the instruction manual and begin databasing in a matter of minutes. More involved use of the program will become evident as the student uses a program more. Usually, students may obtain databases from school or purchase them at minimal cost.

Some libraries (or colleges or universities) subscribe to **RefWorks**, a Web-based database. This is a personal database helping to organize data, format your paper and create your bibliography. It includes choices for bibliographic format and when that data is correctly entered, it will create the bibliography in the desired format. As a Web-based database, it can be accessed from any computer with Internet access. For more information about this database, consult your reference librarian.

## *Word Processing*

Students should use word processing programs to construct papers and theses. Most computers have a word processing program. Writing a paper using a word processor takes most of the drudgery out of the process. It allows for instant corrections as you are typing. This takes the fear out of the process and greatly increases one's typing speed and confidence at the keyboard. Editing can be done directly on the keyboard or from a hard (printed) copy of the text. Words can be changed, sentences moved, paragraphs may be added, deleted or rearranged instantaneously and the revised version can be printed out immediately. Large amounts of text can be stored on floppy disks or CDs rather than on reams of paper and large numbers of index cards. Many word processing packages provide a spelling checker integrated into the software package which will automatically check the spelling of all words in the text. Some programs even offer substitute words to use. Most word processors also include a thesaurus that provides synonyms. One merely points to a word in the text, hits a key and a list of substitutes appear. Most also include spell checkers and grammar checkers. The student should always proof read the document after using the spell checker. A typo may have occurred that is an actual word and thus not corrected by the spell checker. For example, the word **on** may have been typed and the word **no** is the intended word. Since **on** is a word, spell checker does not mark it as a misspelled word.

Also one may use a word processor for other purposes besides composing documents. Footnoting is easy using a word processing program such as *WordPerfect* or *Word*. The program allows footnotes to cross-reference documents in many ways. The reader can be informed to seek additional information on other pages, in other chapters, in other paragraphs and in end notes. An automatic reference numbering system allows the writer to renumber his footnotes automatically as new ones are added or old ones deleted.

As one is writing, key words or phrases may be marked for later use in a table of contents or for indexes at the back of the book. Both *Word* and *WordPerfect* have a feature for outlining that automatically creates the necessary levels using Roman numerals, letters and many subdivisions.

Paragraphs may be numbered for future editing and graphics, charts, spread sheets and pictures may be inserted into text and calculations may be done without leaving the program. As with the databases, some time must be spent learning to use a word processor, but again the time will be well spent. The reason for this will become apparent when one writes just one paper on the word processor.

## Footnoting

Deciding what must be footnoted or cited is a difficult decision. Authors are entitled to credit for their work, just as the student wants a grade or credit for the paper he or she has written. It is unfair, immoral and may be illegal to use information written by another author without giving the appropriate credit to the author. Some

Theft or vandalism of library materials deprives all users. If you see someone stealing or vandalizing library materials, report it to a staff member.

information is common knowledge and does not have to be cited. For example, the name of the 13th president of the United States, dates of important events and other data are so widely known that authors need not give credit. This kind of information, though one has to look it up, need not be cited. Still, specific information, such as an author's written opinion and other unique productions such as research findings should always be cited. On should never copy from another work unless it is made clear that the material is a quotation and the author is cited.

When reusing information from another source, it is still necessary to cite the author even if the words that are used by the student are different. If the idea was found in someone else's work, it must be cited. It is not only ethically and morally an imperative, but copying without citation could result in dire consequences to the student. All colleges have several rules against copying or, as it is called, plagiarism. Students have

**Checking out at the circulation desk.**

been expelled or given a failing grade because their papers had been known to contain material that was plagiarized. A college handbook is a good source of information on the college's policy on plagiarism.

Copying from a source without credit is analogous to stealing. But one can avoid the problem. Whenever there is the slightest doubt as to whether one should cite something, cite it. It is preferable to cite too much than to omit a citation that is necessary.

One simple and widely used method of notation consists of inserting parenthetically the author's last name, a comma and the date directly in the text as needed. For example, a study has shown that boys and girls do not significantly differ in total reading ability at the 8th grade level (Wolf, 1978).

This seems a logical way to cite works by other authors. However, instructors may insist on a particular format for citations and bibliographic listings, and the student should make sure that they use the required format. If the instructor lacks preference, the student could well use the method described above for citations and the bibliographic style that is found after each chapter in this text. Anyhow, one must get the information correctly transcribed the first time, since it may be extremely difficult to find it later. Transcribe the bibliographic information plus the citation onto the first card or into the database exactly as it should appear in the final paper. This will make it easier when the paper is written. Use as many cards as necessary for that source, putting the citation on each card. For example, "(World, 1975)." A numbering system also will be useful with multiple cards.

## Primary Sources

To develop precision in researching a topic the student should use as many primary resources as possible. Primary sources are those that are written or reported by the author. Secondary sources, on the other hand, are reports, abstracts or descriptions based on the primary sources or taken from the primary source. Primary sources may often be more accurate than secondary sources, particularly where the secondary source extensively summarizes the original material. Secondary source writers may misquote, misinterpret or distort the original materials. This usually occurs in reviews of the literature in a particular field. For example, in the *Annual Review of Psychology* the reviewer must abstract one dozen research articles on a topic such as psychotherapy. Often in condensing the findings, gross errors occur as well as subtle differences in meaning.

Researchers should find out whether the information being obtained derives from a primary or secondary source. Detective work should reveal original sources that provide more accurate data. These should be consulted when possible.

## Copyright

Copyright is a means of protecting the rights of authors, composers and artists. Copyright laws protect original works from being copied, except for specific conditions outlined in the law, and insure that the individual creating the copyrighted materials receives payment (royalties) for the sale of his or her works. The copyright law is specific in detailing requirements for receiving a copyright (the copyright office is a part of the Library of Congress), and in the placement of the copyright statement in published materials. To locate copyright information in published materials, look on the title page or the back of the title page for the date. The law is also specific about the conditions for reproducing copyrighted materials and the penalty for violating the law. The law provides for stiff penalties for infringement on the rights of the copyright owners (author or publisher) when copies are made without the written permission of the copyright owner. Today's high quality, rapid photocopying machines provide the means of violating the law, and students and faculty should not make multiple copies of protected materials without permission. A single copy of a page or two of a journal article or a book, to be used for scholarly purposes, is usually permissible. Yet, credit should be given to the author and permission obtained from the copyright owner. This may be obtained by writing the publisher. Under no conditions should multiple copies be made without the permission of the publisher.

## *Term Paper Guides* (see also Chapter 5)

Bolner, Myrtle S. *The Research Process: Books and Beyond.* Rev. print. Dubuque, Iowa: Kenall/Hunt Pub. Co., 1997.

Lunsford, Andrea, and Robert Connors. *The St. Martin's Handbook.* 5th ed. New York: St. Martin's Press. 2003.

*MLA Handbook for Writers of Research Papers,* 6th ed. Edited by Joseph Gibaldi and Walter S. Achtert. New York: Modern Language Association, 2003.

Slade, Carole. *Form and Style: Theses, Reports, Term Papers,* 12th ed. Boston: Houghton Mifflin Co., 2003.

Turabian, Kate L. *A Manual for Writers of Term Papers, Theses, and Dissertations,* 6th ed. Chicago: University of Chicago Press, 1996.

# Appendix:
# Answers to Exercises

## Chapter 1

Each library will differ in layout and regulations

## Chapter 2

1. (A) Q 121 M3
   (B) PE 1625 )87
   (C) AY 67 N5 W7
   (D) JK 516 C57
   (E) AG 5 K315

2. (A) 520
   (B) 599.9
   (C) 599.8
   (D) 000

3. (A) E-F
   (B) L
   (C) ND
   (D) NE
   (E) R
   (F) G

4. (A) 1997
   (B) Lanham, Md
   (C) Z 1209 W83 1988 or E 58 W83 1988
   (D) Wolf, Carolyn E
   (E) 016.970/0049 721
   (F) 2
   (G) Indians of North and South America, 2nd Suppl.
   (H) No
   (I) Scarecrow Press
   (J) Yes

## Chapter 3

The results will vary depending on the library's holdings. If your library does not have any books by Richard Warren, choose another author. Be sure to try question 4 even if your library has no books by Richard Warren. Try accessing another library via the internet and repeat the search for books by Richard Warren. Try accessing the Library of Congress at *www.loc.gov* and search for Richard Warren.

## *Chapter 4*

1. **Last Supper** (LCSH v. 3:3442, 2001)
   BT 420 Here are entered works on the final meal of Christ ...
       UF Jesus Christ — Last Supper
       BT Dinners and Dining in the Bible
       RT Jesus Christ–Washing of the Apostles' Feet
         Lord's Supper
         Maundy Thursday
         Passover in the New Testament
       Last Supper. Room of the (Jerusalem)
         USE Cenacle (Jerusalem)
       Last Supper in Art (NOT subd Geog)
       Last Supper in Literature (NOT subd Geog)

2. Some examples are
   Jewish — Arab Relations (LCSH v. 1: 3178, 2001)
   Arab-Israeli Conflict (LCSH v. 1:302, 2001)

3. For a good example see Arab-Israeli
   Conflict heading in previous question.

4. Answers will vary depending on heading chosen

## *Chapter 5*

1. (A) Poe, Edgar Allan (1,2,4, will vary from library to library. 3. Examples: Dameron, J. Lasley and Irby B. Cauthen. *Edgar Allan Poe: A Bibliography of Criticism, 1827–1967*. And Pollin, Burton R. *Dictionary of Names and Titles in Poe's Collected Works.*

2. (A) Doing a WilsonWeb search in July 2005 of Books in print. (1) 20 Records located. (2) Information in a WilsonWeb entry includes author, title, publisher, year, language, ISBN, Doc type, update codes, accession number, review citation with full text.
   (B) CBI 1990, v. 1:2106 10 entries

3. (D) WorldCat (search in July 2005) Subject search 1130 records. Keyword search 1213 records. Princess Diana (keyword) 1426 records by categories

| | | |
|---|---|---|
| Books 1129 | Scores 21 | Archival 1 |
| Visual 142 | Articles 9 | English language 1190 |
| Sound 95 | Serials 6 | |
| Internet 21 | Computer 3 | |

## *Chapter 6*

1. Have you looked at this book carefully?

2. For example: Morton, Andrew. *Diana: Her New Life.* See *Book Review Digest* 1995 p. 1576 (2 reviews listed).

## *Chapter 7*

Questions 1–10, 13–14 involve the varying resources of individual libraries. For 10 (c) see any of the comparative guides like those published by Barron's or Peterson.

11. (a) Yellow Pages — ads, subject index; Blue pages — government agencies, local, county, state and federal
    (b) Green pages (sometimes green edges) Zip codes, sometimes local street maps
    (c) white pages at the front (sometimes edged in gray)
    (d) city street maps, airport diagrams, tourist attractions, community services, station and theater diagrams

12. A.  McGraw-Hill Corporate Headquarters
    1221 Ave of the Americas
    New York, NY 10020–1095
    212–904–2000
    (examples of sources with this information)
    McGraw-Hill website at *www.mcgrawhill.com*
    Print source — *Headquarters USA* v. 1:702, 2005

    B.  Population of Chicago
    Print source example — *World Almanac* 2004, p. 376. Pop. As of 2002 2,886,251
    Online sources — Try a Google search using Chicago AND population. Numerous sources.

    C.  Canada
    Print source example — *World Almanac* 2004 p. 768–9.
    Population 31,510,000
    Geographical area — 3,851,806 sq miles
    Political leader — 2005 Prime Minister is Paul Martin
    Online — try a Google search for politicians using terms: Canada political leaders

## *Chapter 8*

Questions 1–3, 7 will vary from library to library and from student to student.

4.  v. 56 p. 111
    v. 50 p. 983
    v. 44 p. 950
    v. 39 p. 713
    v. 34 p. 568
    WilsonWeb for 2001 24 records
                  2004 49 records
                  1996 40 records

5.  1996 p. 1118–1119, 10 see also headings, 11 major subheadings and one of these has 5 subheadings. WilsonWeb search (July 2005) for 1990–91 found 211 records, 1996–97 found 339 records and 2004 found 2017 records.

6.  WilsonWeb Search done in July 2005 provides the following:
    Business (2004–05) 306 records
    Education (2004–04) 66 records
    Social Sciences (2004–05) 592 records
    Entries include abstracts and subject headings

## *Chapter 9*

Answers will vary from library to library

## *Chapter 10*

1.  Answers will vary from library to library. See the bibliography at the end of the chapter.
2.  a. For example see *Columbia Granger's Index to Poetry in Anthologies*, 1997, p. 143
    b.  See entries in *Short Story Index* under Chekhov, Anton. A WilsonWeb search done in 2005 retrieves 316 records.
    c.  A WilsonWeb search of *Book Review Digest* (2005) retrieves 6 reviews, some with abstracts and some with full text.
    d.  A ProQuest newspaper search found 4 records (searching by title + movie). ProQuest also provided two suggested subject searches.
    e.  A ProQuest search (in 2005) in the *New York Times*, no date limits, search for Neil Simon reviews retrieves 127 records.
    f.  An InfoTrac search of *Literature Resource Center* retrieves 8 entries. For

an example of a print citation see *Critical Survey of Long fiction* v. 7:3230–28.

g. For example — *Last of the Mohicans*. See *Masterplots* v. 6:3261, 1976.

## Chapter 11

Will vary from library to library
Will vary from student to student

## Chapter 12

1. For some examples see the bibliography at the end of chapter 12.

2. a. Using a keyword search of GPO Monthly Cat (online in July 2005) and no date limits, results in 160 records. Most of the recent documents were from the General Accounting Office and the Congress. House. Committee on Homeland Security

   b. Using GPO Monthly Cat online keyword search Iraq prisoner abuse finds 3 records.

3. Examples of useful print sources: *Congressional Quarterly's Washington Information Directory* and *CQ's Politics in America*.

4. a. Alben W. Barkley — see any general encyclopedia

   b. Use *United States Government Manual* or any encyclopedia.

   c. For example see *Congressional Quarterly's State Information Directory*

5. Answers will vary

## Chapter 13

1. For examples of titles see the bibliography at the end of chapter 13.

2. a-b Will vary from student to student
   c-e Check sources such as *Biography Index, Personal Name Index to the New York Times* or check online sources such as Yahoo! or Google.

3. Check the back of biography Index by occupation.

## Chapter 14

1. See *Thomas Register* or *Hoover's Company, Florida Business Directory* or online search ProQuest ABI/INFORM

2. Online try *Business Index ASAP*. Air bags as subject search finds fewer citations than air bags as keyword search. Check *Business Periodicals Index* either in print or online. ProQuest or firstSearch are other choices.

3. Answers will vary

4. Examples: *Hoover's Handbook of American Business* v. 2:847–8, 2004, online *Reference USA* or try *www.verizon.com*.

## Chapters 15 and 16

Answers will vary

# Index